# GREEN GOVERNANCE AND HUMAN RIGHTS

# GREEN GOVERNANCE AND HUMAN RIGHTS

*Editor*
**P.K. Rajagopal**

KALPAZ

ISBN : 978-81-7835-983-0
Price : ₹850

First Published 2013

*Published by*

**Kalpaz Publications**
C-30, Satyawati Nagar,
Delhi-110052
Ph.: 9212142040
E-mail: kalpaz@hotmail.com

*Laser Typesetting* : Shakun Graphics Delhi-32
*Printed at* : G. Print Process, Delhi

**Cataloging in Publication Data—DK**
Courtesy: D.K. Agencies (P) Ltd. <docinfo@dkagencies.com>

**I. Rajagopal, P. K.**
**Green governance and human rights** / editor, Rajagopal P.K.
p. cm.
Includes bibliographical references.

ISBN 9788178359793

1. Human rights—Environmental aspects—India—Congresses. 2. Environmental law—India—Congresses. 3. Climatic changes—India—Congresses.

DDC 344.54046 23

# CONTENTS

**SECTION-III : CLIMATE CHANGE AND HUMAN RIGHTS**



**SECTION-IV: CLIMATE CHANGE AND FOOD SECURITY**

# PREFACE

Environmental concerns were largely ignored within the conventional governance process. However, the need for conservation of environment had called in for urgent attention of national governments all over the world. The magnitude of the environmental issues required specialized groups within the government machinery with sound knowledge over environment and issues surrounding it. It is in this backdrop that the concept of green governance came into being. Green governance can be defined broadly as the structures and processes that make policies related to environment and oversee the implementation of such policies, apart from acting as advisor on environmental issues to the government. The primary aim of environmental governance is to bring in transparency, accountability and efficiency on issues related to environment. In India, during this period, the Indian judiciary also became. environmentally pro-active and pronounced environment-friendly judgments. For instance, the judiciary brought in the issue of pollution in a big way thereby addressing environmental concerns and rights of the people. The judiciary for the first time brought in the idea of right to life with dignity, thus going beyond the right to life. As a consequence, environmental issues like pollution came under much wider criticism.

In spite of environment related policies in place, there appears to be certain setbacks at the implementation level. One major issue that seems to have been ignored is the livelihoods of the people in granting environmental clearance. As a result, many environmental movements in India today are centred on the livelihoods of the people in the context of dams, industries, nuclear power plants, mining, and other infrastructure projects. Such movements often articulate their demands in the form of rights based upon their lifestyles and livelihoods. The conflict over livelihoods is mainly due to the mis-management in allocating resources like land and water.

In this context, it is pertinent to address people's rights through environmental governance. A strict adherence to people's rights would automatically ensure transparent, accountable and efficient environmental governance. Therefore, environmental governance could be manifested as a means to achieve the fulfilment of rights. A degraded environment either due to cyclone or tsunami or climate change or any other environment disaster would directly or indirectly infringe upon basic human rights.

Proper green governance would also ensure equity and justice that form the basis of modern understanding of human rights. Such human rights based environmental governance would help in sustaining resources for the future. Therefore, it is essential to create reliable and accountable environmental governance structures that would help in protecting and ensuring basic rights like life, health, livelihood, apart from protecting the rights of future generations. The present volume is a modest attempt to highlight some of these issues which deserve special attention and also offers recommendations for improving the existing conditions.

I am graterful to the University Grants Commission for providing financial assistnace to the National Seminar. I would like to thank Dr. M.P. Rajan, Principal, NSS Hindu College Changanacherry for his constant encouragement and inspiration. Heartfelt thanks are extended to my colleagues in the department of political Science Prof. V. Jayaprakash Narayanan, Prof. G. Harikumar, Dr. K. Mohankumar, Dr. Asha. V, Dr. B. Udayanan, Dr. R. Samala, Prof. B. Madhusudhanan, Prof. Suresh Babu, Prof. P.V. Sreejith, Dr. R. Giriji and Shree Kannan for their assistnace in several ways. I extend my heartfelt thanks to all the contributors, without their help this work may not be a reality. Thanks are due to Prof. Sreekala. K. Assistant Professor of History, BJM Government College, Chavara for her suggestions to improve this work. I am very thankful to the Kalpaz Publications for publishing this work. The book is dedicated to Bharata Kesari Mannathu Padmanabhan, pioneer of social reformers in modern kerala.

**P.K. Rajagopal**

# LIST OF CONTRIBUTORS

1. **Prof. N.R. Madhava Menon, Dr. S. Radhakrishnan,** Chair on Parliamentary Studies (Rajya Sabha) Honorary Professor, Centre for Development Studies, Trivandrum.
2. **Dr. Venkateshwaran Lokanathan,** Assistant Professor, Department of Geopolitics and International Relations, Manipal University.
3. **Dr. Kannan C.S. Warrier,** Institute of Forest Genetics and Tree Breeding (Indian Council of Forestry Research and Education) Coimbatore.
4. **Dr. Lekshmi R. Nair,** Faculty Associate IFMR, Chennai.
5. **Prof. Gokul Das N.N.,** Retired professor (Zoology), Sree Krishna College, Guruvayur.
6. **Dr. Joseph Sebastian Thekedam,** Associate Professor St. Berchmans' College, Changanacherry.
7. **Asha Ajith,** Postgraduate Student, University of Kerala.
8. **Muralidharan P.T.**, Associate Professor, Department of Physical Education PRNSS College, Mattanur, Kannur.
9. **Sajin Philip,** Research Scholar in Madras Institute of Development Studies, Chennai.
10. **Dr. Biju Lekshmanan,** Assistant Professor of Politics, Govt. College, Nedumangad.
11. **Dr. Umadevi S.,** Associate Professor in Political Science, Sanatana Dharma College, Alappuzha-3.
12. **Reinhart Philip,** Junior Research Fellow, Postgraduate & Research Department of Political Science, S.N. College, Kollam, University of Kerala.
13. **Dhanasree Jayaram,** Postgraduate Research Scholar, M.S. Geopolitics and International Relations, Manipal University.
14. **Akhila P. Nair,** Research Scholar, M.G. University.
15. **Rose Mary,** Assistant Professor, Department of Political Science, Providence Women's College, Malapparamaba, Kozhikode.

16. **Dr. K.C. Sunny,** Dean, Professor and Head, Dept. of Law, University of Kerala.
17. **Sreekala K.L.,** Asstt. Professor, N.S.S. Training College, Changanacherry.
18. **Dr. K. Mohankumar,** Associate Professor Politics, NSS Hindu College, Changanacherry.
19. **Dr. S.R. Jitha,** Associate Professor in Political Science, Sree Narayana College, Chengannur, Alappuzha, University of Kerala.
20. **Biju Kumar A.,** Department of Aquatic Biology and Fisheries, University of Kerala, Thiruvananthapuram.
21. **Dr. V. Asha,** Associate Professor, Political Science, NSS Hindu College, Changanacherry.
22. **Dr. Pramod Gopinathan,** Associate Professor, Chemistry, NSS Hindu College, Changanacherry.
23. **Dr. K. Unnikrishnan,** Associate Professor, Physics, NSS Hindu College, Changanacherry, Kerala.
24. **Dr. R. Samala,** Associate Professor, P.G. Department of Political Science, N.S.S. Hindu College, Changanacherry.

# SECTION-I

# ENVIRONMENT AND HUMAN RIGHTS

# 1

# Global Warming, Climate Change and Human Rights Protection

*Prof. N.R. Madhava Menon*

## A Word of Appreciation

I am delighted to be a participant in a Seminar discussing a problem of global significance to life in Planet Earth. Let me congratulate the post-graduate Department of Political Science of NSS Hindu College, Changanacherry for having taken the initiative to look at the problem across disciplines and professions keeping the individual rights in focus.

I sincerely believe inter-disciplinarity is the key for growth of knowledge in the future and this seminar is truly inter-disciplinary in content and organisation. The theme of the Seminar includes science, economics, politics, management, international relations, human rights and many more branches of knowledge. Naturally, the solutions to the problem may also vary between engineering solutions, economic solutions, political solutions, management solutions, legal solutions and, if I may say so even spiritual solutions! If the experts drawn from these and other disciplines participating in the Seminar could collectively identify and prioritise the solutions in the context of India's development, we will have contributed to the education and mobilisation of public opinion and the articulation of public policies to meet the challenges of climate change.

I have pleasure in inaugurating such an important conference.

## A Necessary Follow-up in Academic Pursuits

Let me suggest to the Principal and Faculty of NSS Hindu College that modules developed out of the deliberations of this Seminar be included in the programmes of study offered by every department of this college and others under NSS management and is made compulsory reading of students in every course they offer be it in social science, basic sciences, management or whatever. This is the minimum that we can do as academicians in disseminating knowledge which affects not only the current generation but also future generations everywhere in this beautiful world.

It was last week (October 12) that newspapers reported the results of a study conducted by the National Institute of Oceanography in Goa in which it was found that all the three oceans surrounding the Indian sub-continent recorded an increase of temperature of up to one degree and it is increasing steadily year after year, possibly 3 to 4 degrees higher in the next 50 years! It is predicted that this would lead to large scale migration of fish and aquatic life away from Indian Ocean, Arabian Sea and Bay of Bengal. Further, it has already started sending the rain-bearing clouds emanating from the Bay of Bengal away from its regular route across India denying the rains particularly in Southern States. Drought and scarcity of water is the long-term prospect of this phenomenon. We need to build awareness about this phenomenon which affects our lives and livelihoods among all sections of society, particularly the educated elite. The problem is not only about human rights but also about **human responsibilities in** containing actions tending to climate change and **environmental degradation**.

## What is Climate Change and How does it Happen?

**Climate change is** the product of **industrial revolution** and the spectacular developments of science and technology in the post-industrial era. **Industrial revolution** and technological developments did give freedom and leisure, material comfort and a better life to people. At the same time it ignited the quest for exploitation of natural resources for insatiable consumption of energy and mass production of goods and services. The pattern of development was soon found to be unsustainable not only because natural resources are limited but also due to the after effects of such development for life on Earth. The Nicolas **Stern Committee Report** (U.K.) after studying the problem of **global warming** and world economy pointed out that at the current rate of consumption of resources and energy available on the planet, mankind would require more than one planet for survival. **The Stern Committee Report** therefore stressed on reduction of **green house gas** emissions by remodeling life style and by transmitting from a **carbon economy** (energy derived from hydro-carbon) to a non-carbon economy (renewable energy). How does Global Warming and threat of climate change occur? Use of hydrocarbon which is a finite natural resource for energy used in motor and air transport leads to toxic emission of carbon dioxide and other **greenhouse gases** into the atmosphere. This leads to **global warming** a scientific phenomenon influencing climate change and ecological imbalance which, in turn, jeopardizes environmental security, food security and sustainable development across nations, developed and developing. It is estimated that nearly 80 per cent of global warming is caused by hydrocarbons and 20 per cent by deforestation. With increase in number of cars, airplanes, refrigerators, airconditioning equipments etc., it is said, irreparable damage will be caused to the ozone layer protecting earth and maintaining life. More and more countries in the name of development are repeating the same pattern adopted by the Western industrial nations nearly a century ago.

It is said that the unplanned growth of **urbanization** and migration of people to cities and towns that is now happening in India is making the cities vulnerable to the effects of climate change. By 2020 the urban population is expected to exceed the rural folks in India. This process will increase the emission of greenhouse gas into the atmosphere contributing to climate change and climate change-induced disasters like unexpected flooding, sea level increase etc. Nobody wants to stop urbanization as it leads to economic growth and reduction of poverty. But there is a price to pay for this. According to reports every one per cent increase in the density of urban areas would reduce the carbon monoxide level by 0.7 per cent unless urban and climate change policies are balanced at the level of municipalities and corporations on the basis of a sustainable growth pattern. It is easily said than done. The pressures of urbanization and the lobbies which stand to benefit from the process are least bothered by **greenhouse gas** emissions and the disasters that are waiting to happen.

At the international level, the politics and economics of development followed by the developed nations seek to deny the same privileges to the developing ones. Negotiations on environmental management and sustainable development continue indefinitely in world forums with no one wanting to limit one's right to exploit natural resources or to moderate consumption of energy at sustainable levels. The crisis is getting aggravated day by day and the solutions lie in paper only. This is the tragedy of the situation silently engulfing the whole of mankind towards a certain disaster being created by man himself.

## How does Climate Change Impact on Human Rights?

The **Universal Declaration of Human Rights** and the two Covenants on Civil, Political as well as Social, Economic and Cultural Rights direct State Parties to ensure that individuals enjoy the basic rights promised under these instruments. It involves both negative and positive obligations on the Governments which circumscribe the power of State authorities in organising governance including developmental activities. The core obligations in this regard are written into the Bill of Rights of the Constitutions of most countries and mechanisms for remedying violations are also provided in it. In this scheme of things, right to life, right to livelihood, right to health, right to food and right to clean water, air and environment are inalienable rights of individuals and protecting them are constitutional and international obligations of States. In other words, if Governments allow so called developmental activities which endanger health security, **food security, environmental security,** access to clean air and water and sustainable life, they run the risk of violating human rights for which they are liable under municipal and international law. When it happens in mass scale as in the case of unplanned urbanisation, indiscriminate industrialisation and uncontrolled deforestation leading to **emission of greenhouse gas** and **climate change**, we call it mass torts or man-made disasters. When one-fourth of world population living in Europe and America are consuming three-fourth of energy resources to live a life of unlimited comfort, we call it exploitation of the worst kind violating the right to sustainable development of the people in the rest of the world. This is what the **Stockholm Conference** discussed and Brundtland and Human Development Reports warned the world community. A number of Conventions and Protocols have been negotiated to moderate and limit activities resulting in greenhouse gas emission; however, greed and urge to dominate lead nations to find ways to disregard obligations under climate change treaties.

Within the country, civil society organisations are using the political, legal and judicial forums to agitate against State policies which they contend as unsustainable and violative of human rights. In fact, much of environmental standards of governance has been evolved through **public interest litigation** and **judicial activism** in support of an expanded conception of right to life. However, Governments also have obligations under Millenium Development Goals and under Directive Principles of State Policy under the Constitution. In discharging those obligations, industrialisation and urbanisation become inevitable and, in the absence of appropriate technologies, Governments succumb to the use of cheap technologies which are energy-intensive and carbon-based. In short, the debate is around choice of evils as all development activities involve paying a cost in terms of environment and resources.

## Human Rights-Friendly Solutions to Climate Change Challenges

Obviously the easy solution to fight climate change is to give up activities which lead to emission of greenhouse gas. This retards development and eradication of poverty. Therefore the solutions lie in the economics and politics of development policies and governance. This was evident when Parliament recently discussed the Nuclear Liability Bill and the Land Acquisition Bill.

The alternate strategy is to find scientific and engineering solutions based on clean energy. People may have to go by public transport instead of cars or walk or cycle the distance as they did in the past. Waste disposal has to be scientific and environment-friendly. People will have to moderate their consumerist greed of air travel and air-conditioned comfort in their homes and offices and depend on renewable sources of energy. Individual rights will have to subserve collective rights and material pleasures will have to be moderated for sustainable life-supporting common good. In short, individual rights will get protected only by seeking collective action and common good. Interest of each nation will find protection only when the interests of other nations are equally protected. As one writer reminded, "... Dominant Western Cultures must learn to live simply so that others can simply live" (Prof. David Bennet in The Cindrella Syndrome).

In conclusion, one would recommend what Mahatma Gandhi had preached and practiced since the beginning of the 20th century which is summarised by Mr. Satya Narain Sahu in his insightful article "Gandhian Engineering – A Key to Survival" :

> *"Mahatma Gandhi was far ahead of his times in grappling with challenges to planet Earth arising out of a life style which multiplied wants and desires and left no stone unturned to satisfy them. At a time when mankind is facing the dangerous prospects of getting annihilated due to accelerating pace of global warming, it is important to re-discover Gandhiji's ideas and put them into practice".*

Quoting Ms. Patra Kelly, one of the founders of the Green Party of Germany, Mr. Sahu wrote :

> "... *We have been greatly inspired by Mahatma Gandhi. That is in our belief that a life style and method of production which relies on endless supply of raw materials and which use those raw materials lavishly, also provide motive force for violent appropriation of raw materials from other countries. In contrast, a responsible use of raw materials as part of an ecologically-oriented life style and economy reduces the risk that policies of violence will pursue ... such a vision provides the remedy to create a new civilisation the foundation of which is based on discipline, restraint and morality*".

The sum and substance of **sustainable development** according to **Gandhi** is that "earth has enough for fulfilling everybody's need but not anybody's greed". Share more and consume less is the mantra for sustainability. Will the world listen to Mahatma Gandhi's strategy for survival in the face of the impending disaster brought about by climate change?

# 2

# Environmental Security and Climate Change: Challenges for Policy Formulation

*Dr. Venkateshwaran Lokanathan*

In a globally competitive world, from the dominant neo-realist perspective, modern states, in their interactions with one another, have always sought to maximize their interest by increasing their power and influence over one another. Interestingly, the 21st century has witnessed the emergence of an interconnected world, fueled by the advent of the World Wide Web and advances in technology. Simultaneously, the advent of globalisation, characterised by cross border interactions, has widened the traditional boundaries of competition, challenged competency and increased the urge for technological innovations. Crucially this has led to the globalisation of even local problems. An offshoot of this development is the wider ramifications posed by challenges like climate change which transcend the traditional boundaries of States. Climate change-related issues are becoming a larger part of international relations and as global problems, they need global solutions. This will require States to adopt a neo-liberal perspective based on cooperation and coordination of consensual policies. However, there are significant roadblocks to finding effective answers, partly as the result of a long-standing trust deficit between states.

## The Complexities over Terminology

One such challenge has to do with the terminology currently in use, which is often confused or inaccurate. The definition provided by the **Inter-Governmental Panel on Climate Change** (IPCC) and the **United Nations Framework Convention on Climate Change** (UNFCCC) is a significant representation. **The UNFCC** defines **climate change** as –

"means a change of climate which is attributed directly or indirectly to human activity that alters the composition of the global atmosphere and which is in addition to natural climate variability observed over comparable time periods".[1] In comparison, the IPCC definition states – "Climate change refers to a statistically significant variation in either the mean state of the climate or in its variability, persisting for an extended period (typically decades or longer). **Climate change** may be due to natural internal processes or external forcings, or to persistent anthropogenic changes in the composition of the atmosphere or in land use."[2] Interestingly, the **UNFCCC** specifically focuses on human induced climate change while the **IPCC** provides a wider connotation by drawing the distinction between changes in climatic patterns due to human interference and natural causes. There is, hence, an urgent need for clarification as to whether efforts are being largely addressed towards understanding natural causes or human induced or both when it comes to changes in patterns of climate. Addressing this will go a long way in providing clarity in understanding the problem and thereby making efforts towards solving it more effectively.

What needs to be clearly at the outset is that climate change is only one component of the larger problem of direct, man-made environmental change. The emerging patterns of climate change and its impact on the environment will have serious consequences for the international community in the future. The pace at which the International environment has evolved over the last century has been rapid. Humans are making direct and major alterations to the environment creating considerable concern over its sustenance in the long term. As the boundaries of the carrying capacity of the planet are being pushed, a smaller degree of environmental variation has larger implications. In the more recent past, massive population increases have had a dramatic effect on global sustainability. At the turn of the 20th century, there were around 1.65 billion people on the planet. The first decade of the 21st, has already seen this jump to seven billion. The result will be an increased usage of groundwater, cutting of forests for human habitation, increased migration from rural to urban areas thereby creating social and cultural disruptions, land abuse leading to increased soil erosion, environmentally unsecure and faulty development of infrastructure and ultimately a changed environment.

There is an urgent necessity to explore the various ways by which climate change will affect **geopolitics** and its corresponding influence on foreign relations, national security and economic policies. Crucially, this needs to encompass an assessment of the impact of climate change on traditional borders of nation states. There are critical questions that require attention – One, will the impact of climate change lead to a potential loss of complete sovereignty for a nation state in the future? Second, what are the larger implications for the connectivity and infrastructure of nation states? What becomes clear is that understanding the complexities of the geopolitical/geostrategic implications of climate change will provide crucial impetus for nation states, obsessed with state sovereignty and territorial integrity, to cooperate in an effort to address this issue effectively.[3]

## Warming Planet: The Domino Effect

It was the Club of Rome, an informal organisation established in 1968, which for the first time in a book titled **The Limits to Growth** published in 1972, expressed increasing concerns over the sustenance of the planetary resources in the face of growing demands fuelled by a burgeoning population. Subsequently, the **Stockholm conference** of 1972 highlighted the importance of sustainable development keeping in mind environmental concerns. Although the **Brundtland report** and the IPCC assessment reports of 1990 and 1995 highlighted varying concerns over increasing global temperatures, it was the Third Assessment Report of the IPCC in 2001 that significantly highlighted the emergence of global warming due to a combination of natural variability and human interference. Based on observed, including palaeoclimatic data, it dwelt at length over an increase of approximately 0.6 degrees Celsius over the 20th century in global average surface temperature since 1861. It also inferred that extreme warming had occurred during the periods from 1910 - 1945 and 1976 - 2000 and identified the 1990s as the warmest decade of the 20th century. Significantly, it observed that the three hottest years since 1861 was in the first decade of the 21st century. The report also observed that the average surface air temperature over the Indian subcontinent indicated a slight warming trend by 0.2 degree Celsius to 0.4 degree Celsius in mean annual temperature over the last century. This warming was noted during the post-monsoon period (October – December) and the winter season (January – February).[4]

## Decreasing Sea Ice

Sea ice plays a critical role in the natural maintenance of climate. It acts as an effective insulator by decreasing the amount of heat lost from oceans to the atmosphere. It also reflects a lot of solar radiation back into space there by playing a critical role in maintaining the thermal budget of the earth. The bacteria in the sea ice are also critical to the food chain of different marine species. Additionally, sea ice plays a vital role in converting complex organic matter back to $CO2$. Crucially, satellite data has indicated a decrease of about ten per cent in extent of snow cover since the 1960. There is similar inference based on ground data which indicates a reduction of about two weeks in the annual duration for lake and river ice cover in the mid and high latitudes of Northern Hemisphere over the 20th century. This is accompanied by widespread retreat of mountain glaciers in non-polar regions. The sea ice extent has decreased by 10 to 15 per cent in the north hemisphere spring and summer since 1990. There are also records of a 40 per cent decline in artic sea ice thickness during late summer to early autumn in recent decades.[5]

## Melting Glaciers

Mountain regions from the Andes to the Himalayas are warming faster than global average under climate change. Ice will turn into water and glaciers in the process will slowly reduce to being lakes. Glaciers ranging from Chile and Argentina to Alaska are showing double the rate of melting since 1975. There have been reports that the average temperature in the Himalayan region has risen by one degree Celsius since the mid-1970s. There are some 20,000 glacial lakes spread across varying altitudes across the Himalayas. There is increasing concern over increasing human activity on glaciers including the Gangotri which might result in major meltdown by 2023.

The environmental degradation of **Siachen**, a 76 km long river of ice which feeds river Nubra that in turn flows into Indus, due to its militarisation is a growing cause of concern. It is estimated to have receded by nearly 800 meters over the last 20 years. The Space Applications Center (SAC) of the Indian Space Research Organisation (ISRO) and the Snow and Avalanche Study Establishment (SASE) of the Defense and Research Development Organisation (DRDO) have analysed the effect of melting glaciers in Beas and Baspa basins in Himachal Pradesh on the winter stream run-offs during December using WiFS data of Indian Remote Sensing Satellite. The research has indicated an overall increase in stream-runoff by 75 per cent since 1966. A steady rise in global temperature has led to a steady rise in stream run-off. Warmer winters are also causing snowmelt and retreat of snow cover especially in the months of December and January at altitude of 5400 m. The data of available temperature in the two towns of Manali and Shimla in Himachal Pradesh have confirmed the unusual warm winter. It has also indicated a fall in precipitation and considerable decrease in snowfall since the 1990s.

The **glacial lakes** in Nepal and Bhutan, for example, are filling rapidly with water due to the melting of glaciers and surrounding snow areas. One such example is the Tsho Rolpa Lake in Nepal which has grown from 0.23 sq km in the 1950s to 1.8 sq. km in the first decade of the 21st century. Once peak levels are reached, it will burst banks suddenly and travel many kilometers downstream thereby causing flooding, acute shortage of drinking water, increase in threat from water borne diseases and silting in the surrounding hydro power plants. Flooding of this Tsho Rolpa Lake, for example, will affect 10,000 people upto 108 kms downstream.[6]

The **Imja Glacier** Lake, another case in point, is situated at an altitude of 5100 m above sea level. The lake is about 600 meters wide at the centre and up to 96.5 meters deep in some places. It is growing by 47 meters a year and stretches for 1.5 miles down from the glacier spawning three small ponds. The chunks of ice falling due to the melting of surrounding glaciers can cause the lake to break through its walls of glacial debris known as moraine. This could release a deluge of water, mud and rock for almost 100 kilometers swamping houses and fields leading to the loss of valuable land. The International Centre for Integrated Mountain Development has begun making efforts to decrease water level by 30 m and also a warning system for surrounding villages. However, mobilizing engineering equipment and expertise to lakes including the high costs involved at such high altitudes makes the task of meeting such challenges extremely daunting.[7]

## Rising Sea Level

The rising sea level is another indicator of global warming. Based on tide gauge data – 0.1 to 0.2 meters rise in global average sea level estimated during the 20th century. Although there have been no specific trends in global rainfall, it is believed to have increased by half to one per cent per decade in the 20th century. There has been also a two to four per cent increase in frequency of heavy precipitation events in the mid and high latitudes of northern hemisphere in the last half of 20th century. Simultaneously, the El Nino and South Oscillation have been reported to be more frequent, persistent and intense since mid-1970s as compared to the previous century. The breakup of ice shelves by itself is a natural process of renewal. However, the cause for alarm in recent years is the size and rate of production of icebergs. In April 2002 a 500 billion tonne chunk of Larsen B ice shelf that was 200 m thick with a surface area of 3,240 sq broke off km in Antarctica in the Weddell Sea due to sharp rise in temperature by 2.5 degree Celsius over the last 50 years. Similarly, the National Ice Centre, Maryland had spotted the collapse of the Ross Ice Shelf in Ross Sea in May 2002. Both the collapses were identified to a process of calving in which constant motion of polar ice cap fractures the ice into fragments. These huge icebergs may float loose into the sea and result in further breakups in the Antarctica thereby sending huge icebergs into the Southern ocean. Further, it may lead to disintegration of other sections of ice shelves in the fringes of Antarctica's continental ice cover and can lead to melt down of grounded West Antarctic ice sheet in the longer term. It is assumed that these developments could cause the World's oceans to rise up to Five metres m, affecting marine life and lead to the deep ocean circulating system slowing down the production of smaller amounts of dense oxygen-rich sea water.[8]

## Challenges to National Security and Policy Formulation

There is no doubt that environmental change could cause a redrawing of the physical map of the globe. As has occurred during past climatic shifts, there will be flooding of some areas while others will emerge from the melting of ice which might open up previously non-navigable sea lanes. This can open up potential conflict situations in an era of international law, in which political boundaries are closely and rigidly tied to physical ones especially when it comes to maritime borders which, legally, are often determined by coastlines. If so, a host of global political, economic and security issues would emerge. The ownership of strategic sea lanes might come into dispute. Remote island-based military installations and the right to locate them in those regions could be lost. Nations could find that their offshore resources are now in international waters. Debates between neighbours over tiny rocks anchoring vast maritime claims could intensify. Only around 160 of the potential 365 or so maritime boundaries worldwide have been agreed.[9]

The UN Convention on the Law of the Sea (UNCLOS), which came into force in 1994, attempts to create norms for determining boundaries[10], and the International Tribunal for the Law of the Sea (ITLOS) is designed to be a forum for resolving disputes.[11] So it is unfortunate that many of the assumptions of geographical and hydrological stability on which UNCLOS is based might be compromised by climate change. UNCLOS freezes coastlines and borders at a specific point in time until challenged or revised. That leaves many grey areas when physical boundaries dramatically shift and change, for example, as a result of flooding. When such challenges are made, it could eventually result in foreign policy and security concerns.

It was only as recent as April 2007, that the United Nations Security Council (UNSC) debated 'climate change' for the first time.[12] Subsequently legislation was introduced in the United States asking for a National Intelligence Estimate on the security implications of 'global warming'. The Center for Naval Analysis convened Military Advisory Board in a study entitled National Security and the Threat of Climate Change noted: 'Projected climate change poses a serious threat to America's national security ... **Climate change acts** as a threat multiplier for instability in some of the most volatile regions of the world ... Projected climate change will add to tensions even in stable regions of the world.'[13] Critically, by broadly labeling most environmental change-related security issues as being the result of '**global warming**' or '**climate change**', the international community is inadvertently limiting the range of possible responses, and potentially adding further confusion to an already complex problem.

## Access to Vital Resources – Water Stress and Food Security

In many regions, it will become increasingly difficult to guarantee the basic necessities of life, in particular water, food and shelter. This can lead to increased regional conflict, massive migration causing social and cultural disruptions and more opportunities for extremist ideologies and anti-social elements.

The glacier freshwater lakes in the Himalayas provide water directly to Bhutan, Nepal, Afghanistan, Bangladesh, Pakistan, China and India and are the sources for rivers including the Mekong, Ganga and Indus. Now, with all the glaciers showing alarming signs of melting, it puts close to half of the world's population under threat from flooding of their lands in the short run to droughts, water and power shortages in the long run. Sea level rise will accentuate this situation further by inundating the land near the coastlines and will contribute towards increasing salinization of the freshwater. All this, combining with other environmental change factors such as abuse of land and deforestation, could contribute to destabilizing the region by large-scale migration and through aggressive competition between countries for access to water resources.

India and China are two countries that depend heavily on agriculture making a significant contribution to their respective GDPs. This sector also employs a huge workforce there by contributing to employment and poverty alleviation. Additionally, the agriculture sector also depends on the monsoons to a large extent. The stress over water resources and the rising sea levels when combined with increasingly erratic patterns of rainfall will have a direct impact on food security. Scarcity of water will significantly affect irrigation, while rising sea levels will inundate fields near the coastlines. Additionally, the threat of flooding from swollen rivers due to the melting of glaciers in the short run and its drying up in the long run is ever present. The lingering social effect of increased poverty in the already suffering countryside, accompanied by increased migration to the urban areas, has been compounded by a failure of effective state response. The issue of farmers committing suicide because of heavy debts is now a constant feature in political debates in India.[14]

Other regions of the world are also getting affected by similar concerns. In 2006, climate conditions and beetles wrecked crops in Australia, Ukraine, Argentina and North America, driving wheat prices to a ten-year high. In the end, it is all likely to just make it even harder on poor people in rich countries and on poorer countries already suffering agricultural deficits. That could potentially lead to instability within and between nations, and formulation of policies with an objective to create preferential relationships with reliable agricultural producers. In 2005, a drought in Spain and Portugal destroyed nearly half of the cereal crop in Spain and led to a war of words between both countries over access to water resources.[15]

## Melting of the Arctic Ice: Emergence of New Transportation Routes

The changes in temperature are expected to be relatively small over the oceans as compared to land, as the oceans can absorb a lot of heat. The Arctic ice, however, being light-coloured, reflects sunlight. As the ice starts to melt, less of this ultraviolet light will be reflected back into space and more solar radiation will remain trapped at the surface. Additionally, the warming of the surrounding waters can also contribute to faster melting at the ice edge, and this is further accentuated as the ice pack is at a lowered elevation. It has been noted that the sea ice is melting earlier in the spring and freezing later in the autumn, and its thickness is decreasing.

The Hadley Centre for Climate Prediction and Research in the United Kingdom, which is measuring the rate of melting in the Aretic, predicts that the ice cap covering will disappear around September 2079. It has already noticed the shrinking of the area covered by the Arctic ice by 20 per cent since the 1950 and the average winter thickness reduced by 40 per cent since 1970.[16]

RosHydroMet, Russia's hydro meteorological agency has projected a winter temperature increase of upto four degrees centigrade along Russia's Arctic coast by 2040. Base temperatures near minus forty degrees centigrade, however, mean that the winter ice of the coastal sea and rivers and temperatures will continue to be a challenge. Still, such a change in temperature would be significant, because it would lead to a shorter and less extreme winter in the North, with less time for ice to spread and thicken. Warming in the southern Arctic region of the watershed, estimated at two degrees centigrade, will gradually increase growing periods and lead to the melting of permafrost, slowly moving northward the accessibility of lands.[17]

The absence of ice covers can lead to the expansion of sea which in turn can increase evaporation thereby inducing more rainfall and with decreasing warm currents in the Gulf Stream around the British Isles potentially leading to freezing temperatures will pose a complicated challenge for Europe.

Additionally, the warming of the climate will affect polar bears and seals and can increase the growth of plankton thereby enhancing the fish population in the region.[18]

Interestingly, the melting of the Arctic ice is also opening up access to oceanic resources including the economic potential of offshore oil and gas deposits which were earlier trapped under the sea ice. The US Geological Survey estimates that the Arctic contains up to 30 per cent of the world's undiscovered gas and 13 per cent of the world's undiscovered oil resources. It has also projected over 60 per cent of the total resources (equivalent to about 412 billion barrels of oil) to be located in Russian territory, with all but a very small percentage on shore or inside the EEZ. The area of greatest potential is in the Kara Sea basin, with smaller, yet still respectable, prospects in the Laptev and East Siberian seas. Advanced offshore techniques, including remote-exploration technology, directional drilling that allows a single well site to reach through the sea floor to tap deposits many kilometers away, and seabed-based production technologies, among others, are making development in the Arctic seas more attractive.[19] Russia has long been a major producer of oil and gas from land-based resources. Now the resources of the Arctic continental shelf are drawing increasing attention. Deposits in the Barents Sea are already being developed, with other known deposits in both the Barents and the Kara seas being eyed for future exploitation.[20]

One of the many geopolitical results of this melting ice is that shipping routes through the Arctic will become more viable. It will open up the entire Northwest and Northeast Passage thereby shortening distance for ships between Europe and the Far East. Travelling between Asia and Europe through the Northwest Passage, which is mostly in Canada but might also include the waters of the United States, Denmark and other nations, is faster, and cheaper, than the current route through the Panama Canal. Russia is already making increasing use of its territorial Northeast Passage. It is using powerful ice-breakers to cut through thick layers of ice during summer and winter to escort ships.

Interestingly, while Canada claims that much of the Northwest Passage is part of its internal waters, a claim with a sound legal basis according to UNCLOS, the United States claims that the route is actually an international strait, open to free passage for all. Frequent flare ups between Canada and the United States over passage rights in the Bering Strait had resulted in the Arctic Cooperation Agreement in 1988 which stated that the US would ask permission before sending icebreakers through the passage but that, when so asked, Canada would give permission. The agreement, however, did not last and there have been various protests from Canada from time to time over passage of US and Russian submarines through the region. Although, Canada's claim is legally strong, the changing conditions caused by climate change create uncertainty and give an opening in which international politics can outflank international law.[21]

China is displaying a real interest in the Arctic, as attested by its applying for observer status at the Arctic Council in 2008. The Chinese Government has also allocated more resources for research in the arctic. Since China's economy is reliant on foreign trade, there are substantial commercial implications if shipping routes are shortened during the summer months each year. Nearly half of China's gross domestic product (GDP) is thought to be dependent on shipping. The trip from Shanghai to Hamburg via the Northeastern Sea Route—which runs along the north coast of Russia from the Bering Strait in the east to Novaya Zemlya in the west—is 6400 kilometers shorter than the route via the Strait of Malacca and the Suez Canal. Moreover, due to piracy, the cost of insurance for ships travelling via the Gulf of Aden towards the Suez Canal has increased significantly. Hence, it is striving to position itself so that it will not be excluded from access to the Arctic.[22] Up until now, China has adopted a wait-and-see approach to Arctic developments, wary that due to its size and status as a rising global power, any active overtures would cause alarm in other countries. Chinese officials are therefore very cautious when formulating their views on the Arctic. They stress that China's Arctic research activities remain primarily focused on the climatic and environmental consequences of the ice melting in the Arctic. However, in recent years Chinese officials and researchers have started to also assess the commercial, political and security implications for China of a seasonally ice-free Arctic region.[23]

India also began its Arctic research programme in August 2007. The National Centre for Antarctic and Ocean Research, an autonomous institution under the Ministry of Earth Sciences, based in Goa, has been coordinating India's polar research.[24] In July 2008, India established its own research station 'Himadri' at the Arctic at Ny-Alesund in Norway.[25]

It was not until a comprehensive law of the sea was negotiated and implemented in the 1982 UNCLOS that rules applicable to the Arctic were agreed upon. Other laws and agreements, including the 1990 US - USSR Maritime Boundary Agreement, the 1995 Fish Stocks Agreement, and conventions and guidelines of the International Maritime Organisation, have further extended the legal regime of the Arctic. The Arctic Council, established in 1996, provides a forum for collaborative study of issues of sustainable development in the Arctic. The Ilulissat Declaration of 2008 commits the five Arctic coastal States (Russia, the United States, Canada, Norway, and Denmark) to resolve issues through diplomatic channels.

However, it is already evident that the opportunities this new route opens up will increase tension between States. Several sovereignty issues have yet to be resolved: Russia and Norway have complex boundary and resource access issues to resolve, the United States may challenge some of Russia's claims of internal waters along the Northeastern Sea Routes, and the Commission on the Limits of the Continental Shelf has yet to decide whether to recommend recognition of Russia's expansive claim to much of the seabed on the Asian side of the Arctic. They are currently working to resolve their boundary in the Barents Sea and sovereignty issues around the Svalbard Archipelago. The increasing military importance of an ice-free Arctic is indeed reflected in decisions during recent years by all five littoral States to strengthen their military capabilities in the Arctic.

At present, the Arctic shipping season is of unpredictable length, dependent on changing climate patterns and sea and ice conditions that require ships designed specifically for passage through icy waters. The transport routes will not appeal to major shipping firms as a regular route until more experience is gained and the route is upgraded with modern aids to navigation, port facilities, and search-and-rescue capabilities. Over time, those developments, with or without further retreat of the polar ice, will make the Northeast Passage more attractive, particularly as the number of ice-capable vessels increases. By 2050, the sea route is likely to be a regular shipping route, beginning with seasonal service based on ice-class vessels and expanding as climate and ice conditions allow. As the Arctic becomes more accessible, the northern coast of Eurasia may take the place of Harold Mackinder's "geographical pivot", as both a route of passage and an area of exploitable resources.[26]

## Altering Coastlines: Impact on State Sovereignty

One of the more significant long term physical impacts of climate change is the rise in sea levels. As sea levels rise, coastlines will alter and low lying islands may become uninhabitable. Inhabitants may have to be evacuated as salt water infiltrates groundwater, killing vegetation and animals and leaving those without desalination plants also without fresh water. There is a lot of uncertainty about how quickly this is happening, as protective barrier coral reefs seem to be trying to grow to keep pace with rising waters. Yet as water temperatures increase, the coral, which is temperature-sensitive, may die off. It is very likely that eventually at least one entire nation will have to be completely resettled.

It is worthwhile to note here that Article 1 of the **Montevideo Convention** on Rights and Duties of States details that a state to be recognised must have a permanent population, defined territory, a government and the capacity to enter into relations with other states. The last two qualifications are relatively easy to maintain, even in exile, assuming other states will continue to recognize the dislocated nation as a state. However, the first two, a defined territory and a permanent population, are complex issues that need to be address in a detailed manner.[27]

Tuvalu, with a population of 11,000 people approximately, is made up of a string of atolls in the pacific with the highest point only 4.5 m (15 feet) above sea level, making it extremely vulnerable to flooding. There is serious concern that rising tides and sea level will submerge the land and poison supplies of freshwater making the islands inhabitable. It is not just the shoreline that is at the mercy of high tides, reaching over three meters, but also water surging up from underground through the coral on which the islands are built. The IPCC has forecast the rise in tides by another half meter. In the space of an hour, all the lowest areas of the island, including the runway, which is a vital lifeline to the outside world, are flooded.[28] In October 2011, Tuvalu declared a state of emergency because of a severe shortage of fresh water. The nation, which normally expects to get 200 mm to 400 mm of rainfall every month, had not received rains for over six months. People were advised to not drink water from wells and neighbouring New Zealand was requested to provide water supplies and desalination units. Fearing that increasing emissions of harmful greenhouse gases into the atmosphere by nations could wipe it of the map, Tuvalu has aimed to depend on renewable sources, especially wind and solar power, to meet its energy requirements by 2020. By going carbon neutral in an effort to reduce **greenhouse** gas emissions to zero, Tuvalu hopes to set an example for other nations to follow in the future.[29] If Tuvalu does indeed go under water, the core question for external policy formulation will be - Can a nation exist without a physical state? Will it lose its seat in the United Nations (UN)? Will its current maritime exclusive economic zone revert to international waters? Will any nations assist in relocating its population? Can its people be shifted to another existing or artificial island nearby?

As with Tuvalu, the Indian Ocean nation of the Maldives is composed entirely of low-lying coral atolls. The IPCC has predicted that if the sea level rises over two meters, it will inundate nearly 50 per cent of Maldives. Its president, Mohamed Nasheed, has been actively trying to secure a home for his citizens should evacuation prove necessary including land purchase. Another option is to use the value of national sovereignty to "pay" for relocation. In that model, neighbouring India, for example, might take in the Maldivian immigrants in exchange for India being able to extend its national waters to include Maldivian waters. The proceeds from this extended EEZ (fisheries rights, seabed mining, etc.) could be used to resettle and set up a trust fund for Maldivian immigrants. Maldivians could also get preferential access to the waters for economic development and, should the islands ever re-emerge, resettlement could be possible. The advantage for India would be an orderly settlement of relatively wealthy immigrants, and an extension of its coastal security zone.[30]

Another interesting case in point is the low-lying UK territory of Diego Garcia in the Indian Ocean Chagos archipelago that is used as a base by the US is at threat from rising seas. If Diego Garcia is lost to the sea, will the UK also lose exclusive access to that crucial tract of ocean and, in the process, lose a valuable bargaining chip with the United States? Will the US look to shift its base to another island nearby which could cause potential concerns for other rising powers in the region? Kiribati is another small island country that is also facing the threat of existence due to rising sea levels. Interestingly, because its islands are well scattered over a large section of the Pacific, it has a maritime exclusive economic zone approximately the size of India. If it does submerge in the future, it could lead to increased jostling among major powers including China, India and the US for seabed mining rights, shipping lanes and geostrategic positioning.[31]

These dangers are not restricted to the small low lying islands. As around two-thirds of the world's population live near the coast, it is not surprising that 16 of the world's 19 largest cities including cities such as Shanghai, Mumbai, London, Washington and Paris are under threat from sea level rise. Additionally, sea-level rise compounds the effects of storm surges and other extreme weather events. India's naval bases situated around the Indian Ocean rim including Mumbai, Cochin, Karwar, Vishakhapatnam; the Joint Forces Command in the Andaman and Nicobar Islands and the Car Nicobar Air base will be adversely affected by tropical cyclones or tsunamis. China's investments in deep water ports and refueling stations in Gwadar, Hambantota, Chittagong, Sittwe and Kyaukphyu along vulnerable coastlines will also be susceptible. There are also long-term destabilizing consequences for internal security implications. For example, the on-going social disruption caused by the Katrina refugees is most obvious in neighbouring Houston. According to the National Hurricane Center, New York City is the fifth most vulnerable place in the US. The risk area includes coastal New York, New Jersey and Connecticut, an area with a combined population of around twenty million. Manhattan is only about three meters above sea level, with critical regional infrastructure, such as airports, even lower-lying. A major climate vulnerability study on the region for the US government's Global Change Research Programme has warned that by the end of this century, flooding may occur at least once every decade for two-thirds of transportation infrastructure facilities with elevations at or below ten feet above sea level. This sort of vulnerability leaves nations open to international pressure, uncontrolled population movement and economic stress.[32]

## Exclusive Economic Zones: Potential Conflict Areas

Under the law of the sea, an **exclusive economic zone** (EEZ) is a sea zone over which a state has special rights over the exploration and use of marine resources, including production of energy from water and wind. It stretches from the seaward edge of the state's territorial sea out to 200 nautical miles (370 km) from its natural coast. The exception to this rule is if a country's zone is adjacent and also overlaps against the zone of another country, in which case they usually split the difference equally and any point within an overlapping area defaults to the nearest state. States also have rights to the seabed of what is called the continental shelf up to 350 nautical miles (648 km) from the coastal baseline, beyond the EEZ.[33]

**The United Nations Environment Programme** (UNEP), University of Dhaka, and the World Bank have published a map that shows the potential impact of a one and a half-metre sea-level rise that could affect 15 -17 million people and 12 to 15 per cent of agricultural land, which is a loss of one per cent of national rise production in Bangladesh.[34] The Survey of India has been recording the sea level across 23 ports in east and west coast of India. Tide Gauge records indicate a rise of the sea level in the Bay of Bengal by 10 to 25 cms over the last century. More worryingly, the sea level is expected to further rise by another 50 cms at the turn of the 22nd century. However, drawing analysis from these data becomes complicated substantially as the region is also experiencing high subsidence due to the seismic activities of the Indian plate on the eastern boundary. Additionally, there is high sedimentation rate which means that particles in suspension will settle out of the water in which they are entrained, and come to rest against the coastline barrier. This would indicate that some of the areas along the coastline will also be expanding.

It is quite possible that rising sea levels may not flood Bangladesh, but, according to the IPCC, storm surges and cyclones in the Bay of Bengal are predicted to increase in intensity, causing flooding. Those two factors of environmental change alone have the potential further to exacerbate the two major international issues that climate change in Bangladesh might aggravate: increasingly desperate environmental refugees pushing towards India and tensions over maritime exclusive economic zones in the Bay of Bengal.[35]

One such hotly contested island in the Bay of Bengal was the New Moore Island or the Sheikh Mujib Island. Claimed by both India and Bangladesh amidst speculation over the existence of oil and natural gas, it was in a geostrategic position, at the mouth of the Hariabhanga or Haribhanga River, the boundary between the two countries. Recently, it was discovered that New Moore Island had disappeared, probably due to a combination of rising sea levels, changes in monsoonal rain patterns which altered river flows and land subsidence. The problem of land loss, with other islands such as Lohachara and Ghoramara in the Sundarbans region eroding potentially leading to maritime zone loss, is likely to be a prominent feature in the near future.

Changes to maritime zones based on changing coastlines might also affect Bangladesh's ability to exploit offshore resources. The coastline of Bangladesh is extremely difficult to define as it is considered to be extremely fluid with liquid mud. Determining a maritime boundary becomes very complex especially as Bangladesh shares the arc of the Bay of Bengal with India to the west and Myanmar to the east. Its maritime claim is shaped like a triangle, squeezed on both sides by its neighbours as it extends further out to sea. The bay itself is suspected of containing considerable hydrocarbon deposits, making offshore maritime claims particularly valuable. Flooding is a serious yearly phenomenon in Bangladesh, with water levels rising by between 13 centimeters and two meters. If its coastline were to retreat dramatically, in theory its maritime border would retreat commensurately, potentially completely squeezing it out of zones that are rich in hydrocarbons.

Similarly, it was reported in September 2009 that despite existing on maps for centuries, the tiny island of Bermeja, in the Gulf of Mexico, could no longer be found. The existence of Bermeja Island was crucial as Mexico was involved in a dispute with the United States to lay claim in the hydrocarbon-rich waters of the Gulf. It could by laying claim to the Island extend its maritime border by another 80 kms. The Mexican Government made numerous attempts by sending out expeditions to find the missing Island and even accused the United States of plotting its submergence. The US was quick to respond that since there was no island in sight, Mexico's claim over the extended area was invalid.[36]

Another case is the US–Cuba border which was agreed by a bilateral treaty in 1977 to be renewed every two years. The problem with the agreement reached is that the US shoreline that is used as a base measurement is down in the Florida Keys, an extremely low-lying region, while Cuba itself is relatively mountainous and not as likely to lose ground to rising sea levels. So, leaving the Bahamas aside, the hypothetical question is, if the Florida coastline retreats up towards the middle of the state, and Cuba stays more or less as it is, should the border be moved to reflect the new midpoint? That would put the entrance to the Gulf of Mexico in Cuban waters and, while southern Florida would be submerged, it would still be an impediment to shipping, meaning traffic would have to loop down through Cuban waters. Given that the boundary is confirmed bilaterally every two years, there might be a case under international law for Cuba or the United States to seek a renegotiation on the grounds that reality has changed as a result of sea-level rise. But it is likely to be international politics and security concerns, rather than international law, that will determine whether the boundary changes or not.[37]

From a **neorealist perspective**, the modern state views sovereignty and territorial integrity as the focal ingredients of increasing power and maximizing national interest. However, it has been clearly established that the emerging environmental changes pose a significant challenge to these concepts in the 21st century. If champions of environmental changes focus on highlighting the possibility of increasing conflicts over altering coastlines and maritime boundaries becoming a reality, states might be forced to eventually make an effort to cooperate and address these challenges in an effort to secure themselves from potential conflicts in the future. Instead merely expressing concerns over the sustainability of the environment for future generations will be dismissed by states, striving to compete furiously in a rapidly competitive world, as plain utopian or idealist pleas.

## References

1. United Nations Framework Convention on Climate Change (1992), Article 1, Clause 2, FCCC/INFORMAL/84 GE.05-62220 (E) 200705, p. 3 , See http://unfccc.int/resource/docs/convkp/conveng.pdf, accessed on 2 November 2011.
2. IPCC Fourth Assessment Report (2007), Working Group I, Annex II, Glossary, p. 78, See http://www.ipcc.ch/pdf/assessment-report/ar4/syr/ar4_syr_appendix.pdf, accessed on 25 September 2011.
3. See Cleo Paskal (2007), "How climate change is pushing the boundaries of security and foreign policy", Energy, Environment and Development Programme EEDP CC BP 07/01, Chatham House Briefing Paper, June, pp. 2-3, http://www.chathamhouse.org/publications/papers/view/108552, accessed on 18 September 2011.
4. Sushil Kumar Dash *Climate Change: An Indian Perspective*, Center for Environment Education, (India: Cambridge University Press, 2007), pp. 78-79.
5. *Ibid*, pp. 80-81.
6. *Ibid*, pp. 82-83.
7. See Suzanne Goldenberg, "Glacier lakes: Growing danger zones in the Himalayas", The Guardian, 10 October 2011, http://www.guardian.co.uk/environment/2011/oct/10/glacier-lakes-melt-himalayas?newsfeed=true, accessed on 11 October 2011.
8. n. 4, pp. 83-85.
9. n. 3, pp. 3-4.

10. United Nations Convention on the Law of the Sea (1982), Preamble, See http://www.un.org/depts/los/convention_agreements/texts/unclos/preamble.htm, accessed on 13 October 2011.
11. International Tribunal for the Law of the Sea, See http://www.itlos.org/index.php?id=15, accessed on 13 October 2011.
12. United Nations Security General Debate (2007), "Secretary-General calls for unity against climate change, better access to resources", 17 April, See http://www.un.org/Docs/sc/search2007.shtml, accessed on 8 October 2011.
13. Center for Naval Analyses (2007), Military Advisory Board Briefing, "National Security and the Threat of Climate Change", April, See http://www.cna.org/sites/default/files/Climate%20Change%20Briefing.pdf, accessed on 5 October 2011.
14. Cleo, Paskal, *Global Warring: How Environmental, Economic and Political Crises will Redraw the World Map*, (Canada: Key Porter Books Limited, 2010), pp. 144-148, 150-157.
15. *Ibid*, pp. 60-63.
16. "The Future of Arctic Marine Navigation in Mid-Century", Scenario Narratives Report, Global Business Network, May, 2008, See http://www.institutenorth.org/assets/images/uploads/articles/GBN-AMSA Scenario Narratives Report FINAL May 08 v1May.pdf, accessed on 30 September 2011.
17. "The Future of Arctic Marine Navigation in Mid-Century", Scenario Narratives Report, Global Business Network, March, 2008.
18. Arctic Marine Shipping Assessment, The Protection of the Arctic Marine Environment (PAME), "The Future of Arctic Marine Navigation in mid-21st Century", April 2007, See http://www.institutenorth.org/assets/images/uploads/articles/AMSA Interview Highlights.pdf, accessed on 30 September 2011.
19. See Linda Jakobson, "China prepares for an Ice-free Arctic", SIPRI Insights on Peace and Security, n. 2010/2, March 2010, http://books.sipri.org/files/insight/SIPRIInsight1002.pdf, accessed on 1 October 2011.
20. See Caityln L. Antrim, "The Next Geographical Pivot – The Russian Arctic in the Twenty-first Century", Naval War College Review, Summer 2010, http://www.usnwc.edu/getattachment/f8217b41-afd2-4649-8378-7b6c8a7e61d2/The-Next-Geographical-Pivot—The-Russian-Arctic-in, accessed on 3 October 2011.
21. See George A. Backus and James H. Strickland, "Climate derived tensions in Arctic Security", Sandia Report, n. SAND2008-6342, September 2008, http://est.sandia.gov/earth/docs/Tensions_in_Arctic_SecurityFinal.pdf, accessed on 25 September 2011.
22. See Frederick Lasserre, "China and the Arctic- Threat or Co-operation Potential for Canada", CIC China Papers, n. 11, June 2010, See http://www.opencanada.org/wp-content/uploads/2011/05/China-and-the-Arctic-Frederic-Lasserre.pdf, accessed on 25 September 2011.

23. See Dr. Vijay Sakhuja, "China- Breaking into the Arctic Ice", ICWA Issue Brief, http://www.icwa.in/pdfs/ib%20%20dr.pdf, accessed on 23 September 2011.
24. See Amitav Ranjan, "Next stop, next year: India in the Arctic", The Indian Express, 5 October 2006, http://www.indianexpress.com/news/next-stop-next-year-india-in-the-arctic/14133/, accessed on 18 September 2011.
25. See P. Sunderarajan, "New Indian research station at the Arctic", The Hindu, 2 July 2008, http://www.hindu.com/2008/07/02/stories/2008070253572000.htm, accessed on: 18 September 2011.
26. n. 20.
27. Seventh International Conference of American States, Montevideo, Uruguay December 26, 1933, See http://untreaty.un.org/unts/60001_120000/18/31/00035536.pdf, accessed on 21 September 2011.
28. British Broadcasting Corporation, (2009) – "Tuvalu vows to go carbon neutral", 20 July, See http://news.bbc.co.uk/2/hi/asia-pacific/8158604.stm, accessed on 15 September 2011.
29. See British Broadcasting Corporation, "Tuvalu declares emergency over water shortage", 3 October 2011, http://news.bbc.co.uk/2/hi/asia-pacific/8158604.stm, accessed on : 10 October 2011.
30. Columbia Law School and Republic of Marshall Islands Co sponsored Conference on "Threatened Island Nations: Legal Implications of a Changing Climate", http://www.law.columbia.edu/centers/climatechange/resources/threatened-island-nations, May 23-25, 2011, accessed on : 16 October 2011.
31. See Cleo Paskal, "Strange case of the disappearing islands", April 2010, http://www.nzherald.co.nz/world/news/article.cfm?c_id=2&objectid=10635956, accessed on: 7 October 2011.
32. See Cleo Paskal, "From constants to variables: how environmental change alters the geopolitical and geo-economic equation" International Affairs, October 2009, URL: http://www.chathamhouse.org/publications/ia/archive/view/163045, accessed on: 10 September 2011.
33. United Nations Conventions on the Law of the Sea, Preamble, Exclusive Economic Zone, Part V, Article 55 – 75, See http://www.un.org/depts/los/convention_agreements/texts/unclos/part5.htm, accessed on 23 November 2011.
34. n. 3, pp. 4-5.
35. n. 4, pp. 115-116.
36. n. 31.
37. n. 14, pp. 45-46.

# 3

# Environmental Rights, Human Rights and Sustainable Development

**Dr. S.R. Jitha**

*The issue of the relationship between environment and development is not of recent in origin. In ancient times Plato was concerned about environmental degradation and he said the environment had been turned into bones of wasted body: richer and softer parts of the soil having fallen away and the mere skeleton being left.*

**Human Rights and Environmental Rights** have many close affinities and the protection of one is essential for the realisation of other and for achieving sustainable development. The late twentieth century has witnessed an unprecedented increase in legal claims for both human rights and environmental goods. Almost all nations in the world have constitutional and statutory provisions to safeguard the fundamental rights of their citizens as part of human rights protection. Environmental degradation, depletion of natural resources, pollution of water bodies, lack of proper waste management and the deteriorating health level of people have prompted many nations to come out with legal frameworks to protect the environment at all levels.

**Human Rights** are the basic rights and **freedom to** which all are entitled. These rights are inherent to all human beings, whatever be the nationality, place of residence, sex, national or ethnic origin, colour, religion, language, or any other status. All are equally entitled to human rights without any discrimination. So **Human Rights** are those rights which are inherent in our nature and without which one cannot live as a human being (Daren 2005: 399). Equality and Justice are at the heart of all human rights. It includes adequate and decent food, water, health, freedom from slavery, fair treatment under law, shelter etc. All these rights are interrelated, interdependent and indivisible. These rights enable a person to develop his personality and lead a decent life on earth. Under the shadow of human rights all people are entitled not to starve, not to suffer from preventive disease, to have opportunity to better their economic condition, to have access to knowledge and information and to decide on anything that affect their life (Anita *et. al.* 2003: 4).

These basic human needs and values are at the foundation of universal ideas of human rights and which is in Article (2) of the Universal Declaration of Human Rights (UDHR 1948), which states:

> *"Everyone is entitled to all the rights and freedoms set forth in the Declaration, without distinction of any kind such as race, colour, sex, language, religion, political or other opinion, national or social origins, property, birth or other status. Furthermore, no distinction shall be made on the basis of the political jurisdictional or international status of the country or territory to which a person belongs, whether it be independent, trust, non self governing or under any other limitation of sovereignty."* (UNPI 2005)

**Environmental protection** and human rights protection have many commonalities. Environmentalists and human rights activists work together towards common goals. It is quite natural that environmental degradation or pollution has its repercussions on environment as well as human rights. This is because many of the environmental rights are part of human rights. **The Right to Life** becomes meaningless in the absence of a clean and safe environment. The nature of environment and human rights problems are similar in all countries. Such common concerns include water pollution, *i.e.* lack of access to drinking water, pollution of water resources, pollution due to toxins; air pollution that includes industrial air pollution, emission of sulphur and nitrous oxides, carbon dioxide and CFC emissions; land pollution; pollution due to dumping of waste, deforestation; destruction of ecosystems and biodiversity etc. In all these cases the destruction of natural resources invariably affects the very basic fabric of human rights.

When the environmental groups work for sustained utilisation of natural resources, for the greater commo. good and enjoyment of basic environmental rights of present as well as future generations, the human right groups argue for the welfare of the present generations and equitable distribution of available resources in the process of guaranteeing their basic rights. Thus, the focus of environmental groups is mainly intergenerational, *i.e.* distribution and enjoyment of natural resources in a sustainable developmental paradigm which meets the needs of the present generation without affecting the needs of the future generations to meet their own needs (WCED 1987: 43). The focus of human rights group is mainly intra-generational, criticizing the environmental movements for disregarding immediate human needs in the quest to protect bios, natural resources and basic needs of future generations.

The Constitution of India provides amble provisions for the protection of human rights and environment. A separate part (Part III) has been provided for the protection of basic rights, not only of the citizens but also of other population (it depends). As per the Directive Principles, the state is obliged to protect the environment, forest and wild life (Article 48A). It is the fundamental duty of the Indian citizen to "protect and improve the natural environment including forests, lakes, rivers and wild life" (Article 51A). Besides this, many environmental laws were enacted with the purpose of controlling pollution and promoting environmental conservation, which includes: Wildlife Protection Act, 1972; Water, Prevention and Control of Pollution Act, 1974; Forest Conservation Act, 1980; Environment Protection Act, 1986; Factories Act, 1987; and the Green Tribunal Act 2011).

During 1980's there underwent a sea change not only in administrative and legislative activities but also in judicial decisions. The Supreme Court of India widened the ambit of Article 21 (No person shall be deprived of his life or personal liberty except according to procedure established by law) to include Right to Safe Drinking Water, Right to Health, Clean Environment and so on. Maneka Gandhi's case was a starting point in this regard. In Francis Coralie case (AIR 1981), the Supreme Court ruled that **right to life is not** confined to mere animal existence, but extends to the right to live with basic human dignity. In Rural Litigation and Entitlement Kendra *vs.* State of Uttar Pradesh, the Supreme Court of India extended the scope of Article 21 to include the right to live in a healthy environment. The court upheld the right of people to live in a healthy environment with minimal disturbance to ecological balance (AIR 1985). This got concretized in Chhetriya Padushan and Subash Kumar cases, where the court declared (latter case) that "right to life enshrined in Article 21 includes the right to enjoyment of pollution free water and air for full enjoyment of life" (AIR 1991). By adopting international principles such as polluter pays principle, precautionary principle, sustainable development principle, public trust doctrine and the principle of absolute liability, the Supreme Court consolidated its position in strengthening "Right to Healthy Environment" concept under Article 21.

The landmark in the field of legal decisions was the Narmada Bachao Andolan *vs.* Union of India (AIR 1991a). In this case the Supreme Court recognized the relationship between the quality of human environment and the enjoyment of basic human rights:

> *"Water is the basic need for the survival of human beings and is part of right to life and human rights as enshrined in Article 21 of the Constitution of India. ...it is a matter of great concern that even after half a century of freedom, water is not available to all citizens even for their basic drinking necessity violating human rights resolution of UNO and Article 21 of the Constitution of India."*

Here comes the importance of environment-friendly development, popularly known as sustainable development. The term 'sustainable development' in place of development has become increasingly popular in discussions among all the social scientists, organisations, statesmen, politicians etc. (Allam & Stein 2004: 5). The industrial-technological-economic development registered by human kind during the past 100 years has not proved to be a real development in so far as it has created imbalances in the environment as well as among the nations. Degradation of environment resulting from unprincipled and excessive exploitation of resources of our planet earth has threatened to negate and has already adversely affected the development registered by various societies.

**Sustainable development** stands for sustainability and it represents an approach to development which is concerned with such fundamental concerns like poverty, environment, equality, democracy, development and peace (UNESCO 2010). The Brundtland Commission on Environment and Development defined sustainable development as *the development that meets the needs of the present generation without compromising the ability of the future generations to meet their needs* (WCED 1987: 43). The four indicators of sustainable development includes:

(1) Development in no way should lead to environmental degradation;
(2) Development should be in tune with the health of land, water, air, forests and other natural features of planet earth;
(3) The earth and its resources are the common possession of our civilisation and benefits must be shared equally; and
(4) Development in the present should in no way hinder or damage the developmental needs and abilities of the future generation.

**Sustainable development** involves the concept of "prudent management of available global resources and environmental capacities and the rehabilitation of the environment previously subjected to degradation and misuse" (Johan 2003: 15). It is the duty of the bureaucracy to ensure that development in no way should lead to environmental degradation and the development should be in tune with the health of land, water, air, forest and other natural resources. They also have to ensure that development should benefit all classes of people living in all parts of the world.

**Sustainable development** encompasses a number of principles: Basic needs of life should be available to all human beings; Consumption of natural resources should be utility based. Economic growth should be made within the safeguarded interest of the future generation to come; Ecological process should continue unabated; The development and maintenance of environment should run simultaneously; Regional imbalance in conservation of nature should be minimized or removed; International fraternity should be united to fight the menace of pollution; A long term view should be adopted for a better relation between human and species generation. Sustainable development thus is a moderate position between *extreme of no growth verses unlimited growth* and is based on the use of renewable resources in harmony with ecological system. It is moderate in the sense that there is no restriction on using the resources for development. However, there is restriction in using the resources exhaustively. Therefore sustainable development should *address* effectively environmental degradation.

The dominant development model of our time is 'economic globalisation'. Key to globalisation is commodification. New commodities are created with the expansion of markets to new geographical areas and new sectors that may not yet have been marketised. For the profit of multinationals the 'free gifts' of nature – water, air and other natural resources have been commodified and commercialised. Commodification of water is a direct assault on the commons and is striking at the roots of **sustainable development**. Profit driven exploitation of water has resulted in environmental degradation round the planet. Commodification seriously affected the availability, accessibility (both physical and economic) and quality of water, which are considered as the indicators of human right approach to water. Commodification of water hampers human rights as it denies common man access to safe drinking water. When the exorbitant increase in water prices directly affects the current generation, depletion of water affects the future generation by its scarcity. So it is clear that commodification of water resource is against the principle of sustainable development.

The Draft **Water Policy** of India 2012, failed to address the question of water security. It opened up the doors of water supply across the country to domestic and foreign companies, by advocating corporatization and private sector participation. A situation is emerging in which instead of providing assured drinking water, the right to purchase bottled water is being pushed in (*The New Indian Express* 2012: 8). This is a clear **violation of the human right** to water together with violation of judicial interpretation making right to water a fundamental right under Article 21 of the Indian Constitution (AIR 1991). Instead of opening the doors for free trade in water, the government must first assure availability of safe drinking water and take steps to conserve water sources and ensure its equitable resources.

For **sustainable development** and the protection of environment, waste management is necessary. In India, cities and towns generate 50 million tonnes of solid waste and 38 million litres of sewage every year. Local bodies entrusted with the task of disposing it have neither resources nor capability to do that resulting most of these wastes get dumped up and untreated. This not only has a hampering effect on the environment but also on the human right to health. Environmental degradation due to accumulation of waste materials results in the outbreak of diseases like plague, chikungunya, dengue and jaundice. Fall in waste managements normally affects the dual cardinal rights to pollution free environment and right to health. These interrelated rights can be protected only through better waste management. Development and economic growth of a society or nation lead to increased accumulation of different types of waste. There should be efficient system of waste management. Reducing and recycling are effective alternative to disposal.

India has some of the most impressive legislative acts on environmental issues in the world. But lack of resources, training, corruption of officials and lack of will often conspire to delay in implementation. Unsustainable development for immediate and narrow economic benefits have proved to be a havoc in many areas and thereby affecting the human rights of people generations after generations. Mega dam projects have evacuated a number of villagers and tribals from their home land and deprived them right to property, livelihood and culture. Pollution and other environmental harm have affected the agricultural lands and brought drought and climate change. It is very clear that only when environment is respected and the human life is in harmony with nature the people can get everything from nature for their happiness. When human beings tried to became the masters of the nature, all sorts of exploitations and the consequent sorrows followed. Thus, it is evident that only through sustainable development; human rights can be ensured forever. All efforts should be made to conserve natural resources and use renewable sources of energy as far as possible. Efforts such as effective rain water harvesting, solar and biogas plants, micro hydro electric projects etc. should be implemented at the government level. Big projects are not the only way to effect big development. Instead of that a series of small dams and bunds that require much less investment and cause minimum displacement is beneficial to human community as a whole.

## References

1. AIR (1981): *Francis Coralie Mullin vs. The Administrator, Union Territory of Delhi*, SC 746.
2. AIR (1985): *Rural Litigation and Entitlement Kendra vs. State of Uttar Pradesh*, SC 652.
3. AIR (1991): *Subash Kumar vs. State of Bihar*, SC 420.
4. AIR (1991a): *Narmada Bachao Andolan vs. Union of India*, 2 SCC 718.
5. Allam, Ahmed; Stein, Josephine (2004): "Science, Technology and Sustainable Development, A World Review," *Inderscience*, Vol. 1, No. 1.
6. Anitha, Cheria Edwin and Sriprapha, Petcharamesree (2003): *A Human Rights Approach to Development: A Source Book*, Books for Change.
7. Darren, Bryne J. (2005): *Human Rights: An Introduction*, Pearson Education India, New Delhi.
8. Johan, Rockstrom (2003): *Rethinking Water Management: Innovative Approaches to Contemporary Issues*, Earthscan, London.
9. *The New Indian Express* (2012 July19): *Editorial*, Kochi.
10. UNESCO (2010): "Teaching and Learning for a Sustainable Future," *UNESCO-UNEP.*
11. UDHR (2012): *Universal Declaration of Human Rights*, United Nations.
12. UNPI (2005): "The United Nations and Human Rights," *The UN Department of Public Information*, New York.
13. WCED (1987): *Our Common Future*, Report of the World Commission on Environmental and Development, Official Records of the General Assembly, Forty-second Session, Supplement No. 25 (A/42/25).

# 4

# Environmental Governance in India and Climate Change

*Dhanasree Jayaram*

*"There is now general agreement that the environment cannot be protected by perpetuating the poverty of developing countries. Their basic concern is with development and this is as it should be. But it is also no longer acceptable to take as given that a certain degree of environmental degradation and over-exploitation of natural resources in the cause of promoting growth is inevitable."*

***— Dr. Manmohan Singh, Prime Minister of India***

The issues of **environmental governance** especially with regard to climate change have gained salience in India in the past one decade. Any country's **environmental governance** does not stop at the duties and decision-making of the policy-makers; it extends to different levels – individual, community, State Government, Central Government and agencies, and international treaties. In this closely-knit system, the judiciary plays an important balancing role at all the levels.[1] However, this paper would concentrate more on the policy-making loop and its relationship with the rest of the system in terms of environmental governance and climate change policy. In this context, the issues of climate change and energy management would be discussed as the energy requirements of the country have been rising rapidly and at the same time the impacts of climate change have been worsening across the world. India has to grapple with the consequences of climate change on the one hand and the costs of mitigation and adaptation on the other. The question is whether the country should focus on alleviating poverty or on mitigation of climate change. The need of the hour is to understand that it is not a question of either-or; it is to synchronize alleviation of poverty and prevention of environmental degradation and regard development as the most important adaptation strategy; this could happen only if development is sustainable and not consumerist.

## CLIMATE CHANGE AND ASSOCIATED ECONOMICS: CENTRE TO THE ISSUE OF ENERGY MIX

### Climate Change and Energy Management: 'Two Sides of the Same Coin'

India's climate change policy is heavily contingent on its energy mix. India's energy policy in turn is driven by a number of factors including environmental concerns. First, any growing economy can sustain its growth only if it has a reliable supply of energy, usually in the form of electricity, gas and petroleum products. Second, the energy supplies are essentially strained by increasing household incomes. Third, over-reliance on imported resources including gas, crude oil, petroleum products and coal is a direct offshoot of negligible domestic reserves of fossil fuels. Fourth, the urge to adopt cleaner and efficient fuels and technologies emanates from the awareness of the environmental impacts of meeting energy requirements. Therefore, any policy that is implemented to mitigate climate change has a direct bearing on the energy policy of the country and vice-versa. According to an **International Energy Agency** (IEA) report (2007), coal/peat accounts for nearly 40 per cent of India's total energy consumption, combustible renewables and waste 27 per cent, oil nearly 24 per cent, natural gas six percent, hydroelectric power almost two per cent, nuclear nearly one per cent, and other renewables less than half per cent.[2] When talking about India's climate change policy, besides the energy mix, it is equally important to emphasize on its heavy dependence on imports to meet its energy demands for two reasons. First, India's financial resources are being exhausted for buying fossil fuels, which not only augments emissions but also reduces investment in the renewable energy research and development (R&D). Second, owing to lack of self-sufficiency, India might end up depending on the industrialized countries and other emerging economies for renewable technology in future. India's growth is theoretically and practically, therefore, determined by factors such as international markets, availability of global energy reserves, production capacities and geopolitics. Among the renewable energy sources, hydroelectric power has an installed capacity of nearly 38,000 MW, wind power has over 12,000 MW and solar power has nearly 18 MW. The share of renewable energy in installed capacity has grown from 9.7 per cent in

2009 to close to 11 per cent in 2010. In addition, the country has in excess of four million family-size biogas plants installed. The total projected capacity by the end of 2022 in wind power is 38,500 MW and solar power is 20,000 MW.[3] Most of the policies formulated by the Government of India in the field of renewable sources of energy are contained in the Five Year Plans brought out by the Planning Commission, especially the 11$^{th}$ Five Year Plan (2007-2012) and the other plans are enshrined in the Integrated Energy Policy approved by the Planning Commission in 2006 with the broad objective of meeting energy demand "at the least cost in a technically efficient, economically viable and environmentally sustainable manner."[4] **Nuclear energy** has become one of the major poles of the climate change debate especially in a country like India as it is not only being earmarked as a source of energy that could fulfil the electricity demand of majority of the population but also a primary source of mitigation of climate change. It is very clear from the country's establishment's gesture of showing green signal to the controversial Jaitapur plant on the 25th anniversary of the Chernobyl disaster that nuclear energy will certainly be on top of the agenda at least in the next 20 years.

## The Environment versus Development Debate

One aspect of India that needs to be understood lucidly is the basis for the existence of a whole range of poles in the country. The administrators have to grapple with three issues on each side of the divide while formulating climate change policy. On the one hand, the growing challenges from climate change are immense and the scientific predictions do not seem quite bright either; internationally, the pressure on India is rising to take multiple steps forward to address climate change and to reach a viable international treaty that would facilitate free flow of adaptation and mitigation funds into India; the dreams of achieving 'sustainable development,' which the establishment claims is entrenched in the Indian ethos, are contingent on the country's environment-friendly policies in the current scenario. On the other, a significant population of the country still subsists below the poverty line and thus, the rich-poor divide needs to be bridged; the middle class is growing at a rapid pace and their energy demands are escalating at an even faster pace; the so-called 'bane of democracy' as some would call it or 'realpolitik' as others would, requires the political class to be more concerned about the fulfilment of the immediate needs than the consequences of the current policies that could unravel themselves much later.

It has been noted that one of the major factors that has led to a decline in the foreign direct investment is the negative role played by the Ministry of Environment and Forests under the erstwhile minister, Mr. Jairam Ramesh. These sentiments were expressed at Davos 2011, in which a few foreign companies had expressed concerns about the stalling of various projects such as Posco, Vedanta etc. Some of the Indian politicians also alleged that his actions were partly responsible for a 36 per cent dip in the FDI in April-September 2010.[5] The Prime Minister himself has re-articulated India's age-old stand on this debate by stating that "poverty is the biggest polluter"[6] and that there needs to be a balance. This debate dates back to the days of Indira Gandhi's reign; when India was asked by Ronald Reagan in the early 1980s to "pull up its boots," Mrs. Gandhi retorted that India was not in a position to pull up its boots as the Indians did not have boots.[7] As a case in point, nearly 400 million Indians are reported to be without electricity.[8] Not only is part of the population cut off from the oil network, but also the country has one of the world's highest taxes on fossil fuels. The social repercussions of development and industrialisation such as displacement, shoddy compensation etc., therefore, have taken precedence over environmental ones. It is this amalgamation of social and environmental issues that has ensured indirect environmental justice to some extent. At the same time, **Environmental Impact Assessment** (EIA) has also been held responsible for the stalling of most of the developmental projects in the Northeast, a part of India that is said to be alienated from the rest of the country primarily due to lack of development. Dr. Manmohan Singh has asserted time and again that no regulatory framework should take the form of license permit raj that could take India back to the pre-liberalisation era.[9] Environmental concerns, thus from being a non-issue, has indeed turned into a 'thorn in the flesh' of the successive Indian Governments.

## ADAPTATION AND MITIGATION OF CLIMATE CHANGE: INDIA'S STRATEGY

### Stepping Stones to Climate Change Policy-Making

On the front of climate change policy front, the Government is focussing mainly on energy efficiency, energy conservation, renewable energy, afforestation, wasteland development and fuel substitution. The integration of climate change and sustainable development strategies is institutionalized through Ministry of New & Renewable Energy, the Bureau of Energy Efficiency, and the Technology Information, Forecasting and Assessment Council (TIFAC). The other institutions created by the

Government of India to not only measure climate change but also to brainstorm solutions include the National Committee to Assess the Impacts of Climate Change and the Prime Minister's Council on Climate Change. The former includes meteorologists, climate modellers, energy economists, representatives of key Ministries etc. and it is chaired by the Principal Scientific Advisor to the Prime Minister.

The institutionalisation is the first step towards mainstreaming; the next step would undoubtedly be designing the policy framework. It is the 'perspectival' number-game that has yet again played a crucial role in the stage of policy-formulation. This chronicle is essentially centred on the dispute between quantum emissions and per capita emissions. **The Green House Gas** (GHG) **emissions** are recorded to have increased at a compounded annual growth rate of 4.6 per cent excluding the agriculture sector.[10] The 2007 GHG estimates also make India the fourth largest emitter[11] and it is expected to become the third largest emitter of energy-related $CO_2$ by 2015 as per the predictions of the International Energy Agency.[12] Yet India's per capita $CO_2$ emissions are approximately one tonne per annum, compared to a world average of four tonnes per annum. This is the reason why Prime Minister Manmohan Singh has upheld that India's per capita GHG emissions would not exceed those of the developed countries even while pursuing pro-development or pro-growth policies.[13]

## Labyrinth of Perceptions and Incongruities

One of the important distinctions that the Indian establishment has stressed on is the one between climate change and climate resilience. While it clearly lays out the policy for climate resilience (that is governed by natural phenomena mostly) based on meteorological measurements, it lacks expertise on climate change as of now. India stands by the belief that climate change is not just an anthropogenic phenomenon[14] and at the same time, it blames the industrialised countries squarely for climate change. In short, India is still in the process of conducting climate change-related research and arriving at convincing conclusions. As far as the understanding of the public about climate change is concerned, a recent global public opinion poll revealed that only 19 per cent of Indians "believe that global warming is sufficiently serious and pressing problem to merit taking immediate action as it involves significant cost" in comparison to 42 per cent of Chinese and 43 per cent of Americans.[15] Therefore, the underlying fact is that India is yet to mainstream climate change in its policy in true spirit and letter.

Before going into the specifics of these policies, it is imperative to understand India's position on mitigation and adaptation. The concerned authorities do not see much of a difference between the two as according to them, both are complementary to each other; any mitigation strategy could also contribute to adaptation efforts and vice-versa. Though the country's focus is more on adaptation as of now, mitigation is not being overlooked. Majority of the policies and funds are oriented more towards climate resilience than climate change, that is, strategic knowledge, disaster preparedness and rehabilitation. "Adaptation has to be part of the way we live. We have to make up for the loss and make sure that loss does not happen in future," says Dr. Indrani Chandrasekharan.[16] Yet again, the two biggest factors that determine India's adaptation and mitigation strategies are – a booming economy and the increasing number of extreme weather events. But the unfortunate part is that as far as climate change is concerned, there is no sector-wise estimation of the capital that would be required for mitigation purposes. Since India does not have an obligation under any international agreement to take actions for mitigation, it needs to focus more on the adaptation front according to majority of the policy-makers. In fact, defence is not even earmarked as one of the sectors in the list of emissions inventory; defence has been identified as one of the biggest energy consumer in the world and every single developed country has been focussing equally on reducing emissions from the defence sector. In India, the Ministry of Defence (MoD) does not even have an environmental policy for the country's armed forces in place. Even in the area of adaptation, the country is purportedly in the process of assessing the risks of climate change and the plausible adaptation strategies.

## Policies and Prospects Galore

India has undertaken a series of actions and enacted a series of policies, which not only call for poverty alleviation but also ecological sustainability, regulatory and voluntary mechanisms and efficient strategies among others. **The National Action Plan on Climate Change** (NAPCC), approved by the Prime Minister on 30th June, 2008, is the core of India's climate change policy at the domestic level. Under its umbrella, the Government of India has adopted eight National Missions – **National Solar Mission, National Mission for Enhanced Energy Efficiency (NMEEE), National Mission on Sustainable Habitat, National Water Mission**, National Mission for Sustaining the Himalayan Ecosystem, National Mission for a Green India, National Mission for Sustainable Agriculture and National Mission on Strategic Knowledge for Climate Change. The most ambitious Mission that the Government of India has launched in the past few years is the Jawaharlal Nehru **National Solar Mission** (2010) under the brand name, "**Solar India**," which intends to deploy 20,000 MW of solar power by 2020 through a three-phase approach.

Some of the States have also introduced **State-specific Action Plans on Climate Change** (SAPCC). The Delhi Plan (2009-2012) gives an idea of what the Delhi Government has done and what it will do in future to complement the steps being taken by the Central Government under the aegis of the NAPCC. It takes account of the green agenda of the State, especially in the areas of air pollution, water, noise, municipal waste and greening. One of the concerns of the Delhi Government has been the paucity of the supply of natural gas that could come in the way of functioning of the natural gas-based power plants that have replaced the coal-based power plants. The promotion of solar heating devices, Compact Fluorescent Lamps (CFLs), Compressed Natural Gas (CNG) and bio-fuel, greening, waste-water treatment and reuse, generation of electricity from municipal waste, environmental education and training have been initiated by various governmental agencies.[17] Gujarat is one of those States which has even allocated a budget to invest substantially in the Clinton Climate Initiative for setting up of a 3000 MW Solar Park, other green solar projects, Jyotigram Yojana to reduce electricity transmission losses, Bus Rapid Transit System which has already received accolades worldwide for its services in Ahmedabad and is now being planned in Surat and Rajkot, state-wide drinking water grid, planting of mangroves etc. It is also the first State to form a separate climate change department.[17] Therefore, like the NAPCC, the SAPCCs have also largely been a mixed bag. At the outset, these plans seem to be restricted to low-hanging fruits which cannot be effective in the long-run and could be too little even in the present. One needs to go deeper into the impact of the actions such as the impact of the metro transport system on the number of private vehicles on the roads of Delhi or the impact of the closure of coal-based power plants on the Government's policy of regulation of electricity consumption patterns of the population and accordingly draw estimates of what could be in store for India in future, with and without large-scale use of green technology across the spectrum.

The Government has taken several steps to remove barriers that earlier restricted private players from exploring, extracting, converting, transmitting and distributing primary and secondary energy. Some of them include Electricity Act 2005, Tariff Policy 2003 and Petroleum & Natural Gas Regulatory Board Act 2006. Also, the promotion of use of renewable energy sources was reinforced by the introduction of feed-in-tariffs in 2008, Rural Electrification Policy 2006 and the New and Renewable Energy Policy 2005. Blending of ethanol with gasoline is being not only encouraged but also authorised across the country as evidenced by the Government's decision in 2003 to authorize a five per cent blending of ethanol with gasoline in nine States and 4 Union Territories in 2003, which was extended to 20 States and 8 Union Territories in 2006.[18] On the flip side, there are reports which indicate a certain rollback on the part of the Indian Government on the front of **bio-fuels**, especially jatropha due to lower production of jatropha seeds, rising food prices, fear of diversion of land for **bio-fuels** and its impact on food production, and the purported negative consequences of first generation bio-fuels on the environment. Based on these reasons, the erstwhile Minister of Environment and Forests, Mr. Jairam Ramesh rejected Executive Secretary, Christiana Figueres' suggestion that India should "explore business possibilities of jatropha plantations for **bio-fuels**" with private bio-fuel companies backed by the International Air Transport Association (IATA) in 2011.[19]

In addition, the Government has also taken steps to bolster disaster management efforts especially in terms of response to extreme weather events, such as infrastructure design, communication networks, protection of coastal areas, health care services and capacity building both at the regional as well as state levels. The Government has been pumping lot of funds into the development of arid-land crops and pest management; drought proofing programmes by which the adverse effects of drought on production of crops and livestock could be curtailed; these are the Crop Insurance Scheme and the Credit Support Mechanism that insures farmers against climate risks and facilitates extension of credit to farmers respectively.

## Future as Viewed through the Present

One of the biggest steps that India has taken in the post-Copenhagen scenario is to form an Expert Group on a Low Carbon Strategy for Inclusive Growth. The interim report of the Group under the Chairmanship of **Dr. Kirit Parikh** has come up with a series of options that could reduce India's emission intensity over a particular time frame. According to the report, the Government could bring down the emission intensity of India's GDP by 23 to 25 per cent over the 2005 levels if it adopts 'Determined Efforts' and 33 to 35 per cent over the 2005 levels if it adopts 'Aggressive Efforts' by focussing on the sectors of power, transport, industry, buildings and forestry.[21] While the former stresses on the strengthening and upgradation of the existing policies and the ones which are in the pipeline, the latter emphasizes on the introduction and implementation of new policies. Apart from the fact that the report fails to deviate from the 'business-as-usual,' it also does not look forward to decrease the electricity demand of the country. **Dr. Kirit Parikh**, on the other hand, defends the report by saying that it emphasizes on moving away from the 'business-as-usual' scenario; however, the fulfilment of ambitious targets requires huge amount of money.[22] It is extremely important for the Planning Commission to retrace steps to its Integrated Energy Policy report that gave equal importance to both increasing energy efficiency as well as decreasing the energy intensity. India's policy-makers promote energy efficiency as a short-term measure in order to bring down the energy intensity. They deem energy efficiency as the way forward and therefore, the key is to be as efficient as possible through technical progress and innovation. As **Dr. Parikh** observes, "Energy efficiency makes activities more profitable; the economy grows faster and the energy consumption increases. However, the energy intensity decreases."[23] There is a section of economists according to whom energy efficiency reduces demand in the course of time. It is believed that energy efficiency essentially leads to reduction in wasted energy besides the fact that the consumers would be expected to use lesser amount of energy to achieve the same level of utility. There are two sides to this debate. First, according to the '**Rebound Effect**,"[24] as the demand as well as the cost of using the particular resource decreases there would be a rebound in demand. Second, according to the "**Piggy Principle**,"[25] the consumers would rather try to achieve a higher utility at the same expense. Moreover, there is a limit to which energy efficiency can be increased and the energy demand would only increase with the increasing population.

Unfortunately, even the data presented in the report has come under the scanner for various reasons. First, the data generators are mostly government statistical agencies; however the estimates are generated by non-governmental agencies that may or may not be cross-checked before being used for framing policies. These non-governmental agencies could even be influenced by external entities in terms of financial and political agencies that could be detrimental to the country's interests. Second, as a report of the Centre for Science and Environment reveals, the data is "weak, outdated and not referenced." The review also concludes that the projected 2020 performance "has already been achieved or will be achieved soon" in some sectors while in others, the projected 2020 performance is "overly ambitious and will be difficult to achieve."[26] Yet it is also necessary to acknowledge that India is the first non-Annex I country to update its GHG Emissions Inventory. The Planning Commission has also defended itself by stating that the figures cannot be inaccurate since most of them are an outcome of mapping by the satellites. The future of climate change policy depends to a great extent on the subsequent reports of the group.

In the past two years, India has also shown commitment to levy carbon tax that would eventually contribute to a National Clean Energy Fund. Besides, it has also implemented various other measures such as the Bachat Lamp Yojana (Clean Development Mechanism Programme of Activity for mass distribution of CFLs), the setting up of a REDD+ (Reducing Emissions from Deforestation and Forest Degradation) Technical Group, the Solar Energy conclave that discussed the financial and technical aspects of the National Solar Mission for an effective implementation, among others.[27] The reality is hard to gauge with very little transparency on the findings of the conclave since the ambitious targets set by the Government could be achieved only if the investment is increased manifold. The Government's initiative to increase the forest cover by five per cent has reportedly failed; it could meet only one-third of the target. One could also argue that the Government should instead be commended for 'maintaining' the forest cover despite immense pressure from various quarters.

## Costs of Mitigation of Climate Change for India

The impact of $CO_2$ emission reduction strategies will come at a cost if India does not change its strategy in a manner that balances the growing population and the escalating needs of its population. Studies show that it could even lead to lower GDP and higher poverty. As per a study, "A 30 per cent $CO_2$ reduction over a period of 30 years using annual emissions reduction targets leads to a fall in GDP of four per cent and raises the number of poor by 17.5 per cent in the 30th year (that is, if 2000 were taken as the baseline, these changes would occur by 2030)." If a cumulative emission reduction target of 30 per cent is taken into consideration, then the fall in GDP would be 1.4 per cent and the increase in the number of poor would be 6 per cent by the 30th year. Moreover, the compensation for the loss in welfare would require immense capital inflows ($278 billion for annual reduction and $87 billion for cumulative reduction). However, it has been found that tradable emission quotas could make India carbon-efficient as India could transform itself from a net seller in the first 25 years to a net buyer in the later years.[28]

The best way to deal with the costs is to enhance the role of the Clean Development Mechanism (CDM) and Technology Transfer. India could also contemplate emissions trading as one of the options towards achieving obligations towards reducing GHG emissions. It is considered one of the most cost-effective incentive-based approach; however, a national-level emissions trading mechanism can only sustain itself if it is linked to the global/regional emissions trading mechanism. Also, there is a fear that it could get converted into a license raj system wherein the Government intrudes in the system in terms of not only setting the standards and monitoring, but also giving permit to the industries. At the same time, there is apprehension among the policy-makers about the benefits of the carbon trading system for the developing countries as it is contingent to a large extent on the competitiveness of the market, existence of future markets and the mechanism by which carbon is bilaterally traded in a project-by-project basis as envisioned under the CDM.

## The Saga Continues...

As far as India's energy management is concerned, India's fossil fuel consumption has increased manifold over the years and it is high time that the country shifts focus to renewable energy sources so that the next generation does not become a victim of the current generation's 'unsustainable' policies. Moreover, India's geography allows it to utilize various renewable sources of energy such as solar, wind and hydro. On paper, it is the lack of resources and increasing energy demand of an increasing population that have been the biggest stumbling blocks in renewable energy and technology investment. More than these two factors, it is the lack of political will that has retarded the process even though the authorities have shown some propitious signals. Besides, paranoia surrounding privatisation and autonomy have also led to the creation of a vacuum in the arena which the Government is struggling to fill. The costs of adaptation and mitigation are expected to be reasonably high, especially for developing countries like India. When it comes to the achievement of long-term sustainable development, one has to remember that benefits of adaptation and mitigation not only in terms of climate change but environmental degradation in general far outweigh the costs. Relocation of a nation state's critical infrastructure itself could ad infinitum exhaust its financial reserves leaving other development programmes unfinished or crippled. India also has to get itself out of the labyrinth of perceptions and definitions in order to boost its ethos of sustainable development rather than replicating the Western model of economic development blindly.

India is on the right track in what appears to be the Asian century as North America and Europe have already plunged into deep economic crisis. If India wishes to be a global power in the making as labelled by many analysts, it has to show more responsibility and character. Reports disclose that in 2010 developing countries invested more in renewable energy than the developed countries, especially Brazil and China. South Africa is also getting ready to launch its **South African Renewable Initiative** (SARI) despite financing concerns and other obstacles.[29] Therefore, it is imperative for India to pull up its socks and increase its renewable energy investment so that it does not lag behind the rest of the emerging economies in the world. Despite having a huge and flourishing Information Technology (IT) sector, very few innovations have been made on the front of renewable energy technology in the country. When there are no dearth of IT brains in the country, nothing should stop the Government from taking advantage of them and find long-term solutions. The policies framed by India tend to focus more on the low-hanging fruits and at some level, the loopholes in them could be exploited by the "growth-first stonewallers" to thwart the efforts of the "progressive realists" and the "progressive internationalists."[30]

## REFERENCES

1. Group Captain Manoj Kumar VSM, *Environment Change and National Security* (KW Publishers Pvt. Ltd. in association with Centre for Air Power Studies, New Delhi: 2011), p. 206.
2. Energy Information Administration, "India Energy Data, Statistics and Analysis – Oil, Gas, Electricity, Coal," *Country Analysis Briefs* (U.S.A. August, 2010), p. 1, see http://ei-01.eia.doe.gov/emeu/cabs/India/Background.html, accessed on 3 February, 2011.
3. See, "Renewable Energy in India: Progress, Vision and Strategy," Ministry of New and Renewable Energy, Government of India, pp. 8 and 14, http://www.mnre.gov.in/pdf/mnre-paper-direc2010-25102010.pdf, accessed on 15 July, 2011.
4. See, "Climate Change Mitigation Measures in India," International Brief 2, September, 2008, http://www.pewclimate.org/docUploads/India-FactSheet-09-08.pdf, accessed on 23 February, 2011.
5. See, "Davos: Development vs the Environment debate," *NDTV 24×7* (28 February, 2011), http://www.ndtv.com/video/player/ndtv-special-ndtv-24x7/davos-development-vs-the-environment-debate/189398, accessed on 10 March, 2011.
6. See, "Action louder than words," *Hindustan Times* (30 June, 2011), http://www.hindustantimes.com/StoryPage/Print/715796.aspx, accessed on 20 July, 2011.

7. Interaction with Air Commodore Jasjit Singh AVSM VrC VM (Retd), Centre for Air Power Studies, on 6 July, 2011.
8. See, Jeremy Page, "India looks to the sun for ambitious surge in green power," *The Times* (3 August, 2009), http://www.timesonline.co.uk/tol/news/world/asia/article6736726.ece, accessed on 15 June, 2011.
9. See, Manmohan Singh, "We need a regulatory framework that does not become license permit raj," *The Indian Express* (Delhi: 26 July, 2011), p. 11.
10. "Interim Report of the Expert Group on Low Carbon Strategies for Inclusive Growth," *Planning Commission, Government of India* (May, 2011), p. 23, see http://planningcommission.nic.in/reports/genrep/Inter_Exp.pdf, accessed on 20 June, 2011.
11. See, "India: emissions up 58%," *India Climate Portal* (May, 2010), http://www.indiaclimateportal.org/component/option,com_policy brief/view,policybriefdetail/id,24, accessed on 15 June, 2011.
12. See for more information, International Energy Agency, "World Energy Outlook 2007: China and India Insights," p. 3, http://www.iea.org/textbase/nppdf/free/2007/weo_2007.pdf, accessed on 7 February, 2011.
13. Ministry of Environment and Forests, Ministry of Power and Bureau of Energy Efficiency, "India: Addressing Energy Security and Climate Change, October, 2007, pp. 1-2, see for more information, http://www.moef.nic.in/divisions/ccd/Addressing_CC_09-10-07.pdf, accessed on 3 February, 2011.
14. *Ibid.*
15. John Podesta and Peter Ogden, "Security Implications of Climate Change 1: Expected Climate Change over the Next Thirty Years," in Kurt M. Campbell (ed.), *Climatic Cataclysm: The Foreign Policy and National Security Implications of Climate Change* (The Brookings Institution: Massachusetts, 2008), p. 100.
16. Interaction with Dr. Indrani Chandrasekharan, Adviser, Planning Commission, at Yojana Bhawan, New Delhi, on 13 July, 2011.
17. See, "Climate Change Agenda for Delhi 2009-2012," http://publicity.delhigovt.nic.in/public/eng/publication/climateChange0003.aspx, accessed on 9 June, 2011.
18. See, "Climate Change Action & Adaptation," Climate Change Department, Government of Gujarat, http://moef.nic.in/downloads/others/States-SAPCC-gujarat.pdf, accessed on 19 July, 2011.
19. See, "Why India must push for ethanol blended petrol," *Rediff Business* (27 July, 2010), http://business.rediff.com/slide-show/2010/jul/27/slide-show-1-why-india-must-push-for-ethanol-blended-petrol.htm, accessed on 27 July, 2011.
20. Nitin Sethi, "UN official lobbied for private biofuel firms during India visit," *The Times of India* (2 July, 2011), see http://articles.timesofindia.indiatimes.com/2011-07-02/developmental-issues/29729976_1_bio-fuels-jatropha-iata, accessed on 20 August, 2011.

21. See for more information, "Low Carbon Strategies for Inclusive Growth: An Interim Report," Planning Commission, Government of India (May 2011), p. ii.
22. Interaction with Dr. Kirit Parikh, Chairman, Expert Group on Low Carbon Strategies for Inclusive Growth, at Integrated Research and Action for Development, New Delhi, on 19 July, 2011.
23. Interaction with Dr. Kirit Parikh, Chairman, Expert Group on Low Carbon Strategies for Inclusive Growth, at Integrated Research and Action for Development, New Delhi, on 19 July, 2011.
24. Frank Gottron, "Energy Efficiency and the Rebound Effect: Does Increasing Efficiency Decrease Demand?," CRS Report for Congress (Washington, D. C.: 30 July, 2001), see http://www.ncseonline.org/nle/crsreports/energy/eng-80.cfm?&CFID=11262148&CFTOKEN=7028302, accessed on 19 August, 2011.
25. Marco Bertoli, "Energy Efficiency and its Impact on Energy Demand," *OilPrice.com* (28 February, 2010), see http://oilprice.com/Energy/Energy-General/Energy-Efficiency-and-its-Impact-on-Energy-Demand.html, accessed on 19 August, 2011.
26. "Comments of the Centre for Science and Environment on Interim Report of Expert Group on Low Carbon Strategies for Inclusive Growth by the Planning Commission of India," 6 May, 2011, p. 1, see http://www.cseindia.org/sites/default/files/Comments%20of%20the%20Centre%20for%20Science%20and%20Environment%20on%20Interim%20Report%20of%20Expert%20Group%20on%20Low%20Carbon%20Strategies%20for%20Inclusive%20Growth.pdf, accessed on 13 July, 2011.
27. See, "India: Taking on Climate Change, Post-Copenhagen Domestic Actions," Ministry of Environment and Forests (30 June, 2010), http://moef.nic.in/downloads/public-information/India%20Taking%20on%20Climate%20Change.pdf, accessed on 19 July, 2011.
28. Jyoti K. Parikh and Kirit Parikh, "Climate Change: India's Perceptions, Positions, Policies and Possibilities," *OECD* (Paris: 2002), p. 7, see http://www.oecd.org/dataoecd/22/16/1934784.pdf, accessed on 3 February, 2011.
29. See, United Nations Environment Programme, "Global Investments in Green Energy Up Nearly a Third to US$211 billion," http://www.unep.org/newscentre/Default.aspx?DocumentID=2647&ArticleID=8805&l=en, accessed on 28 July, 2011.
30. Navroz K. Dubash, "Towards a Progressive Indian and Global Climate Politics," *CPR Climate Initiative* (Centre for Policy Research, New Delhi: September, 2009), p. 1.

5

# Conservation Strategy of Sacred Groves Functioning as Carbon Sink in a Non Forested Region in Kerala

*Kannan C.S. Warrier*

## Introduction

Patches of vegetation protected on religious grounds are called sacred groves. **Sacred groves occur** in India and in other parts of Asia, Africa, Europe, America and Australia. In India, they are mainly distributed in the states of Andhra Pradesh, Chhattisgarh, Haryana, Himachal Pradesh, Karnataka, Kerala, Maharashtra, Manipur, Meghalaya, Orissa, Rajasthan, Tamil Nadu, Uttarakhand, West Bengal and the Union Territory of Pondicherry. According to the National Environment Policy of India, ancient sacred groves should be treated as possessing "Incomparable Values". They represent the past status of vegetation and biotic as well as biotic diversity of the region and are abodes of rare, endangered and threatened species. Many valuable medicinal plants and wild relatives of cultivated species are present in the groves which may have definite role to play in the future species improvement programmes. The total number of sacred groves in the country is likely to be between 100,000 and 150,000 (Malhotra, 1998) and the latest number of sacred groves known is 13,720 (Malhotra *et al.*, 2001).

## Sacred Groves of Kerala

**Sacred groves of Kerala** are generally referred as ***Kavu*** and they exist almost throughout the state. These groves are generally dedicated to serpent deities (*Sarpakkavu* in south and *Nagam* in north), Goddess Bhagavathy (*Bhagavathykkavu*) or Lord Ayyappa (*Ayyappankavu or Sasthamkavu*). Small groves dedicated to spirits, demons or ancestors (*Yakshikkavu, Madankavu* and *Appoppankavu*) are also common. In north Kerala, certain groves are called as *Daivakkvu* in general where a male God (Vishnumurthy, Siva, Vettakkorumakan, Kshethrapaalan, Gulikan or Kuttichathan) is worshipped. Groves exclusively dedicated to Vettakkorumakan and Gulikan are known as *Kottam* and *Mundya* respectively. **Sacred groves** of the state are mainly owned and managed by ancestral families, cluster of related families, village communities or temple trusts. Some are under the control of **Devaswom Board**, Government of Kerala.

Most of the sacred groves in Kerala are veritable sanctuaries of flora and fauna. Many of them can be seen in combination with sacred ponds and they also act as micro-watersheds of freshwater systems. Some groves give birth to streams and even rivers as in case of river Kavvai originating from Theyyottukavu in Kannur district (Mohanan and Prasad, 2004). A study conducted by the Tropical Botanic Garden and Research Institute, Thiruvananthapuram, Kerala revealed that structurally, the vegetation of the sacred groves is typically of tropical evergreen forest in general with several tiers or types of trees, climbers, shrub and undergrowth. Floristic diversity indices of the sacred groves of Kerala are equal or nearly equal to the forests of the Western Ghats (TBGRI, undated).

An early 19th century census report stated the number of sacred groves in the erstwhile province of Travancore alone in south Kerala to be around 15,000 (Ward and Conner, 1827). There is evidence on the presence of innumerable groves in the erstwhile Malabar (north Kerala) province also (Logan, 1887) and it could be estimated that a minimum of 30,000 groves existed in the state in the beginning of the 19th century (Induchoodan, 1996). However, the changing social values and religious beliefs have resulted in dwindling of these valuable resources. A report in 1995 showed that the total number of sacred groves in Kerala to be around 2000 (Rajendraprasad, 1995). On the other hand, Unnikrishnan (1995) reported the presence of around 10000 groves (*Sarpakkavu*) in the northern districts of Kannur and Kasaragod alone and after five years, he updated the number of sacred groves (*Kavu*) in these two districts to be nearly 1000 (Unnikrishnan, 2004). Balasubramanian and Induchoodan (1999) verified that the number of groves having an area of 200 square metres and above is only 761. Another report revealed that only less than 1000 sacred groves exist in the state and most of them are less than 10 square metres in extent (Mohanan and Prasad, 2004). Though the decline is certain, all the above information indicate the requirement of a comprehensive data base detailing the number, distribution, extent and biodiversity values of these invaluable treasure houses in the state.

## Significance of the Study

Alappuzha is the smallest of the 14 districts of Kerala (1414 km$^2$) with the highest population density (1492 persons per km$^2$). It is a sandy strip of land intercepted by lagoons, rivers, and canals the presence of which has given the appellation "The Venice of the East". **Alappuzha** is the only district in Kerala without natural forests. However, sacred groves of varying size are present in the area, which attract utmost attention as they are the only remnants of natural forests once present. No thorough studies have been conducted to assess the status of the groves present in this region. Therefore, an attempt was made to carry out an in-depth assessment of these natural resource pockets.

## Salient Results of a Case Study

Enumerated 1128 sacred groves and the total area recorded under these groves was 83.55 ha. Nearly 40 per cent of the groves had sacred pond associated with it. Considerable variations were observed with respect to extent of the groves and species composition. Area of these groves ranged from 0.003 to 36 acres. Most of the groves are abode of many endemic and rare plant species. A total of 687 plant species belonging to 493 genera and 127 families have been identified from these groves. Detailed phytosociological studies were undertaken in 24 selected and permitted groves. The major tree associations observed included (1) *Vateria indica – Hopea ponga*, (2) *Vateria indica – Holigarna arnottiana*, (3) *Vateria indica – Hopea ponga - Holigarna arnottiana*, (4) *Quassia indica – Holigarna arnottiana*, (5) *Quassia indica – Hopea ponga*, (6) *Calophyllum calaba – Carallia brachiata*, (7) *Olea dioica – Aporosa cardiosperma – Lannea coromandelica*, (8) *Cinnamomum verum – C. malabatrum – Hopea ponga* and (9) *Artocarpus hirsutus – Hopea ponga – Holigarna arnottiana*. Natural regeneration was mainly observed in *Artocarpus hirsutus, Caryota urens, Cinnamomum malabatrum, Holigarna arnottiana, Hydnocarpus pentandra, Quassia indica, Strychnos nux-vomica, Vateria indica, Adenanthera pavonina and Calamus rotang.*

## Major Threats to Sacred Groves

Many sacred groves in the district face threat due to the dense human population and change in socio-economic status. Break up of ancestral joint family system to nuclear families is the major reason for deterioration of these valuable resources. The family member who receives the portion of the land harbouring sacred grove would clear the vegetation by transferring the deities of the grove to selected temples in the State after offering expensive special rituals. Sacred groves are hence destroyed by sacred ways. **Sanskritisation** and changes in beliefs also attribute to this denudation. People strongly prefer to follow idol worship and for them, most of the tree species or vegetation in the groves are of no economic use. However, there are exceptions where the natural vegetation is preserved understanding its ecological importance. 'Ulladans', the tribal community of the district who are permitted to access the groves, collect canes and firewood indiscriminately. Overexploitation of the resources by them has lead to its retrogression to a great extent. Removal of litter along with the seeds from the floor has also resulted in retrogression by hindering the natural regeneration process. Exotic weeds namely, *Mikania micrantha, Lantana camera* and *Chromolaena odorata* overgrow the native species and play a major role in degradation. Various ways to conserve these valuable resources have also been discussed.

## Conservation Strategy

Sacred groves require complete protection from human interferences and are the only way to preserve these priceless treasures of nature. The small number of 'Ulladans' settled in the district generally do not maintain their traditional tribal way of life and have become one with the rest of the society. Hence, they can be made aware of the importance of the vegetation system and the rational and sustainable exploitation of the resources. People who clear the grove after transferring the deities to the serpent worship **temples for** various developmental activities should also be sensitized to avoid further damage. Officials of Forest Department, Research Organisations, **NGOs** and Educational Institutions should take lead in imparting knowledge on the functional role and importance of sacred groves. They also should help in ecological restoration of the retrogressing sacred groves by way of selecting and planting suitable plant species. The temple authorities can play a major role in conserving the existing sacred groves by not accepting the transfer of deities from these groves to the temple. In general, each sacred grove was found to possess its own unique biological, ecological, cultural and economic dimensions. A detailed database on important sacred groves containing all the vital information including soil type, nutritional status, flora, fauna, plant associations, population structure, cultural and religious aspects and management operations will help in prescribing site specific conservation strategy. Like any growing natural vegetation, sacred groves can also perform the function of carbon sequestration and contribute substantially towards the reversing the process of climate change. Financial supports / rewards to the individuals and trusts maintaining these groves will go a long way in preserving them intact for posterity.

## References

1. Balasubramanian, K. and Induchoodan, N.C. 1999. Can the endemics of the sacred groves in Kerala withstand human onslaught? In: Kumaravelu, G. and Chaudhuri, K.K. (eds), *Endemic and Endangered Plant and Animal Species of Eastern and Western Ghats*. Tamil Nadu Forest Department, Chennai, pp. 59-64.
2. Induchoodan, N.C. 1996. *Ecological Studies on the Sacred Groves of Kerala.* PhD Thesis. Salim Ali School of Ecology and Environmental Science, Pondicherry University, Pondicherry.
3. Logan, W. 1887. *Manual of the Malabar District.* Govt. Press Madras (Reprinted in 1906) pp. 185-186.
4. Malhotra, K.C. 1998. Anthropological dimensions of sacred groves in India: an overview. In: Ramakrishnan, P.S., Saxena, K.G. and Chandrashekhara, U.M. (eds), *Conserving the Sacred for Biodiversity Management.* Oxford and IBH, New Delhi, pp. 423-438.
5. Malhotra, K.C., Gokhale, Y., Chatterjee, S. and Srivastava, S. 2001. *Cultural and Ecological Dimensions of Sacres Groves in India.* Indian National Science Academy, New Delhi and Indira Gandhi Rashtriya Manav Sangrahalaya, Bhopal, 34 p.
6. Mohanan, C. and Prasad, G.A. 2004. The sacred groves of Kerala and their conservation. In: *Workshop Papers, National Workshop on Sacred Groves*, 16-18 September 2004, Kozhikode, Kerala. Ministry of Environment and Forests, Government of India and Department of Forests and Wildlife, Government of Kerala, pp. 44-55.
7. Mohanan, C. and Prasad, G.A. 2004. The sacred groves of Kerala and their conservation. In: *Workshop Papers, National Workshop on Sacred Groves*, 16-18 September 2004, Kozhikode, Kerala. Ministry of Environment and Forests, Government of India and Department of Forests and Wildlife, Governmnet of Kerala. pp. 44-55.
8. Rajendraprasad, M. 1995. Ph.D Thesis. University of Kerala, Thiruvananthapuram.
9. TBGRI, Undated. Available on the web:http://www.btisnet.nic.in/tbgri/page3.htm. Accessed on 7th April, 2004.
10. Unnikrishnan, E. 1995. *Utharakeralathile Visudhavanangal – Oru Paristhiti – Nadodisamskara Padanam (Sacred Groves of North Kerala – An Eco-Folklore Study)*. Jeevarekha, Thrissur, Kerala, 229 p.

11. Unnikrishnan, E. 2004. An ecofolklore inquest of sacred groves of north Kerala as centres of excellence in *in situ* conservation. In: *Workshop Papers, National Workshop on Sacred Groves*, 16-18 September 2004, Kozhikode, Kerala. Ministry of Environment and Forests, Government of India and Department of Forests and Wildlife, Government of Kerala, pp. 56-60.
12. Ward and Conner. 1827. *Geographical and Statistical Memoir of the Survey of Travancore and Cochin States.*

# 6

# Environmental Governance in India: Role of Local Self-Government Institutions

*Dr. Rose Mary George*

**Abstract**

*Environmental governance is significant at the academic and empirical level as it is critical to the management of natural resources. Natural resource management was highly decentralised and community oriented during pre-British India. While the colonial regime centralised the management through nationalisation the post-colonial globalised regime tries to privatise the natural resource management which is encountered by movements towards decentralisation. This paper is an attempt to explore the transformation of the resource management regimes in the light of the increased role of LSGIs. The first part of the paper deals with the historical developmental pathway of environmental governance in India while the second part deals with the role of Panchayats in managing resources.*

In traditional societies formal institutional environmental governance was absent since resources were owned by no one but belonged to everyone. Resource scarcity was not experienced and all natural resources were freely available to all which reduced the scope for conflicts and institutions of management. This governance system sometimes referred to as the **Open Access Regime**. As the human population increased, demand for the natural resources and their products increased which called for certain institutional governance by means of communalisation or nationalisation. Before the intervention of state communal arrangements came into practice, in which there exists certain formal communal institutions for the exclusion of non-users. Resources are classified as public property or state property since its nationalisation. Parallel to nationalisation the process of privatisation also took place in India which allowed treating resources as private property.

A property governance regime is a system or set of institutional arrangements or working principles of rights and duties characterising the relationship between co-users to one another with respect to the basic management of resources. The basic requirement of a property governance regime is an authority system or institutional arrangements like central, state or local governments/resource development committees/ user groups that can guarantee the rights of the users (Marothia, 2005). The institutional arrangement define who can control the resource and how the techniques are applied and effective functioning of these system depends on the existence of appropriate institutions either local and informal or community–based and government sponsored (Bromley, 1991). As happened elsewhere the absence of environmental governance in India demanded for a coordination system especially when the resource becomes scarce, either due to deterioration by natural process or due to destruction by lack of maintenance. Under these circumstances free riding becomes an effective means to capture the resource. In other words each resource user places his self-interest above the community interest and use more and more till the resource is completely degraded.

The primary governance model in India came into existence before state intervention. Communal arrangements came into practice, in which there exist certain formal communal institutions for the exclusion of non-users. In this system the resources were identified as communal or collective property (property of an identifiable group) and the governance regime was known as Communal or Collective Property Regime. In this system of governance user rights for the resource are controlled by an identifiable group and are not privately owned or managed by governments; there exists rules concerning who may use the resource, who is excluded from using it and how the resource should be used (Berkes, 1989). Here community based resource governance system prevails over property where individuals have claims on collective good as members of a recognized groups. This group of local people provides the work team for the ownership, control, maintenance and equal distribution of the concerned property, which is assigned to them. Generally, these governance systems are working at the village and sub-village levels share a common culture, knowledge of the resource. As such, these systems are not only means of livelihood but also a way of life (Singh, 1994).

Finest examples for **community management** can be traced back to Pre-British South India where communities managed water collectively through a system called '**Kudimaramath**' (self-repair). In this system a peasant paid 300 out of 1,000 units of grain he or she earned to a public fund and 250 of these units stayed in the village for maintenance of commons and public works. Later these units went straight to the East India Company and maintenance revenue was lost; as a result the commons systems were destroyed (Shiva, 2002). An increasing number of scholars are in support of collective management like Elinor Ostrom, who wrote extensively on this subject. **Vadana Shiva** in her book 'Water Wars' certifies that the Chobala Pond in Mundalana village is still communally maintained and serves the water needs of ten villages.

Though state intervention reduced the scope for communal arrangement, still collective governance systems can be seen in the management of forest resources, irrigation, etc. In the working of Water User Associations (WUAs) under Participatory Irrigation Management (PIM) principles of collective property regime can also be found. Water User Associations are new forms of farmer's organisations in irrigation management aiming better participation and efficiency. Andhra Pradesh is the first state in the country to enact the Andhra Pradesh Farmers Management of Irrigation System Act, 1997 (APFMIS Act), making the formation of WUAs mandatory for management of irrigation. In these projects the local communities/resource user's group and state or local government share the responsibility of managing water resource distribution within a command area beyond the outlet of the water distribution network, by combining appropriate institutional skills of local resource users and technical, administrative and financial resources available from the state (Marothia, 2005). These formal institutions are creating for effective management and conflict resolution to ensure environmental justice by equitable distribution of resources. Generation and accumulation of power is present in this system. Different from this formal arrangement an informal communal property regime without formal institutions can be seen, in places where water is shared as a common good. The cooperate use of one well, pond or (temple ponds, panchayat ponds and wells) or an aquifer between the villages or among these villages themselves is an example for an informal communal property regime. Apart from formal institutions power generation is absent in this system.

In state property regime, the secure claim rests with the government; ownership, control and the responsibility for equal distribution is held by the nation-state. The government fully acquires a resource by nationalisation and manages it as state property or public property or state intervenes in the existing resource management system by imposing certain rules and regulations to prevent exploitation. The government then needs to develop and establish an apparatus or administrative machinery to provide for the governance of the resource (Singh, 1994). Many developed and developing countries, especially socialist countries were followed the path of nationalisation including India. In India much of these processes have started with British rule. Though these policies were not suit to the interest of the local indigenous people, they have not changed yet. For instance in the wake of nationalisation, state intervention resulted in implementing major and minor irrigation projects which have improved the egalitarian distribution of water. But lack of transparency and unaccountability of bureaucracy are the main hindrances in the successful operation of nationalised projects.

In private property regime the claim rest with the individual or group who use the resource; property is amenable to private appropriation only and user rights are highly exclusive (Bromley, 1989). Many scholars are of the view that the problems of free-riding and tragedy of commons can be resolved by enforcing private property regimes, because the resource becomes private property. In India cases of privatisation of common resources has been enforced through both legal and illegal means, by land reforms and encroachment respectively (Singh, 1994). When the user uses the common property according to his need private property regime starts to prevail until the state or community intervenes through well defined laws and regulations or unwritten laws among the neighbours started to rule. In contrast to community management or state management, rules and regulations to prevent overuse is absent in this system, as such exploitation through monopolisation would become the natural consequence.

The contemporary western view is in favour of privatising the resources and private property regime is taking hold in a global level. The privatisation agenda has found its way into several national policies across the globe since globalisation became the catch words of superpowers. Market-oriented policies have developed by the state in order to cope with the **Structural Adjustment Programmes** (SAPs) as part of the **neo-liberal economic policies**. Consequently, the state is being put under pressure by these international policies is trying to readjust to this new situation by privatising its goods and services. The state is developing new ways and means to commercialise its goods including common properties. Indeed much of the privatisation policies have their origin in the process of globalisation and related dynamics of liberalisation and privatisation (Finger and Allouche, 2002).

Contemporarily, the private ownership-based water management systems are penetrating extensively into the rural and urban areas. While the penetration in urban centers is largely through the privatisation of water supply system, water privatisation in rural areas have a different pattern. The limited water supply institutions of the state governments and local self-governments notwithstanding the water supply and distribution system in the Indian rural areas was mostly organised in community lines. Henceforth, water privatisation in rural context refers mostly to the official issuance of extraction rights of ground and surface water to private monopolies. The interest of the poor section is slightly accommodated in such contexts and they are ousted from the mainstream political system and the new private property resource governance regime. They have emerged as a new class of marginalised sections and united under a common platform to fight against the globalised forces.

## Protest Movements

It is true that grassroot based struggles of local people against the exploitation of natural resources has not been an isolated phenomenon. Beginning from the colonial times, the endeavours of the Indian state to take control over the natural resources had met with protest of the local population. While protests against the British state were largely subsumed by the national independence struggle, the post-independent phase witnessed the emergence of numerous protest movements. The post-independent Nehru government embraced a developmental scheme that gave primacy to the implementation of big projects such as dams, to facilitate agricultural production. Industrial plants also found prominence in the nation-building project. Mass displacement and deforestation was the detrimental impact of most of these projects and there were significant protest at the local level. The fact that the most anti-environmental programmes implemented by the post-independent Indian state did not meet with immediate local opposition probably because of ignorance and lack of political consolidation. Again green revolution was characterised with the exorbitant use of artificial fertilisers and it had proved to be detrimental to the land and water resources. However, the rationale of increasing food production to combat the existent food shortage was more or less appreciated by the Indian people.

Rather 1970s witnesses the emergence of a wide spectrum of movements that can be clubbed under the category of environmental movement. It is during this period environmental issues emerge across the world emerged as an important aspect which no national government can afford to neglect while framing its development policies. In a sense, the Indian movements like Chipko and Narmada indebted heavily to the settling in of environmental consciousness across the globe. This is regardless of the fact that the Indian state took a pessimistic attitude towards the shooting up of environmentalism and environmental consciousness across the globe. Eventhough there is considerable differences with regard to the nature of environmentalist groupings emerged in 1980s and 1990s, there is lot much in common between these groups. It is clear that the movements spurred due to poor environmental governance and failure to accommodate the local interest. In the case of societies with limited integration with the market processes, for example a greater portion of the Indian society, private ownership had not been the dominant mode of protecting the resources within a given locality. A wide array of social practices was prevalent all over the country aimed at protecting and ensuring the sustainable use of common resources. In the meanwhile it should be noted that most of the community ownership systems existed in India were of exclusionary in nature, from the time when the caste-based access regime prevailed in India over centuries.

The prevalence of caste system affected detrimentally the public access to resources in a multitude of ways. For instance a greater number of the Indian population was denied access to public water sources due to their lower caste origin. There are lots of documented instances in which the higher castes population deny the right of lower caste people to access village ponds, public wells, etc. The CSDS (Centre for the Study of Developing Societies) survey in 1996 identified shortage of drinking water as the most important problem faced by the rural people of India. Moreover, there were also documentations regarding the existence of segregation within the lower caste groups. The fundamental point is that notwithstanding the existence of socially determined modes of resource ownership there are widespread occurrences of exclusion on the basis of caste, gender, etc. However, the post-colonial Indian state had initiated steps to strike down the anti-egalitarian bias of the Indian social system. In addition to abolishing the practices of caste system, the modern capitalist Indian state had strived for ensuring state control over the resources. In a sense, the interventions of the post-colonial state have ensured the public access to common property that was essential to the livelihood requirements. But it should be noted that the state failed in its attempt to accommodate the local interest under state property regime.

## Relevance of Local Self-government Institutions

The **community management systems** had not been wiped out by the intervention of the state through legislations and other forms of surveillance tactics. The best example in this regard is the water scenario in India. Ever since the initial years of independence, the successive governments have enacted a wide array of legislations to regulate the control and use of public water resources in an egalitarian manner. However, various types of community based local resource management systems still proved to be critical for the Indian population. Many hybrid varieties of resource management systems originated in the due course. By hybrid varieties the author meant the new patterns of resource management patterns which are evolved out of the state intervention in the existent community management regime. Because state intervention found to be ineffective in places where community systems are highly dominant and efficient. In many places these systems merged together and provided new models of semi-governmental arrangements varying in the degree of state involvement. These governance models accommodative of the local interests reflects the importance of local self-government institutions in managing natural resources.

For instance community based institutions such as *Pani Panchayats* and Van Panchayats are functioning in India years ago. The *Pani Panchayat* experiment was begun at Naigaon, Maharashtra with active involvement of local communities under the leadership of Shri. Vilasrao Salunke. The movement of equitable water rights, which was popularly termed as **Pani Panchayat**, spread all over Maharashtra and to many other Indian states. In Orissa the government has taken up the PIM, covering all the irrigation projects in the state. The Orissa Farmers Management of Irrigation Systems Act 2002, called The Orissa *Pani Panchayat* Act came into being in 2002. As first step a part of the network of the canal system was handed over to the farmers for its Operation and Maintenance (O&M) through *Pani Panchayat* or WUAs. The farmers were helped to organise water distribution in their jurisdiction, resolve disputes, if any, and adopt their own crop planning, etc. (Mahapatra, 2006). In the case of Van Panchyats it is found that, grassroots organisations have tremendous potential in ensuring people's participation. Studies shows that due to over-centralisation and beaurocratic control it cannot function effectively (Saxena, 1997).

The *Jalanidhi* project in Kerala also provides a central role to the grama panchayaths in implementing community based water supply projects. This model has demonstrated successfully an equitable, inclusive and decentralised delivery system to a certain extent. *Jalanidhi* is expanding all over Kerala for large water supply schemes with more involvement of grama panchayaths. Community based organisations are engaged in protecting sacred groves and community lands could also be found in many parts of the country. The recent emergence of Participatory Irrigation and Forest Management systems is another instance in this regard. Under **Participatory Irrigation Management** (PIM) farmers involve in planning, design, construction, operation, maintenance, monitoring and evaluation of the irrigation system.

## Constraints over Power

The passing of **73rd amendment** can be viewed as a culmination of many attempts towards empowering the panchayats in India. After this amendment the states too have passed conformity legislations to meet their legal obligations. These acts have passed with a view to ensure more people's participation in planned development, local government affairs, preparation of plans and implementation of schemes for economic development and social justice. Though there are constitutional provisions for empowering the panchayats, its efficient functioning depends on the devolution of powers and resources. Despite the fact that the panchayats in India performed better in achieving political participation, economic development and social recognition after the 73rd amendment they are still embedded with problems like illiteracy, bureaucratic control, elite capturing, lack of financial resources and powers, etc. In addition to this, the absence of regulatory power over the natural resources poses another threat to its local autonomy and stability. The resource monopolies took control over natural resources like sand, water, soil, etc. and violated the human rights.

Kerala centered around the discussions related to decentralisation in India for about a decade. Because the state achieved a unique place in experimenting with decentralisation. **The Kerala Panchayati Raj** Act, 1994 (KPRA) is a milestone in its attempt towards decentralisation in the rural level. But the instance of Perumatty Grama Panchayat prompted a serious discussion among academia regarding the validity of **Kerala Panchayati Raj Act** in the context of executive and judicial interpretations and moreover regarding the power of panchayats in protecting natural resources. Perumatty panchayat got wide attention as it presents a unique fight against an MNC, Coca-Cola, where water rights of the people get violated by the uncontrolled extraction and pollution of ground water by its plant in Plachimada. The posture of Kerala judiciary and state government in this issue questions the validity of 73rd amendment and reflects the extent of decentralisation in Kerala society. The panchayath faced many hurdles in its fight against an MNC. The Kerala High Court (KHC) in one of its judgment ruled that the "pancahayat has no ownership about such private water resources in effect denying the proprietary rights of the occupier".

This is evident from the **Kerala Panchaythi Raj Act** 1994. KHC pointed out the lapse of a provision in KRPA which identifies the groundwater as a public property and the authority of panchayats over it. Section 218 of the KPRA vested the authority over public water courses in the panchayat. But public water courses include the beds and banks of river streams, irrigation and drainage channels, canals, lakes, backwaters and water courses and all standing and flowing water, springs, reservoirs, tanks, cisterns, fountains, wells, kappuschals, standpipes and other water works. It excludes ground water, because ground water is considered as the sole property of the owner of the land. It should be noted that this lacunae exists regardless of the fact that the Plachimada struggle bring out the various dimensions of the intervention of local self-government in the management of natural resources.

The fight of Perumatty Panchayat points to the importance of amending the **Kerala Panchayati Raj Act** 1994 in such a way that grama panchayats will get more power over natural resources in general and water in particular. Perumatty is the second panchayat in India which fought and won against an MNC. The first case is that of Goa, where a gram panchayat fought against an MNC, DuPont, and made it quit. The fight of Kaledara Panchayath in Rajasthan is the third instance in this context. The disappointing factor is that barring few states the State Conformity Acts have not given panchayats the power to give license to factories and industries. In the case of Goa, Kerala and Rajasthan this power have been diluted and took away by the states themselves.

## Conclusion

Ever since the constitutionalisation of Panchayati Raj system in 1993, majority of the policy makers in India started thinking about the possibilities opened up by the decentralisation of political and economic power. There are lots of policy studies that looked at impact of local self-governments in the socio-economic development at the grassroot level. But there had not been any serious attempt to look into the possibilities opened up by Panchayati Raj institutions in regard to the management of natural resources. Local government can play a vital role in the management of natural resources as it is accommodative of the local interest. The recent development across India in the wake of increased role for local governments with resource management presents a new paradigm shift in the resource governance regime. The potential of local governments have to be explored with a view to protect the natural resource from its possible over exploitation. In the case of Kerala, institutions such as KILA (Kerala Institute of Local Administration) can conduct policy related studies linking resource management with decentralisation processes. In the case of other Indian states where the Panchayati Raj system implemented only in a limited degree, there should be policy related enquiries pertaining what can be done under the existing institutional frame work. Such explorations will amplify the potentialities of LSGIs in natural resource management.

## References


1. Berkes, Fikret (ed). (1989): *Common Property Resources; Ecology and Community–based Sustainable Development*, London: Belhaven Press.
2. Bromley, Daniel W. (1992). *Making the Commons Work; Theory, Practice and Policy,* California: ICS Press.
3. KRPA (1994), *The Kerala Panchayati Raj Act, 1994*, The Law Department, Government of Kerala, Secretariat.
4. Mahapatra, Sushanta Kumar (2006), 'Functioning of Water Users Associations or Pani Panchayat in Orissa: Principle, Procedure, Performance and Prospects', Research Paper, in workshop 'Water, Law and the Commons', International Environmental Law Research Centre (IELRC), 8-10 December 2006, Delhi.
5. Marothia, Dinesh. K (2005), 'Institutional Reforms in Canal Irrigation System', Lessons from Chattisgarh, *EPW*, June 9, 2005.
6. Ramulu, C. H. Bala (2003), 'Water Resource Management Reforms in Andhra Pradesh', *The Indian Journal of Public Administration*; Special number on Water Resource Management: Issues and Strategies, Vol. XLIX: 475 - 488.
7. Ravi Raman K. (2007), 'Plachimada Resistance: A Post-development Social Movement Metaphor', in *Aram Ziai, Exploring Post-development: Theory and Practice, Problems and Perspectives*, Routledge, London and New York.

8. Ravi Raman K. (2005), 'Corporate Violence, Legal Nuances and Political Ecology: Cola War in Plachimada', in *Economic and Political Weekly,* June 18.
9. Shiva, Vandana (2002). 'Water Wars, Privatization, Pollution and Profit', New Delhi: India Research Press.
10. Singh, Katar (1994). *Managing Common Pool Resources; Principles and Case Studies*, New Delhi: Oxford University Press.

# 7

# Environment Development and Human Rights Concern: The Case of Adivasis of Kerala

***Dr. Biju Lekshmanan***

**Abstract**

*Climate change poses a severe threat to humanity especially the structurally disadvantaged sections of the society, more particularly the Adivasis. As you know climatic change is the historical result of grabbing the fossil fuels by the global elites. The far reaching consequence of the climatic change has been a subject of discussion all over the world. In many areas in India, especially in Kerala the adivasis and other indigenous peoples are struggling to save their natural resources from deforestation and from further expansion of mono-crop plantations. Many are searching for ways to effectively adapt to erratic rainfall, drought and other projected impacts of global warming, and for ways to mitigate its cause.*

*Several alternatives have been developed all over the world to tackle the consequences of climatic change at globally and locally. But some of these efforts have negative consequences and pose threat to the livelihood of the indigenous people especially the Adivasis.*

*The paper looks into the impact of REDD and REDD Plus and how the Forest Policy of the government of India adversely affects the livelihood of the Adivasis in India in general and Kerala in particular. Land grabbing and consequent alienation from homeland and displacement are the major human rights issue among the Adivasis.*

*The paper also looks into the potential impact of climatic change on the ecosystem and tribal communities and their livelihood practices. It also discusses the values of the traditional knowledge and the adaptation practices of the Adivasis for their survival and the preservation of ecosystem and sustainable agriculture.*

## Introduction

Climate change poses a serious threat to the lives and livelihoods of all people. The historical result of the grabbing of fossil fuels by global elites, climate change today is already devastating the lives of millions. But what few realise is that some of the methods proposed for tackling climate change can themselves have very destructive effects. In the guise of dealing with climate change, powerful interests are continuing to grab resources. Poverty among adivasi and indigenous women, and thus their comparatively greater vulnerability to climate change, has now become embedded in the structural inequalities of the larger, external social, political and economic institutions that determine legal rights and ownership, and economic livelihood options.

A new international climate scheme called **"Reducing Emissions from Deforestation and Degradation of forests" (REDD)** is a part of international negotiations around climate change. REDD basically is a scheme intended to channel money from rich countries to developing ones for the purpose of protecting their forests. Unfortunately, REDD and its latest avatar, REDD-plus, have become part of the Copenhagen Accord.. While it sounds wonderful on paper, REDD is actually a facade for what will become a massive land grab - with devastating consequences in India and around the world.

## Incidents of Land Grabbing in the Guise of Afforestation

Afforestation programmes usually take place on forest land classified as "degraded forest", or on revenue "wasteland" in case of compensatory afforestation. However, the Forest Department classifies all forest land that has less than a certain percentage of tree cover as degraded forest. Hence grasslands, village fallow lands, grazing areas, and lands that forest dwellers are cultivating (but do not have recorded rights on), but which are recorded as forest land, are all hence classified as degraded forest.

Plantations on such lands have hence become a standard method by which the Forest Department establishes its control over them. Further, in case of "**compensatory afforestation**" *i.e.* plantations meant to "compensate" forest destroyed for projects etc. the Forest Department frequently takes over revenue lands and notifies them as protected or reserved forest, even though these lands too may be grazing areas, common lands etc.

After the passage of the **Forest Rights Act 2006**, the Forest Departments of many States have increased plantations on people's lands in order to block them from claiming rights. Most evictions after 2006 have been linked to plantations. Some examples: in Khammam District, Andhra Pradesh, 10,000 hectares of forest land were allocated for compensatory afforestation. The land included the community lands of the Konda Reddi adivasi community, who protested against this land allocation (which was made without consulting or even informing them).

In several cases in Rajnandgaon, in 2008, forest dwellers were evicted from their lands in order to use the lands for plantations.

Under the 2006 **Forest Rights Act**, communities have rights to all these items as well as the right and power to manage such "community forest resources". The Forest Department, however, is now using compensatory afforestation to get these lands under its sole control. This directive is clear evidence of that, for it states that precisely such community lands should be used for compensatory afforestation and subsequently converted to reserved forests. This directive is in force till date.

In the **Copenhagen Accord** that India and other countries agreed upon in Copenhagen, repeated references are made to a scheme called "**REDD plus**". Paragraph 6 of the Accord says:

> *"We recognize the crucial role of reducing emission from deforestation and forest degradation and the need to enhance removals of greenhouse gas emission by forests and agree on the need to provide positive incentives to such actions through the immediate establishment of a mechanism including REDD plus, to enable the mobilisation of financial resources from developed countries."*

"**REDD plus**" has been left undefined. In fact, the negotiations have left the question of what kind of forest protection will be financed, and how this financing will be done, open for further discussions. As per its earlier submissions, the government of India wants to: Include afforestation and plantation programmes in this scheme, so that they are eligible for receiving money.

Despite the **Forest Rights Act of 2006**, the legal rights of adivasis and forest dwellers are still not being recognised. For instance, rights to minor forest produce, grazing areas, community forests etc. have hardly been recognised anywhere in the country. Without legally recognised community forest rights, it will be easy for companies and the government to grab and sell community forests and resources for REDD credits. The negotiating text of December 15th also only "encourages" countries to respect forest rights rather than requiring them to do so.

If, as the government is demanding, afforestation is made part of **REDD**, these dangers increase. **Afforestation programmes** often take place on cultivated lands (including shifting cultivation fallows), village commons, community pasture lands etc. that actually belong to and are being used by people. Such programmes are already leading to evictions of people and/or displacement from their livelihoods across the country. They also often involve destroying biodiversity rich natural open forests and grasslands; REDD would encourage this, since it does not distinguish between plantations and natural forests.

In October 2008, the Standing Committee on Environment and Forests sharply criticized such programes, saying "**afforestation** ... deprives forest dwellers and adivasis of some or all of theirlands and impacts their livelihoods and basic needs – for which they are neither informed, nor consulted, nor compensated." Till date, however, no Central afforestation programme has included even a reference to forest rights, leave alone complied with legal requirements.

In the meantime, the government continues to run such programms through the administrative scheme of '**Joint Forest Management**' – where forest guards control the 'participatory' bodies. These programms often cause divisions and conflict in the community, while ignoring people's actual legal rights. Institutionalisation of such programms through REDD will cause even more conflict and marginalisation of forest dwellers.

Hence, at present, it is important to call upon the Government of India to:

- Withdraw its submission of June 2009 supporting the inclusion of afforestation programmes in REDD and stop supporting carbon trading as a mode of financing REDD; India should instead support forest protection internationally by demanding that:
- The rights of indigenous people and forest dwelling communities should be made binding.
- Free, prior informed consent of the local community must be a precondition for any interventions for reducing deforestation

or undertaking afforestation. Community control over forests should be central to international talks on forest protection.

- Industrial monoculture plantations should not be part of any agreement.
- Private companies should not be involved in the management or control of forests.
- Implement the Forest Rights Act in full and ensure recognition of all community rights.
- Make all afforestation and forestry projects subject to the control of the gram sabha, to be undertaken only with its consent and under its supervision, as recommended by the Standing Committee on Environment and Forests.
- Recognise and respect forest dwellers' community rights to protect and manage forests.
- Make forest diversion and afforestation subject to a democratic process, including the consent of the local community, as recommended by the Standing Committee on Environment and Forests.

## Climatic Change and the Adivasis

The tribals and Adivasis had confronted the extremes of climatic change for generations. The adivasis are heterogeneous communities that have had historically different relations to land and forests. Wayanad has the highest percentage of indigenous population in Kerala – 15 per cent of the total district population and 35 per cent of the total adivasi population of Kerala. **Indigenous people** (adivasis) constitute 1.01 per cent of Kerala's population. The incidence of land alienation is the highest in this district (Mohandas 1992) and it is the major site of the ongoing struggles for land. Major communities found in the district are Paniyan (44.77 per cent), **Mullu Kuruman** (17.51 per cent), **Kurichian** (17.38 per cent), **Kattunaickan** ( 9.93 per cent), Adiyan (7.10 per cent) and **Urali Kuruman** (2.69 per cent). They can broadly be categorized into three viz., agricultural labourers, marginal farmers and forest dependants. Paniyan and Adiyan communities who were traditionally bonded labourers and Urali Kuruman, traditionally artisans, constitute the major part of agricultural labourers.

Over the years, they developed a large arsenal of practices to survive and adapt to an increasingly dangerous climate. Since these people depend on natural resources, they have a keener knowledge of how to adapt to the changing environment and climate. They observe climate change and react to it positively by making use of their traditional knowledge and ancestors' rich experiences. They use diversified adaptation strategies to survive and ensure their food security. For example, the tribals in Wayanad, Kerala have ensured their food security even in the years of heavy rain and flooding and in years of severe drought.

Over the decades, the people like this have developed certain agricultural practices and varieties of paddy seeds that can withstand flooding for more than two weeks and can be sown and raised when there is no rain. They have also developed farming practices to produce the rice in any climate conditions. All over the world tribal people survive drought and flooding, marrow-freezing cold and searing heat. They prosper by drawing on the lessons from traditional knowledge and the rich experiences of their ancestors. What is the lesson we can learn from this? In order to survive in the changing climate conditions, we have to develop diversified adaptation strategies suitable to every land and region. This age-old wisdom is what the tribal people practice and preach.

- In drought conditions the adivasis use traditional seeds like *Mulanpuncha*, *Kalladian* and *Onavattam*. The night moisture is sufficient for them to germinate. After a month or so, when there is a little rain the crop takes advantage and grows well.
- The adivasis know which seeds to use during drought conditions and which during flooded conditions. They know that some paddy fields will remain inundated with water even if there is less rain.
- The adivasis also have their own ways of knowing when there will be floods and when drought. For example, if certain mushrooms grow in abundance before the rainy season it signifies that there will not be enough of rain forthcoming. (More information has to be gathered on all this).
- The **Kurichya tribe** has a lot of expertise in paddy. They hang the seeds in straw bundles and preserve them. The straw controls the temperature and allows the seeds to breathe.
- The adivasis have identified 72 wild varieties of food producing plants. These include edible leaves, tubers, mushrooms, fruits, etc. They are now promoting the cultivation of 6 varieties of wild tubers on tribal lands.
- The experience of the **adivasis shows** that frequent use of wild mushrooms prevents breast cancer.

- The women of the **Kattu-nayakar** tribe have a low incidence of uterus related problems because of the consumption of *kattu chaimbu*, or wild taro.

## Local Ecosystem, Resource Management and Livelihood Practices

Adivasis look at land as an ecosystem, which integrates the physical, biological and spiritual spaces of their existence. Their struggle has been primarily around the control of this space for their survival. Women play a historical role as seed creators, preservers of animal and plant genetic resources and organisers of family and community.

There are several changes in biodiversity and natural resources, which are linked to the development paradigm. 20 years ago there were more than 60 diverse food crops across the Adivasi areas. But the agricultural policies of the government pushed the people to grow mono crops or plantations for an outside market. This has resulted into the loss of biodiversity, food and forest produce. Erratic rainfalls have resulted in lower yields. The farmers who have practiced their traditional wisdom appear to be in a dilemma as to whether to follow their traditional practices or to respond to changing weather patterns.

## Conclusion

**Sustainable agriculture**, and harvesting or cultivating non-timber forest products, are critical aspects of many adivasi and indigenous people's livelihoods. Maintaining indigenous peoples' legal control and sustainable use of natural resources in their ancestral domains can provide significant benefits in terms of climate change adaptation and mitigation.

Legal control and sustainable use of natural resources improves their livelihoods, thus increasing their hundreds of millions of indigenous women and men throughout the world manage their forests and crops sustainably, and in this way contribute to the sequestration of greenhouse gases. However, maintaining control over their land and forests in the face of colonial and corporate attempts to nationalise or privatise them has been a historic struggle.

Their **sustainable agriculture** and forest use can help to reduce deforestation and also promote land rehabilitation, water conservation and increased biomass production. However, the success of their sustainable practices rests in large part on maintaining inclusive relations among community members that bolster the strength of the entire community when faced with external pressures such as privatisation and globalisation. The sustainable management of natural resources is negatively affected when women have limited rights to manage and control land, and to participate in the community governance of forests.

## References

1. Bates, Crispin 1995. "Lost Innocents and the Loss of Innocence": Interpreting Adivasi Movements in South Asia.' In R.H. Barnes, Andrew Gray and Benedict Kingsbury (eds), *Indigenous Peoples of Asia*, 103-119, Michigan: The Association for Asian Studies, University of Michigan.
2. Bijoy, C.R. and Ravi Raman K. 2003. 'Muthanga: The Real Story – Adivasi Movement to Recover Land', *Economic and Political Weekly*, 38, May 9.
3. Gray, Andrew 1997. 'Who are Indigenous People?' In S. Buchi, C. Erni, L. Jurt, C. Ruegg (eds), *Indigenous Peoples, Environment and Development: Proceedings of the Conference*, Zurich, May 15-18, 1995, 15-18, Copenhagen: IWGIA-International Work Group for Indigenous Affairs.
4. Kjosavik, Darley Jose and N. Shanmugaratnam 2004. 'Integration or Exclusion? Locating Indigenous Peoples in the Development Process of Kerala, South India', Forum for Development Studies, 31 (2): 232-273.
5. Kunhaman, 2003. Pranthavalkaranavum swathwapunarnirv achanangalum. In Dileep Raj (ed), *Thandedangal: Kerala Samoohapadam Muthanga Samarathinushesham*, (Malayalam), 57-67, Kottayam: D C Books.
6. Mohandas, M., 1992. Impact of New Settlers in the Western Ghat Region on the Socio-Economic Conditions of the Tribal Population: The Case of Wynad District in Kerala, Trichur: College of Co-operation and Banking, Kerala Agricultural University.
7. Ravi Raman, K. 2002. 'Breaking New Ground: Adivasi Land Struggle in Kerala', *Economic and Political Weekly*, March 9, 37: 916-918.

# 8

# Corporate Environmental Liability : The Case of Bhopal Gas Tragedy

*Dr. K. Mohankumar*

The National Newspapers on 22 Feb 2012 have reported that the Union Sports Ministry has written to the International Olympic Committee (**IOC**), urging it to cancel the sponsorship of **DOW Chemicals** for the London Olympics. The Ministry had asked the Indian Olympic Association (**IOA**) to convey India's protest over the IOC and the London Games being associated with a company which is the successor of Union Carbide, which in turn was held responsible for the unprecedented gas tragedy that occurred in Bhopal in 1984. The IOC contended that DOW did not have any connection with the gas tragedy and had supported the Olympic movement for over thirty years. DOW is a World wide Olympic partner and part of its funding goes to the National Olympic Committees including IOA.[1] (Indian Olympic Association)

Even as DOW Chemicals has resisted all compensation claims with regard to the Union Carbide gas leak disaster in Bhopal, it found the money to hire an intelligence research firm to intensively monitor all NGOs and activists working on the issue. Recently Wikileaks has released a cache of 5.5 million emails from the Texas-based intelligence company Stratfor, which revealed that regular monitoring reports of NGO activity as well as media coverage were sent to DOW and Union Carbide communication directors. Dow Chemical, which bought Union Carbide in 2001, insists that it bears no responsibility to compensate victims or clean up the contaminated site of 1984 disaster. However, the emails prove that it is still very much invested in monitoring the fall out of the disaster, and its impact on DOW's image.[2]

The Union Carbide India Limited (**UCIL**) was established in 1934 when the **UCC** (Union Carbide Corporation) became one of the first US companies to invest in India. The Bhopal plant was built in late 1970s.

The plant produced pesticides for use in India to help the country's agricultural sector increase its productivity and contribute more significantly to meet the food needs of one of the world's most heavily populated regions.

The plant was sanctioned by a government under pressure to industrialise despite the fact that the support systems were missing. The government of Madhya Pradesh used everything in its power to scale down the magnitude of the crisis. UCC financial team reported that a large volume of water was introduced into the MIC (methylisocyanide) tank and triggered a reaction that resulted in the gas release[3]. A committee of experts for the Government of India arrived at the same conclusion.

In March 1985 Government of India enacted the **Bhopal Gas Leak Disaster Act** that enabled the Government of India to act as the legal representative of the victims, in claims related to the disaster.

Legal proceedings were initiated against **UCC** by GOI in the New York District Court on April 18, 1985. Judge Keenan of the Court ruled that the more convenient forum for trail would be India since the **UCIL** is a separate entity owned, managed and run exclusively by Indian citizens. As a result the scene was shifted to the District Court of Bhopal in 1986. **The District Court ordered** a payment of Rs. 350 crores which was modified to a sum of Rs. 250 crores by the High Court of Madhya Pradesh. In order to circumvent what was described as a lengthy legal battle, the **Supreme Court of India passed an order** on 14 February 1989 directing both parties to arrive at an overall settlement of 470 million US dollars, to be paid as compensation of UCC and a termination of all civil and criminal proceedings against them.[4] Within ten days of the order UCC and UCIL made full payment of 470 million dollars to GOI. Later in April 2007 the Supreme Court reaffirmed the adequacy and finality of 1989 settlements.

The settlement was described as a sell out, a betrayal, a second **catastrophe**. Why did the government of India agreed to a paltry sum of 470 million US dollars when the original demand had been 3000 million US dollars?[5] The Bhopal litigation hinged on two important factors – compensation and liability.

A settlement may be preferable to a long-drawn litigation, but the Government of India's strategy has failed miserably to ensure justice. **The Supreme Court** has lost an opportunity of advancing human right jurisprudence from the third world view point and failed to meet the expectations of the people of India. It has not given ruling on Union Carbide's liability. It was an instance of lost opportunity to the **Supreme**

**Court as** this case was concerned with the legal limits to be determined in the vital interests of the protection of the constitutional rights of the citizens and of the environment.[6] It was concerned with the permissibility of the ultra hazardous technologies and to prescribe absolute and detterent liability if harm is caused by the hazardous process.

Through the settlement, the Indian Government seems to permit new investments in hazardous industries, provided that the investors are willing to bear the social costs resulting from their activities. It is a greed that an amount of 470 million dollars is not likely to have a deterrent effect on a multinational with more than 10 million dollars in total assets.

It is also contended that it is not the amount of compensation that is important. What is important is the need for establishing culpability and fixing liability.[7] If American corporations profited from doing business abroad, they had the moral responsibility of providing justice for any resulting mishap. It was this responsibility that the settlements undermined. The Legal liability of UCC for the gas leakage has not been established by the **Supreme Court**. It has absolved Union Carbide from the damages that may be proved against them in future.

It was believed that the UCC could not have agreed to any negotiated settlement without termination of criminal proceedings and it was Government of India which itself agreed without complaint in the termination of criminal proceedings.[8]

By choosing to ignore the long term effects of **Methyl Iso cyanide** (MIC), the Government of India wittingly or unwittingly strengthened the hands of UCC. It kept hidden from the world the fact that MIC caused chromosomal aberrations and that it attacked the immunological system making the victims vulnerable to life threatening diseases.[9]

The Government could not explain why rules and regulations that were meant to restrict the activities of a foreign company failed to do so. Why did the government grant license to set up the MIC unit when detailed technical information was not provided. The question of liability involved another question of what should be the nature of relationship between the big corporations and the government. It was seen that here it worked within the framework of mutual dependency where considerable power was exercised and regulations overcame by the company. UCC was permitted to use its technical know how on lesser safety measures.[10]

The final tragedy of the **Bhopal settlement** was that no proper system had been evolved, where by the settlement money would reach the gas victims in a fair and equitable way. 3 December 2011 marked the

27th anniversary of the Bhopal Gas Tragedy. Five organisation working for the survivors blocked the rail tracks in Bhopal. The protestors were agitating against the government's allegedly false figures on deaths and injuries caused to people in the 1984 gas leak disaster, presented in a petition pending before the Supreme Court. Government records showed 5,295 deaths, 4902 with permanent disability and 5,27,894 with minor injuries. The protestors claim that till 2009, 22719 people died, 508437 people became permanently disabled and 33781 received severe injuries.

The **settlement** did not discuss the severe consequences of the Gas leakage. Scientific analysis of samples of soil and water collected in around the factory by **Green Peace** in 2002 revealed severe chemical contamination of the soil and ground water in the area where thousands of people live. At least one person a day still dies from gas exposure related diseases and hundreds of families living near the site still use the poisoned water. The crisis persists even after 27 years of its occurrence. It was the **state-multinational nexus** and the shortcomings of Indian judicial system that allowed UCC to escape from the liabilities.

## References

1. *The Hindu*, Kochi, 22 February 1012.
2. *Ibid.*
3. Suroopa Mukherjee in Suman Gupta, Tapan Basu, Subano Chatterji (ed), *Gloablization in India: Contents and Discontents*, 2010, Pearson, Delhi, pp. 37-38.
4. *Ibid,* pp. 38-39.
5. *Ibid,* 39.
6. Upendra Baxi, 'The Bhopal Award: Another calamity for Gas Victims', *Times of* India, Bombay, Feb 16, 1989.
7. Dharmendra, S. *Sengar, Environmental Law*, 2009, PHI Learning, New Delhi p. 185.
8. 'UCC charged with negligence', *Hindustan Times* New Delhi, Nov. 12, 1991.
9. Pushpa M Bhargava, 'The Bhopal Tragedy, A Middle Word', *Economic and Political Weekly*. 1 June 1985.
10. Upendra Baxi and Amita Dhanda, *Valiant Victims and Lethal Litigation; The Bhopal case 1990*, Bombay, N.M. Tripathi Pvt. Ltd.

9

# Environmentally Sustainable Path: A Gandhian Perspective

Dr. R. Samala

Protection of environment is a global challenge. The present environmental crisis is the result of undue exploitation of nature by human beings to serve their selfish ends. The environmental problems such as rapid population growth, production and consumption of resources in a manner causing stress and strain on natural systems like air, water, soil and bio-diversity, unpredictable global climate change, ozone layer depletion and sea-level rise, unemployment, poverty, economic inequality, social injustice, poor condition of villages, problems caused due to urbanisation etc are some of the major challenges facing mankind. These problems are a matter of concern among all statesmen, policy makers, environmentalists, and civil society all over the world.

The concern over environmental issues has been echoed in various **earth summits**. The United Nations Frame work Convention on climate change (FCCC) conference was a land mark in the history of **earth summit**. After this, the world summit on sustainable development took place in Johannesburg, South Africa on 2002.' The Copenhagen summit in 2009 held in Denmark recognised climate change as one of the greatest problem of the present world.[1] The United Nations climate change conference, Durban 2011, delivered a break through on the international communities response to climate change. The outcomes included a decision by participants to adopt a universal legal agreement on climate changes no later than 2015.[2] These conferences brought into limelight the challenges in the field of environment and the concrete action needed to mitigate the issue. In this context the environmentalists all over the world acknowledged that Gandhian insights to environment and sustainable development serve as a guide to understand the problem in a proper perspective. Gandhi's views, on issues relating to environment are clearly based on his toxic approach to life and world view. Here it would be worth while exercise to make introspection and revisit Gandhian values and principles and to understand how relevant these ideas to resolve the complex problem confronting modern world.

## Gandhi as an Environmentalist

Gandhi was not an environmentalist in the present sense of the term. He did not said anything specific on environment degradation because it had not become a problem at that time. But from his writings, speeches and from his way of life we can find everything we need. Many environmentalist acknowledge their indebtedness to Gandhi in understanding the problem from a holistic view. The well known environmentalist Anna Naess mentioned Gandhi in the formulation of the term '**deep ecology**'.[3] In Gandhi's life period there is no serious ecological or environmental issues. But Gandhi was deeply concerned with all problem confronted by humanity. He was strongly against the damages made by modern industrial civilization to the environment which he wrote in '**Hind Swaraj**'.[4] He argued even in 1909 that industrialisation and machines have an adverse effect on the health of people. He was against the use of large scale machinery. He criticised people for polluting the rivers and other water bodies. He criticised mills and factories for polluting the air with smoke and noise. In the place of industrialism he advocated a simple life based on physical labour.

The environmental ethics of Gandhi emerged from his philosophy of life and world view. To him human life cannot be divided into water tight compartment such as economic, political, social, cultural and the like. Human life is an undivided whole. Gandhi said "One's everyday life was never capable of being separated from his spiritual being. Both acted and reacted upon one another".[5] He believed in the unity and oneness of all life and its interconnectedness. This relational world view is equally applicable to animal and plant life. Unity and ones of life is the crux of the Sarvodaya ideology which can be considered as the underpinning of deep environmental philosophy.

To Gandhi in a **Sarvodaya** society there is no exploitation of nature. Everything in the nature belonged to God and therefore it was for his all people as a whole and not for a particular individual or groups that everything belongs. When an individual had more than his proportionate portion he became trustee of that portion for God's people. So when an industrialist or a large scale agriculturalist engages himself in production, he is not the real owner, he is only a coordinator or a manager, since the real owner is god. Therefore these resources are the common property of mankind.[6] Gandhi himself placed before humanity a life style which was in tune with the environment.

## Environmental Ethics and Sustainable Development

The **environmental ethics** of Gandhi is based on the principle of well being of all animate and inanimate beings. Man's progress and the road to development has led to the deterioration of nature. In his quest for fulfilling his needs, he has exploited nature to its maximum. This development is ecologically not sustainable. In the Indian tradition we use the word 'mother earth' to respect the nature. Gandhiji was much influenced by our tradition and stressed on truth and non violence. In the words of Gandhiji "Man has no power to create life; therefore he has no right to destroy life".[7] Man has been endowed with higher faculties so that he can be compassionate to lower beings". To Gandhi, civilization meant not the multiplication of wants, but the deliberate and voluntary reduction of selfish wants. Eradication of poverty and hunger is not merely an intellectual exercise of Science and technology but it also involves the inner purity of mankind. To alter the system it is necessary to alter the paradigm of development and to take cognizance of the spiritual, of the inner voice, of the ethics and values that promote sustainable development. Development is a process that encompasses both the spiritual and material aspects oflife.

In Gandhian outlook the spiritual dimension in consumption and production necessarily brings the ethical aspects of sustainable development. In the sustainable type of interaction between man and nature there exist a spiritual or holistic outlook that guides the relation between human resource and natural resources. In such a system human beings prefer a simple living which fulfils the basic necessities of life and is in tune with nature. It is not a life of poverty or insanity but a meaningful life of fulfilment and happiness. Gandhi visualised a non-violent economic order based on equality and justice. Gandhi's economic ideas revolved around Swadeshi and Khadi. Khadi is not a piece of cloth but a symbol of decentralisation of production and distribution. It stands for a non-rident life style. The application of the principle of decentralisation leads to a life of simplicity in which there is hardly any scope of amassing unnecessary goods in the market.[8] This checks the exploitation of natural resources and helps in maintaining the equilibrium of nature. Thus the natural resources of the earth including the air, water, land, flora and fauna and natural eco systems must be safeguarded for the benefit of present and future generations through an ethically oriented sustainable path.

## Sustainable Development: Gandhian Alternative

Gandhi states that civilization means not the multiplication of wants, but the deliberative and voluntary reduction of selfish wants. A person who believes in non-violence is a spiritual person who is less attached to worldly things and even if he is a wealthy person, he thinks of himself only as a trustee of the properties.[9] Then it should be a meaningful life of fulfilment and happiness. Gandhi was the first man to introduce the concept of service to nature in order to enrich nature. **Sustainable development** is development that meets the needs of the present without compromising the ability of the future generations to meet their own needs. It is a multi-dimensioned concept having a holistic approach. The spiritual, cultural, social, economic, political, psychological, aesthetic, scientific, technological, educational along with the environmental factors constitute it It is an allround human development of an integrated or holistic nature.

The Gandhian model of sustainable development suggests certain steps to attain sustainable life style. A sustainable life style is a living that attempts to reduce an individuals or societies, use of the earth's natural resources and his own resources. For sustainable environment, '**Sustainable agriculture**' should be promoted. We should give up chemical fertilisers and pesticides and substitute them with bio-manures and bio-pesticides. Vermi culture and Vermi composts a must for restoring the healthy of the soil. 'Khadi and Village industries are eco-friendly. They create employment and alleviate poverty. Appropriate technologies should be adopted which are simple and which our villagers are able to comprehend and operate themselves. The use of electricity should be avoided or kept to the minimum use of renewable energy resources. Coal and petroleum are non renewable energy sources and are getting exhausted very fast. Solar energy is limitless and inexhaustible. We can use solar energy for healing and lightning. Water and wind energies can also be harnessed for producing electricity. Tree plantation or 'Sylvi culture' should be promoted; cutting trees for fuel and for the construction of houses is inevitable. Individual should plant two trees for everyone tree we cut. Trees as a source of energy are non-renewable if we only cut them and do not grow them.[10]

Gandhi's philosophy of life provides a sustainable development paradigm which is in tune with nature and eco-system. He himself led a life which was symbolic with environment. Gandhi's whole life was his message and a lesson on "protecting and conserving environment along with the development process" not for the Indians but for the entire world to follow at large. The application of his principle will ensure human progress without harming the progress of future generation. He reminds us that "the earth provides enough to satisfy our needs and not for our greed". It is a fact that man cannot infinitely exploit nature to satisfy his unlimited wants. Each and everyone is compelled to follow a simple and sustainable life style based on minimum human needs. A sustainable life style automatically ensures a sustainable path to development.

## References

1. K.K. N Kurup. Environmental Biology. Arjun Books, Kozhikode–2006.
2. M.P. Mathai, Mahatma Gandhi, World View, Gandhi Peace Foundation, New Delhi–2008.
3. Nirmal Kumar Bose, Studies in Gandhism, Navajivan publishing house, Ahmedabad, 1972.
4. Niraja Gopal Jayal, Pratap Bhanu Mehta (ed), Politics in India, Oxford University Press, 2012.
5. O.P. Ganba, An Introduction to Political theory, Mac millan 2011,
6. Regimol Cherian and others, Green Path to Sustainability. Prospects and challenges, Rajiv Gandhi Chair in contemporary studies, CUSAST, Kochi.
7. Siby K. Joseph, Bharat Mahodaya (ed), Gandhian Environment and sustainable future, Institute of Gandhian Studies, Wardha-2011.
8. T.V. Muralivallabhan, Dimensions of Sustainable Economic development, Uma publications, Alappuzha 2005.

# SECTION-II

# GLOBAL WARMING AND WATER RIGHTS

# 10

# Global Warming and Public Policy Initiatives

*Dr. Lekshmi R. Nair*

## Introduction

Global warming also known as **greenhouse effect** has been one of the most serious environmental concerns of the past few years. According to many recent surveys, global warming has been selected as one of the top environmental concerns by the public (The World's Water 2008-09, 2010). The main greenhouse gases are water vapour, $CO_{2,}$ methane, nitrous oxide, ozone and halocarbons (IPCC, 2007a). The main contributor (four to 36 per cent) of greenhouse gas effect is $CO_2$ which is mainly caused by manmade activities like burning of fossil fuels and deforestation. The main consequences of global warming will be natural disasters like floods, famines, reduction in agricultural output, glacier melting, emergence of new diseases, extinction of species etc. (Sinn, 2007). The consequences of the **global warming** are universally recognized and hence serious efforts are made by all nations to reduce the emission of greenhouse gases especially $CO_2$. The main participants in these efforts are governments and people. In this essay, the public policy actions regarding global warming, the participants in the policy actions, the evaluation of policy, political concerns etc. are critically analyzed.

## The Scope and Nature of the Public Policy Problem

The excessive emission of greenhouse gases due to manmade activities can result in accumulation of heat in the earth's atmosphere leading to a rise in global temperature. This phenomenon is called global warming (Cline, 1992). Among the greenhouse gases, all except methane are originated from manmade activities like fossil burning or electricity generation. Thus power plants are one of the main contributors of this phenomenon. The other main contributors of greenhouse gas emissions include deforestation, burning of gasoline in the engine of vehicles, use of fertilizers in agriculture, burning of organic matter, buildings that require lot of fuels etc. Due to the serious repercussions of the global warming problem concerning both developed and developing nations, it is widely recognised that an internationally integrated approach is needed to tackle this issue. **The Kyoto Protocol based** on the treaty on climate change in the **United Nations Earth Summit** in Rio de **Janeiro, 1992**, called on both the developed and developing nations to formulate local initiatives to reduce the emission of greenhouse gases in all nations irrespective of the costs involved in these efforts (Hass et al, 1992). Both the governments and people can be the participants in the national and regional programmes in this regard.

## The Evolution of Public Policy

The historic treaty produced by the United Nations Earth Summit in Rio de Janeiro in 1992 started the foundation for initiative in reducing the concentrations of greenhouse gas in the atmosphere (Hass et al, 1992). Based on the treaty it was promised that greenhouse gas emission will be reduced all over the world irrespective of the costs involved in these efforts to combat global warming. More than 186 nations were signed in that agreement. Based on the agreement many subsequent rounds of climate negotiations were promised to be held to reduce the emission levels in the levels existing in the 1990s. In 1997, the treaty's implementing protocol, the Kyoto agreement, has delayed after the dilutions at negotiations in Bonn and Marrakesh (Biermann and Brohm, 2005). However, the Kyoto Protocol, in its existing form, restricts only industrial countries except US for emitting greenhouse gases whereas developing countries like India have not taken any major responsibilities for reducing these emissions (Toman et al, 2003). In developing both the **United Nations Framework Convention on Climate Change and Kyoto Protocol**, European Union has a major role (European Commission, 2008).

## Evaluation of Policy, The Actors Involved

Different initiatives were adopted by different nations in response to global warming. For example, UK adopted a domestic target to reduce the emissions of carbon dioxide by 20 per cent by 2010. The other measures in this regard include introduction of a Climate Change Levy, the Renewables Obligation, with tradeable certificates (Renewables Obligation Certificates), R&D tax concessions. From the 2001 election onwards, the Performance and Innovation Unit of the Cabinet Office (PIU 2002), the Energy White Paper (DTI 2003), the Energy Review (DTI 2006) and the recent Stern Review (HM Treasury and Cabinet Office 2006) were published for reviewing policies. In all these reviews, it is assumed that the costs of mitigating climate change are small at around one per cent (Helm, 2005).

In US, climate change policy is considered as a development issue together with many other social issues. The basic objectives of the US climate policy change are to slow GHG gas emissions' growth, major investments in science and technology and institutions and to promote international corporation (Biermann and Brohm, 2005). The US had rejected the Kyoto Protocol in 2001 February and after that, the US government was under severe pressure for taking some action in this regard. Hence, new plan after that commits an 18 per cent of GDP reduction in intensity of greenhouse gas emission. However, this 18 per cent of GDP is very small amount as shown by economic analyses and also lacks any element that would raise the price of carbon emission (Biermann and Brohm, 2005). It is claimed to reduce the cost effectiveness of the plan.

Contrary to the developed nations, India joined with China to oppose the climate change mitigation commitments. They together opposed a discussion of climate change at the UN Security Council. They opposed the argument completely that climate change may have security implications. In addition to the governments, independent groups and the people also can be the participants in efforts to reduce global warming, directly or indirectly. Some of the efforts that can possibly reduce the global warming include planting more trees and developing wasteland, fuel substitution policies, reducing air pollution, promoting renewable sources of energy, reform measures for economy etc.

Since the 1991 Earth Summit at Rio de Janeiro and the Kyoto Protocol in 2005, the Copenhagen conference has been the latest of the UN conferences to achieve an international consensus in dealing with climate change (ACCA, 2009). In 2012, the first commitment under Kyoto Protocol ends and in this context, the aim of the **Copenhagen** conference was to prepare a global climate change agreement from 2012 (ACCA, 2009). Before the Copenhagen conference, five negotiating sessions were conducted by the *Ad Hoc* Working Group on **Long-term Cooperative Action under the UNFCCC** (AWG-LCA) and the *Ad Hoc* Working Group on Further Commitments for Annex I Parties under the Kyoto Protocol (AWG-KP) (IISD, 2009). However, only little progress was made in the AWG-KP since developing nations wanted reduction of greenhouse gas emissions due to their historical responsibilities while the developed nations wanted reduction in this regard by developing nations also to a great extent. Consensus was not achieved under the AWG LCA also though progress was obtained in this regard.

## The Intergovernmental Structure and Political Concerns

Since the developing nations have per capita energy consumption and carbon dioxide emission, which is only one-sixth of the developed nations, they are argued to be not the main contributors of climate change problems (Reddy and Asenza, 2009). At the same time, the developing nations are the most vulnerable ones to the climate change consequences with the limited availability of resources for adaptation to climate change (IPCC climate change, 2007).

Contrary to the developed nations, China and India joined to oppose the climate change mitigation commitments. They together opposed a discussion of climate change at the UN Security Council. They opposed the argument completely that climate change may have security implications. This stand can be argued as legitimate on the one hand based on the burden sharing architecture of the **UNFCCC** and Kyoto Protocol which predicts about the growth of the share of global emissions originating in developing countries to meet their social and development needs' (Toman et al, 2003). In these developing nations, many people are below the poverty line. Hence they are in the fight against poverty and to enhance economic growth and development is argued as the main priority for these nations (Reddy and Asenza, 2009). Based on the differences in the emission of $CO_2$ between developed and developing nations, the UNFCCC has put forward the principle of common but differential responsibility in their policy instruments against climate change. Based on this principle, "developed countries are obliged to lead climate mitigation through national policies, make financial resources available to developing countries to meet the cost incurred in complying with the convention, and promote technology transfer to developing countries to implement the measures under the Convention" (Reddy and Asenza, 2009, p. 52).

On the other hand, this stand taken can be argued as debatable since climate change will affect the poor nations the most. Moreover, in the developing nations, since majority of poor are in rural areas and are dependent on climate sensitive resources, climate change can affect these people badly (Kumar et al, 2001b). According to many reports, between 2004 and 2030 the $CO_2$ emission by the developing nations will increase significantly so that they will be responsible for three quarters of the rise in global emissions and hence they will be ahead of the **OECD nations** in the emission by 2010 (UNFCCC, 2007; Reddy and Asenza, 2009). Reports show that the biggest emitter of $CO_2$ overtaking USA will be China and India will be the third largest emitter overtaking Russia between 2003 and 2030 (IEA, 2005).Thus, the climate change policy has been a challenge to the developing nations.

One main feature of the **Copenhagen conference** was that since it happened along with the global financial crisis, it had to deal with the financial crisis and climate change at the same time (ACCA, 2009). The Copenhagen agreement is not considered as a perfect one though it is considered as an important way to go ahead. The agreement suggested a bottom up approach where there is no quantified emission reduction targets for developing nations or no compromise between US and China (IISD, 2009). Instead, it only suggested need for developed and developing nations to submit their commitments together (IISD, 2009). The most significant feature of the Copenhagen accord however is the provision for short term and long term financing to developing nations by the developed nations through funds like the **Copenhagen Green Climate Fund** and a **Technology Mechanism** (IISD, 2009).

## The Approaches to Policy Setting

Different nations adopted different positions in the conference. While EU and US want the issue to be integrated in the broader framework of international economic agenda, UK ignored the problems like cooperation between nations, cost benefit analysis, attempt for a global agreement etc. Their policy framework was based on low mitigation costs, which was actually obtained to be high in the economic studies. The proposed reduction in **GHG emission** by US is argued to be very low. The developing nations wanted the developed nations to commit for significant reduction in the greenhouse gas emissions based on their historical responsibilities while they were not willing to sign to any binded commitments. Thus, all the countries discussed above adopted different stands with regard to climate policy change. Hence, the Copenhagen agreement is reported as far from perfect (Dvorsky, 2010).

## The Suggested Policy Direction that is Supported by Research

In response to the global warming, global economy seeks to implement this objective through voluntary GHG emission reduction targets. In order to obtain this target of reduction in the emission of Greenhouse gases, a developed country can look for consuming products and processes with high carbon intensities by importing the same from developing countries. As a result, the developing country has to increase its production of the product without having to worry about binding climate compliance (Helm, 2005). Due to the global impact of the global warming phenomenon unlike the other forms of environmental problems, irrespective of their originating place, international collaboration and agreement is needed to tackle the problem.

## Conclusion

Unlike other forms of environmental problems, one main feature of the global warming is that it spreads rapidly irrespective of where they are emitted. Hence this problem affects the global economy in a similar way. In this context, an internationally integrated approach is needed to tackle this problem. In the developing nations, many serious initiatives had been taken to reduce the greenhouse gas emissions. However, with regard to binded commitments, developing nations are still hesitant for any legal agreement even in the latest **Copenhagen Conference** based on the common but differential responsibilities. Since most people in developing nations are below poverty line, the developing nations demand the need for financing in relation to the investment in low carbon economy especially in the light of the recent financial crisis. The developed nations have to support the mechanisms in developing nations to reduce the greenhouse gas emissions through providing technologies and funding.

## References

1. ACCA (2009): *ACCA Position Paper: The UN Climate Change Conference 2009 (COP 15)*, August.
2. Biermann, F. and R. Brohm. (2005). *Implementing the Kyoto Protocol without the USA: The Strategic Role of Energy Tax Adjustments at the Border*. Climate Policy 4: 289-302.
3. Cline, William R (1992) *The Economics of Global Warming*, Washington: Institute for International Economics.
4. DTI (2003), *Our Energy Future—Creating a Low Carbon Economy*, White Paper, CM5761, Department for Trade and Industry, London: TSO.
5. DTI (2006), *Energy Review: The Energy Challenge*, July 11th, Department for Trade and Industry, London: TSO.
6. Dvorsky G (2010) : *Five Reasons the Copenhagen Climate Conference Failed*, http://ieet.org/index.php/IEET/more/dvorsky20100110/, Accessed April 27, 2010.

7. European Commission. (2008). *2020 by 2020: Europe's Climate Change Opportunity*. Communication from the Commission to the European Parliament, the Council, the European Economic and Social Committee, and the Committee of the Regions, COM (2008) 30. Brussels, EC.
8. Hass, P.M., Levy, M.A. and Parson, E.A. (1992) *Appraising the Earth Summit: How should we judge UNCED's success*, Environment, 34(8):12–36.
9. Helm, D. Ed (2005) *Climate Change Policy*, UK, Oxford University Press.
10. International Energy Agency (2005): *World energy outlook*. OECD/IEA, Paris, France.
11. IISD (2009): *A Brief Analysis of the Copenhagen Climate Change Conference-An IISD Commentary*, December, International Institute for Sustainable Development.
12. IPCC, Climate Change (2007): *Mitigation*. Contribution of Working Group III to the Fourth Assessment Report of the Intergovernmental Panel on Climate Change, 2007.
13. Intergovernmental Panel on Climate Change [IPCC]. (2007a). *IPCC fourth assessment report: Working Group I Report the physical science basis* [online]. Available from: http://www.ipcc.ch/ipccreports/ar4-wg1.htm [Accessed 22 May 2009].
14. Kumar, K.S. Kavi, Parikh, J (2001b) *Indian Agriculture and Climate Sensitivity,* Global Environmental Change, 11, pp. 147-154.
15. PIU (2002), *The Energy Review*, Performance and Innovation Unit, Cabinet Office, London, February.
16. Reddy, B.S. and Assenza G.B. (2009): *Climate change – a developing country perspective*, Current Science , Vol. 97, No. 1, 10.
17. Sinn, H.W. (2007) *Public Policies against Global Warming*, CESifo Working Paper No. 2087, Category 8, Resources and Environment.
18. The World's Water 2008-09 (2010): *Top Environmental Concerns of the American Public: Selected Years, 1997–2008*. Retrieved from http://www.worldwater.org/data20082009/Table20.pdf, Accessed October 16 2010.
19. Toman M., U. Chakravorty and S. Gupta (eds) (2003) *India and Global Climate Change: Perspectives on Economics and Policy from a Developing Country*, UK, Oxford University Press.
20. UNFCCC (2007): *Climate change: impacts, vulnerabilities and adaptation in developing countries*. Climate Change Secretariat, United Nations Framework Convention on Climate Change, 2007.

# 11

# Global Warming and the Human Right to Water

**Reinhart Philip**

*Exempting the probability of one more world war, a huge asteroid, or a fatal plague, the only most danger to our planet earth is global warming. Global warming is a global problem that demands a global solution. But the international community has failed to reach at a consensus regarding an action. So it is up to the domestic state systems and its inhabitants to take necessary actions. The effect of global warming is increasing the average temperature of the earth and this unprecedented increase is expected to have severe impacts on the global hydrological system, ecosystems, sea level, crop production and related processes. Freshwater resources are highly sensitive to variations in weather and climate and this will affect the quantity and quality of fresh water, round the planet earth. This has a brimming impact on the human right to water. The present paper is an attempt to analyze the impact of global warming on fresh water resources and on the human right to water together with analysing the role of the state.*

Exempting the probability of one more world war, a huge asteroid, or a fatal plague, the only most danger to our planet earth is global warming. Global warming is a global problem affecting the world round - damage to the aquatic ecosystem in the Murray Darling basin; drying up of Yangtze due to precipitation decrease; warming up of the largest fresh water lake, Baikal; melting up of the glaciers of Himalayas; decline in the area of Lake Chad and extended dry seasons in Africa; damage to the riparian ecosystems in the Elbe region; creation of multi-year droughts in USA and Southern Canada; impairing the non-consumptive water uses in the Mississippi; shrinking of the glaciers of Andes and so on. Warming of the isolated but enormous Lake Baikal (Russia) is a clear signal that climate change has affected even the most remote corners of our planet (Science Daily, 2008).

The phenomenon of **global warming** has its myriad and numerous adverse effects on both the environment and human beings. That effect is extensive and covers every sphere of one's life. The water resources have been heavily affected by the global warming phenomenon. Sea levels have risen, glaciers retreats are taking place often and the most harmful affect is the shrinking of the Arctic Circle. As the effects of global warming are vast and cover every sphere of life, if we do not take note of the alarming rate of its growth, one day or other our earth will perish. Being a global problem, **global warming** demands a global solution or action. But the International Community failed to reach at a consensus regarding an effective action. So it is up to the domestic state systems and its inhabitants to take necessary actions. The state is expected to protect its citizens and make necessary conditions for the enjoyment of their rights. The present paper is (limited to) analyzing the impact of global warming on fresh water resources and on the human right to water together with analyzing the role of the state.

There has been a considerable increase in the average temperature of earth and the average facade temperature of the globe has augmented more than one degree Fahrenheit since 1900 and the speed of warming has been almost three folds the century long average since 1970. This increase in earth's average temperature is called **Global Warming**. Even though there exist divergence of opinion regarding the effects of global warming; more or less all specialists studying the climate record of the earth have the same opinion now that human actions, mainly the discharge of green house gases from smokestacks, vehicles, and burning forests, are perhaps the leading power, driving the fashion.

Scientists all over the world are making predictions about the ill effects of global warming and connecting some of the events that have taken place in the past few decades as an alarm of global warming. The effect of global warming is increasing the average temperature of the earth and is predicted to be about 3° to 5°C by the year 2100. The Intergovernmental Panel on Climate Change (IPCC) projects that the global mean temperature may increase between 1.4 and 5.8 degrees Celsius (C) by 2100 (Jayant et al. 2006: 314). This unprecedented increase is expected to have severe impacts on the global hydrological system, ecosystems, sea level, crop production and related processes. The impact would be particularly severe in the tropical areas, which mainly consist of developing countries, including India. The rise in temperature and precipitation patterns increases the frequency, duration, and intensity of other extreme weather events, such as floods, droughts, heat waves, and tornadoes (Camille & John 2005: 339-44). The total annual power of hurricanes has already increased markedly since 1975 because their average intensity and average duration have increased. While there is increased precipitation in the upper latitudes, there is a decrease in the lower latitudes, including parts of South Asia, an aspect of concern for India. As the temperature of oceans rises, so will the probability of more frequent and stronger hurricanes, like that in 2004 and 2005. When some areas of Earth will become wetter due to global warming, other areas will suffer serious droughts and heat waves. Africa will receive the worst of it, and more severe droughts are also expected in Europe. All these will seriously affect the availability of fresh water all over the world, especially in Africa, where it is already a dangerously rare commodity.

Another important effect of **global warming** is rise in ocean level caused by expansion of water and melting of ice. Observations since 1961 show that ocean has warmed to a depth of at least 3,000 meters and has been absorbing more than 80 per cent of the heat added to the climate system. Smaller glaciers have been de-glaciated by almost 38 per cent in this period. In the Northern Hemisphere, spring and summer sea-ice cover decreased by about 10 to 15 per cent from the 1950s to the year 2000; sea-ice extent in the Nordic seas has shrunk by 30 per cent over the last 130 years (UNEP 2003: 4). IPCC study reveals that melting of polar ice caps has contributed between 0.2 and 0.4 mm annually to sea level rise over the twentieth century and the sea level is predicted to accelerate from 20-30 cm over the twentieth century and to 35-90 cm over the twenty-first century (IPCC 2001). The melting of ice caps will throw the global ecosystem out of balance. Ice caps are fresh water, and when they melt they will desalinate the ocean, *i.e.* making it less salty. The desalinization of the gulf current will "screw up" ocean currents, which regulate temperatures. Temperature rises and changing landscapes in the Arctic Circle will endanger several species of animals. Besides all these salt water intrusion into inland water bodies like ponds, lakes etc. will result in fresh water getting polluted (salty), increasing the grave of fresh water scarcity.

Water the precious gift of nature covers about 71 per cent of earth's total surface. Holding a unique place in the history of mankind, water has many distinct properties that are critical for the proliferation of life on earth. All the major civilisations like Mesopotamia, Egypt, Indus Valley etc. have flourished around rivers and river ways. The success of large metropolis such as London, Paris, New York, and Chicago etc. owes to their easy access to water. From a religious point of view water is considered as a purifier in Christianity, Hinduism, Islam, Judaism and other religions. Water plays an important role in world economy as it functions as a solvent for a wide variety of chemical substances and facilitates industrial cooling and transportation. The role of water in world economy can be understood from the statistics that it takes ten litres of water to produce one litre of petrol, 100 litres of water to produce one kg of paper, 4,500 litres of water to produce one kg of rice and for one tonne of cement, 20,000 litres of water to produce 1 tonne of steel and 40,000 litres to make a car. In United States alone, computer industry is using 1500 billion litres of water a year (Maude & Tony 2002: 8).

According to the United Nations Environment Programme (UNEP), the total volume of water on Earth is about 1.4 billion km$^3$. The volume of freshwater resources is around 35 million km$^3$, or about two and a half per cent of the total volume. Around 30 per cent of the world's freshwater is stored underground in the form of groundwater (shallow and deep groundwater basins up to 2,000 metres, soil moisture, swamp water and permafrost). This constitutes about 97 per cent of all the freshwater that is potentially available for human use. The Earth's atmosphere contains approximately 13,000 km$^3$ of water. The total usable freshwater supply for ecosystems and humans is about 200 000 km$^3$ of water - less than one per cent of all freshwater resources (UN 2011).

Though water has utmost importance and usage, the amount of fresh water available is meager and the world is running out of fresh water. Humanity is depleting and polluting the well spring of life at a startling rate. With every passing day the demand for water out spaces its utility and the demand is growing at more than the rate twice of population increase in the last century (UN 2010). The demand for water has exceeded the supply already. According to the United Nations (UN-Water 2011) 43 countries in the world are currently facing water stress and scarcity and over 700 million people having no access to clean drinking water. The UN Human Right to Water suggests that each person needs 20-50 litres of safe freshwater a day to ensure their basic needs for drinking, cooking and cleaning. But more than one in six people worldwide don't have access to this amount of safe freshwater. By 2025, 1800 million people will be living in countries or regions with absolute water scarcity, and two-thirds of the world population could be under stress conditions. 60 nations will be facing acute water shortage at that time (HDR 2006: 136).

## The Human Right to Water

Water is so important because of the reason that it is needed for sustaining life on earth. Right to Water forms an important part of human rights because of the same reason. No one can secure life and a decent life without access to water. The Supreme Court of India while expanding the scope of Article 21 has included "Right to Pure Drinking Water," as a key right in the Right to Life and Personal Liberty. This signifies the importance of water.

The right to water is receiving increasing attention and recognition by human rights and anti-poverty advocates globally. Proponents argue that the realisation of the right to water is indispensable to the realisation of many other internationally recognised human rights, including the right to food, the right to health, and the right to adequate housing. The UN has recognised Right to Water as an important human right. The rationale for the emergence of the notion of water as human rights stems from the need to secure water for the poor and marginalised sections. Lack of water and sanitation clearly has an impact on the enjoyment of other human rights, such as the rights to education, health and work, which form an essential basis for poverty elimination and human development as well.

## Indicators of Water for Human Rights Approach

There are four indicators of the water for human rights approach - *availability, water quality, accessibility and access to information*. These four indicators have been devised to measure the extent of abidance of countries to the water for human rights approach (UN-Water 2010). The UN concept of water as a human right was used as a tool for the analysis of water delivery systems round the world.

**Availability:** Implies that the water supply is sufficient and continuous for personal and domestic uses, such as drinking, sanitation, washing, food preparation etc. The Human Right to Water suggests that each person needs 20-50 litres of safe freshwater a day to ensure their basic needs for drinking, cooking and cleaning. But in reality more than one out of every six does not have access to these.

**Water Quality:** The water supplied must be clean and safe. There exists WHO Guidelines for drinking water, which guides governments to develop national water quality standards. Water should be of an acceptable colour, odour and taste for each personal or domestic use.

**Accessibility:** Water, water facilities and services must be accessible to every human being. Accessibility includes both *physical* and *economical*. **Physical accessibility** means that water, water facilities and services must be within the safe physical reach for all sections of the population. Sufficient water should be accessible with in the immediate vicinity. Physical security should not be threatened during access to water facilities and services. In case of **economic accessibility** water, water facilities and services must be affordable for all. The charges associated with securing water must be affordable and must not compromise the realization of other rights. Generally, water services are considered to be affordable when they cost no more than 2 percent of the average family income.

**Access to Information:** The public should have access to water data and information. This is needed for planning and sound management of water resources.

## Global Warming and Water Trends

Freshwater resources are highly sensitive to variations in weather and climate. The changes in global climate that are occurring as a result of the accumulation of greenhouse gases in the atmosphere will affect patterns of freshwater availability and will alter the frequencies of floods and droughts. Climate model simulations and other analysis suggest that total flows, probabilities of extreme high or low flow conditions, seasonal runoff regimes, groundwater-surface water interactions and water quality characteristics could all be significantly affected by climate change over the course of the coming decades (Kathleen 2008). As already stated it is mainly by two means global warming is affecting fresh water availability. One is through pollution, *i.e.* the increase in precipitation patterns causing frequent floods, increase in cyclones, tornados and the increase in salinity due to rise in sea level etc. directly or indirectly pollutes the fresh water reserves. Second is through drought, fresh water gets evaporated up or dried up due to severe hot weather conditions.

Drought attributable in significant part to climate change is already causing acute water shortages in large parts of Australia, Asia, Africa, and the United States. California water officials warned that the state, whose enormous agricultural and computer industries are heavily water-dependent, is facing "the worst drought in modern history" (Associated

Press 2009). Shrinking snowcaps are reducing river flows and water supplies across China, India and Pakistan – countries where more than one billion people already lack access to safe drinking water and adequate sanitation. The impact of global warming on water can be studied under the following three heads:

## Increasing Water Demand

The demand for water is increasing day by day and the population growth and economic development are driving significant increases in agricultural and industrial demand for water. Agriculture accounts for more than two-thirds of global water use, including as much as 90 per cent in developing countries. Freshwater consumption worldwide has more than doubled since World War II and is expected to rise another 25 per cent by 2030 (Daniel et al. 2007). Much of the growth is the result of expected increases in the world population from 6.6 billion currently to about eight billion by 2030 and over nine billion by 2050 (Jason et al. 2009: 4).

Global warming will naturally increase the demand for water. Due to prolonged dry periods and severe droughts more water is demanded for agriculture, primarily for irrigation. Secondly the hydration needs of billions of farm animals due to higher atmospheric temperatures demand more water. Water demand in industry will also go up because large quantities of water are needed for industrial cooling due to increased atmospheric and water temperatures.

The most direct impact of the increased demand for water is on its price. When the demand for water is high and its supply less, the more will be its price. Pricing of water is already there and water scarcity is driving shifts toward full-cost pricing aimed at providing economic incentives for efficient water use. In many places, artificially low water prices are rising as subsidies are phased out. In the United States, water prices are increasing to cover the full cost of operating and maintaining water delivery systems such as storage and treatment. In California, for example, the Metropolitan Water District, Southern California's largest wholesale water supplier, raised its price for water by over 14 per cent effective January 1, 2009 (Bradley 2008). According to UN Water (2010), "people living in the slums of Jakarta, Manila and Nairobi pay five to ten times more for water than those living in high income areas in those same cities and more than consumers in London or New York."

Water scarcity, coupled with increased concern among local communities about water withdrawals, will put pressure on local authorities and policymakers to consider water reallocations, regulations, and development of water markets that cap usage, suspend permits to draw water and lead to stricter water quality standards. This will create potential risks for large-scale water users whose historical access to water can be turned upside down by policy shifts and legal rulings.

## Water Scarcity

Water is already over-appropriated in many regions of the world. More than one-third of the world's population, roughly 2.4 billion people live in water-stressed countries and by 2025 the number is expected to rise to two-thirds. Groundwater tables and river levels are receding in many parts of the world due to human water use. In India, for example, farmers are now using nearly 80 per cent of the country's available water, largely from groundwater wells; at current rates, the World Bank estimates that India will have exhausted available water supplies by 2050 (Jason et al. 2009: 6). Regions affected by drought also are increasing. The percentage of global land classified as "very dry" has doubled since the 1970s, including large parts of Africa and Australia (NCAR 2005). Natural water storage capacity and long-term annual river flows are also declining, especially in the Northern Hemisphere, due to glacial/snowcap melting. Glacial melting is one of the reasons that many of Asia's largest rivers are projected to recede in coming decades.

Climate change will: firstly, decrease natural water storage capacity from glacier/snowcap melting, and subsequently reduce long-term water availability for more than one-sixth of the world's population that lives in glacier or snowmelt-fed river basins, including major regions of China, India, Pakistan and the western US; secondly, increase water scarcity due to changes in precipitation patterns and intensity. In particular, the subtropics and mid-latitudes, where much of the world's poorest populations live, are expected to become substantially drier, resulting in heightened water scarcity; thirdly, increase the vulnerability of ecosystems due to temperature increases, changes in precipitation patterns, frequent severe weather events, and prolonged droughts. This will further diminish the ability of natural systems to filter water and create buffers to flooding; fourthly, affect the capacity and reliability of water supply infrastructure due to flooding, extreme weather, and sea level rise. Most existing water treatment plants and distribution systems were not built to withstand expected sea level rise and increased frequency of severe weather due to climate change (Corinne 2008); fifthly, impair non-consumptive water uses, including transportation on inland waterways, tourism sectors and freshwater fisheries.

Water scarcity and unsustainable supply has a hampering effect on the economy. Business will be affected as floods and droughts affect freight transport, like that happened at the Mississippi River in the US and Rhine River in Europe (Jason et al. 2009: 7). Tourism sectors that are dependent on the availability of water or snow are also vulnerable to water scarcity due to climate change. Climate change will concentrate snowmelt and precipitation into shorter time frames, making both water releases more extreme and drought events more sustained. Current infrastructure often does not have the capacity to fully capture this larger volume of water, and therefore will not be able to meet water demands in times of sustained drought. To meet this new and improved infrastructure has to be established which requires millions of rupees.

## Declining Water Quality

Declining water quality is an acute problem around the world, particularly in developing countries where there are notable increases in agricultural and industrial production, coupled with a lack of adequate wastewater treatment. As per the study of **World Water Assessment Programme** (WWAP) every day, two million tonnes of human waste is disposed of in water courses and in developing countries, 70 per cent of industrial wastes are dumped untreated into waters where they pollute the usable water supply (UN 2011a). In many developing countries, waterways traditionally used for drinking water or other community needs have been heavily contaminated. In China, many rivers are so badly polluted that not even industry can use the water and nearly two-thirds of the country's largest cities have no wastewater treatment facilities. Today two and a half billion people, including almost one billion children, live without even basic sanitation. Every 20 seconds, a child dies as a result of poor sanitation *i.e.* one and a half million preventable deaths each year (UN 2011b).

Climate change will no doubt worsen the existing situation. The rise in sea level will contaminate coastal surface and groundwater resources due to sea level rise, resulting in saltwater intrusion into rivers, deltas, and aquifers. As sea levels rise due to climate change, coastal communities could lose up to 50 per cent or more of their freshwater supplies. Other effects include coastal erosion, wetland and coastal plain flooding, and a loss of habitats for fish, birds, and other wildlife and plants. The IPCC notes that as much as 33 per cent of coastal land and wetland habitats are likely to be lost in the next hundred years if the level of the ocean continues to rise at its present rate (Anisimov et al. 2007). Even more land would be lost if the increase is significantly greater, and this is quite possible.

The rise in temperature will lead to more algal and bacterial blooms that further contaminate water supplies. The temperature rise will also affect the aquatic ecosystem. Increase extreme precipitation and flooding, which will increase erosion rates and wash soil-based pollutants and toxins into waterways. This will contribute to environmental health risks associated with water. It is estimated that by 2030 the risk of diarrhea will be up to ten per cent higher in some countries due to climate change (Jason et al. 2009: 7). The marine life is very sensitive to the increase in temperatures and it is expected that many species will die off or become extinct due to the increase in the temperatures of the water, whereas various other species, which prefer warmer waters, will increase tremendously. The most disturbing changes are expected in the coral reefs that are expected to die off as an effect of global warming. Irreversible changes in the ecosystem and the behaviour of animals is also expected. The quality of water will be affected by all these changes.

The impact of global warming on the **human right to water** is clear and evident. Global warming has a severe impact on the availability of clean and safe drinking water. From an abundant supply, water has become a scare resource and the scarcity will mount up with global warming. This will result in lesser consumption of water, which is already there in countries like Mozambique, where people (can) consume only ten liters of water as compared to 200-300 liters a person a day in Europe (UN-Water 2010). The average distance that women in Africa and Asia walk to collect water is six kilometers as against the 1,000 meters envisaged by the human right to water approach. As per the UN-Water estimates, the 884 million people in the world who live more than one kilometer from a water source, water use is often less than five liters a day, when the basic requirement for a lactating women engaged in moderate physical activity is seven and a half liters a day.

Taken together, this means that the world will face vastly increased uncertainty about the availability and quality of water supplies. The warming of the climate system is unequivocal and as it is evident there can be no room any more for skepticism on global warming. Climate change has emerged not only as an important environmental issue but also as a significant political issue at national and global levels. Global warming, being a global problem, needs a global solution. But the North-South divide that exists over the question of reduction in emission of greenhouse gases flops all efforts, including the Kyoto Protocol. An international action to curb global warming effectively cannot be expected in the near future. So what can be done is domestic action to prevent the ill-effects of warming and the protection of indigenous water sources. Governments must build infrastructure to protect coastal areas, improve management of water basins, protect local water springs and adopt new technologies to enhance availability and reliability of water resources.

## References


1. Anisimov, Oleg A. et al. (2007): *Climate Change 2007: Impacts, Adaptation and Vulnerability, Contribution of Working Group II to the Fourth Assessment Report of the Intergovernmental Panel on Climate Change*, Cambridge University Press, Cambridge, 653-88.
2. Associated Press (2009): "California Facing Worst Drought in Modern History," *USA Today*, January 30.
3. Bradley, Fikes J. (2008): "Met Price Hike to Float Local Water Rate Increases," *North County Times*, March 15.
4. Camille, Parmesen and John, Mathews (2005): "Biological Impacts of Climate Change," *Sinauer Associates*, USA, 333-74.
5. Corinne J. Shuster-Wallace et al. (2008): "Safe Water as the Key to Global Health," *United Nations University International Network on Water, Environment and Health*, UN.
6. Daniel, Wild; Carl-Johan, Francke; Pierin, Menzli; and Urs, Schon (2007): "Water: A Market of the Future – Global Trends Open up New Investment Opportunities," *Sustainability Asset Management (SAM) Study*, Zurich, December.
7. HDR (2006): *Beyond Scarcity: Power, Poverty and the Global Water Crisis*, Human Development Report 2006, New York, UNDP.
8. IPCC (2001): *Climate Change 2001: Impacts, Adaptation and Vulnerability*, UNEP.
9. Jason, Morrison; Mari, Morikawa; Michael, Murphy and Peter, Schulte (2009): *Water Scarcity and Climate Change*, Ceres Report, Pacific Institute, Oakland.
10. Jayanth, Sthaye; Shukla, P.R. and Ravindranath, N.H. (2006): "Climate Change, Sustainable Development and India: Global and National Concerns," *Current Science*, 90(3), February.
11. Kathleen, Miller (2008): "Climate Change Impacts on Water," *National Centre for Atmospheric Research*, Colarado.
12. Maude, Barlow and Tony, Clarke (2002): *Blue Gold, The Fight to Stop the Corporate Theft of the World's Water*, Left Word, New Delhi.
13. NCAR (2005): *Drought's Growing Reach*, National Centre for Atmospheric Research, January 10.

14. Science Daily (2008): "Global Warming Affects World's Largest Freshwater Lake," *National Science Foundation*, May 1.
15. UN (2011): "Water Resources," United Nations Water Statistics, *UN Water*, http://www.unwater.org/statistics_res.html accessed on 08-11-2011.
16. UN (2011a): "Water Pollution, Environmental Degradation and Disasters," United Nations Water Statistics, *UN Water*, http://www.unwater.org/statistics_pollu.html accessed on 08-11-2011.
17. UN (2011b): "Drinking Water and Sanitation," United Nations Water Statistics, *UN Water*, http://www.unwater.org/statistics_san.html accessed on 08-11-2011.
18. UN (2010): "Water Use," United Nations Water Statistics, *UN Water*, http://www.unwater.org/ statistics_use.html accessed on 20-12-2010.
19. UNEP (2003): "How Will Global Warming Affect My World?" *A Simplified Guide to the IPCC's "Climate Change 2001: Impacts, Adaptation and Vulnerability,"* France.
20. UN-Water (2011): "Water Scarcity," International Decade for Action, Water for Life 2005-2015, *UN Water*, UNEP.
21. UN-Water (2010): *The Human Right to Water and Sanitation*, Resolution A/RES/64/292, United Nations General Assembly, July 28.

# 12

# Water Pollution – A Challenge to Right to Environment in Kuttanad, Kerala

*Dr. Umadevis*

Human rights are natural rights based on natural law. That is why they are inalienable and unchallengeable. Every individual should have minimal rights as a human being either against the state or political authority or fellow beings. Since they are natural, state and empires are always subsequent to them. So human rights are universal, and must be respected by all societies and governments. The first documentary use of the concept of human rights was in the **Charter of the United Nations**. (Chiranjivi. J. Nirmal, Human Rights in India, Historical, Social and Political Perspectives , p. xxviii) The initiatives for the formation of UNO in 1945 made provisions and suggested to incorporate some of its principles of human rights with the new constitutions of various countries. In 1993 the **UNO World Conference on Human Rights in Vienna**, "all human rights are universal, indivisible and interdependent and interrelated" (Barry e Hill, Steve Wolfson, and Nicholas Targ, Human Rights and the Environment: a synopsis and some Prediction, Institute Natcional de Ecologia). In 1948 the UNO first recognised the existence of human rights, which are those freedoms, immunities and benefits that all human beings should be able to maintain as a matter of right as a social being.

The **Draft Declaration** of Principles on Human Rights and the **Environment** (1994) provided that, 'persons have the right to a secure, healthy and ecologically sound environment. This right and other human rights including civil, cultural economic, political and social rights are universal, interdependent and indivisible' (*Ibid*).

**Right to environment is** the third generation human rights, which is the pre-condition for one of the first generation human rights – right to life. The right to development (material) is another human right to which also right to environment is a prerequisite. So both are equally applicable to present and future generations simultaneously.

Environment is the totality of physical substances and conditions both natural and artificial (human created), including all living organisms in the biotic community, air, water, land, natural resources and climate etc. which affect the entire living beings. The Environmental Protection Act (EPA) in 1986, defines environment includes water, air and land and human beings and other living creatures, plants and microorganisms and properties. (K.K. Sunitha, Environmental Jurisprudence in India: Philosophy and Practice, National seminar on Indian Philosophy: It's relevance in the 21st century - 18th and 19th century, January 2008). The Bhumisuktha of Atharva Veda considers Bhumi, the environment symbolises the three principal components –land, water and air. According to Indian philosophy the environment is composed by "**panchabhoota**"- Akash, bhoomi, water, air and Agni - from which entire living beings including humane coming from, living in and going to!

The right to healthy environment includes the enjoyment of clean water, pure water, and scenic lands, freedom from unwanted exposure to toxic chemicals and other contaminants, secure climate etc. Right to drinking water is important for right to life. A quality drinking water is defined as the water which is free from disease-causing organisms, harmful chemical substances and radioactive matter, taste good, in aesthetically appealing and is free from objectionable colour or odour (Life Water Canada 2007). There is a difference between 'pure water and safe drinking water'-pure water does not contain any minerals or chemicals, and does not exist naturally (**EPA 1999**). Safe drinking water may contain naturally occurring minerals and chemicals such as calcium, potassium, sodium or fluoride which are actually beneficial to human health (UNEP-2008).

Kuttanad is a region located in the coastal low-land of Kerala's well known for its scenic backwaters and paddy fields. It is one of the lowest regions from the sea level (50 km of the area below sea level) in India. It is surrounded by lagoons, rivers and canals. This area forms one of the larger and most complex backwater systems. The geographic characteristic is a system of rivers, rivulet, canals and waterways which is filled with water throughout the year. In this area houses will be surrounded with water throughout the year. It is the region of deltaic formation of the four rivers (Meenachil, Pamba, Manimala and Achankovil). It spreads over Kottayam, Pathanamthitta and Allappuzha districts below the sea level.

**Pollution of water** (both river and well) and the scarcity and sanity of drinking water are shocking issues in this area. About 80 per cent of the people of Kuttanad have no access to clean water. At the same time, other sources of water are unreliable for drinking; the ground water is acidic due to the soil conditions and iron leaching; fresh water from public tap is not frequent; and water supplies from private vendors are extremely expensive. The pollution and unscrupulous urban planning have severely affected the quality and quantity of fresh water supply in this region. According to a survey conducted by the Centre for Water **Resource Development and Management (CWRDM)**, more than 80 per cent of the people in Kuttanad depend contaminated canal water for their daily water requirements. The public water supply network in Kuttanad is failed to meet the popular demand due to several reasons:

1. Supply of drinking water through public taps is highly irregular. It is very frequent in a weak and often for one hour during evening.
2. Officials are not giving enough communications to villagers (leaders) regarding time and quality of water released through the public taps. Since women and children are having the responsibility to collect water from the public pipes which may impose large social burden on them.
3. Public water supply network has limited coverage due to the difficulty in paving pipes across lands and paddy fields.

Due to the above reasons river water has to be used for bathing or washing clothes. In a survey conducted in Kuttanad in 2002 about 7 per cent of the households are using river water for drinking, which is not even suitable for bathing. (Report of the Study conducted by the School of Environmental Sciences, MG University p. 26, Website).

So rain water alone satisfies the quality for drinking water in this area as per the **WHO guidelines.**

According to a study, conducted by **CWRDM**, an average of 2400 Coliforms and e-colis are detected in per 100 ml water. (Reported by India Vision Channel on 13/10/2011) which causes several epidemics and water generic diseases namely, entricfever, typhoid, hepatitis, Weil's diseases, cholera, Japanese encephalitis and amoebiasis (*Ibid*).The major types of bacteria, viruses, prolozoa and worm infections causes Typhoid, cholera and dysentery etc. Well water in sampling contains 1,400 E.Coliforms in 100 ml. of water and river water from the sampling contains 1,050 E.coli. per 100 ml water. So both river and well water are more or less polluted.

Since over 20,000 cases of acute diarrheal disease every year, effective remediation strategies must be put in place immediately (MG University environmental dept study).

## Main Causes for Pollutions

This can be generally categorized in two - human sponsored (both individual and social level) and government sponsored. Pollution from human wastage and animal wastage are extremely high in Kuttanad (Information collected from former NSS Programme Officer who conducted a survey in Kuttanad). The examples for individual sponsored are human wastage from houses, tourists, house boats, hotels and resorts (plastic wastes, food wastes etc.), Increasing usage of chemical fertlisers and pesticides in agricultural sector etc. About 25000 tonne chemical fertilisers, 500 tonne pesticides and 225 crores of material wastes are usually dumping in the water there per year. (Report - India Vision-*Ibid*). Animal enteric bacteria are also polluting the both river and ground water. Lack of adequate waste disposal system and breakage of septic tank are other individual sponsored causes. The population growth is another alarming issue related to human sponsored pollution. Examples for government sponsored are in the name of development unscientific construction works, promoting mechanised maritime facilities etc. The fresh water supply is highly defective due to urban encroachment, land reclamation for agriculture and tourism, fragmentation by transportation routes, intensive agricultural run-offs including fertilisers and pesticides, plastic wards, from hospitals, hotels, house boats etc. There are over 1000 house boats operating here. The food leftovers and plastic waste dumped by tourists and others are causing immense damage to the ecosystem, which in turn will lead to the tourism industry dying a slow death (*The Hindu*, Oct.1st, 2011, Kochi, p. 5). In this region intensive untreated human sewage, progress made in the name of development and modern forms of agricultural activities have caused severe surface water contaminations. The other reasons are reclamations of wet lands for plantations, housing and fragmentations by roads, railway lines etc. Lack of feeling of nature to nature among the people also contributed to the pollution.

**Thannermukkom barrage** is an example for unscientific construction. Recently, our former state finance minister demanded to open the shutter of barrage to let the salt water flow in for cleansing Kuttanad region. The Thannermukkom barrage constructed in 1975 to block the entry of sea water may also have distorted the ecosystem. It is indented for second rice crop in Kuttanadu, what happened is that it has greatly obstructed the water way and made the rivers stagnant leading to severe environmental problems like eutrophication, decline in fish yield from back waters, siltation and water borne diseases. In addition, the stagnant waters are becoming a breeding place for mosquitoes and other germs carrying infectious diseases. (**MSSRF-2007**). It has greatly blocked the water way and made the rivers stagnant due to the absence of third phase of its process. (Reported by Agricultural dept. in *Janmabhumi* (mal) daily 15/10/2011, p. 2).

Further the local environmental condition is more complicated due to regular flooded situation. The region is regularly flooded at a level of 30 cm above from the ground level during the peak of monsoon seasons every year. The epidemiologic studies have indicated that extreme environmental factors are also causing pollution and epidemic outbreaks.

**An over view of Initiatives from the government to ensure right to healthy environment.**

A new provision has been added by the Parliament with the constitution in 42nd Amendment which carries the spirit of Indian Philosophy to respect the nature or environment. The highest court of appeal in India, has taken several proactive role in ensuring these constitutional provisions and the formulation of laws for the purpose of securing clean and healthy environment to each and every citizens of the country. Even though several provisions in the constitution, only because of the failure from the part of other two branches of government, the judiciary is compelled to enter and tackle the problems. This is reflected from an observation made by the Chief Justice B.N. Kripal "it has frequently fallen to the judiciary to protect environmental interests, due to the sketchy input from the legislature and laxity on the part of the administration". Then the Supreme Court of India has linked the human right to environment with right to life (Art. 21) and made actionable under Art. 32 and Art. 226. In a writ, (Subhash Kumar Vs. State of Bihar) (AIR1991, SC, 420), the Supreme Court of India affirmed that the constitutional right to life includes "the right of enjoyment of pollution free water and air for full enjoyment of life". In the writ named Vellore Citizens welfare forum Vs Union of India {(1996) 5 SCC 647}, Justice Kuldip Singh said "in view of the constitutional and statutory provisions ...... the Precautionary principle and Polluter Pays Principle are part of the environmental law of our country. The Supreme Court of India has interpreted this principle as that absolute liability for harm to environment extends not only to compensate the victim of pollution but also the cost restoring the environmental degradation. Besides there were various High Court in India went ahead and enthusiastically declared that the right to environment was included in the right to life under Art. 21. (P. Leelakrishnan, Environmental Law in India, Butter worths 2002).

Water Acts have been enacted by the government (both centre and state governments). **The Kerala State Pollution Control Board** has enacted 4 Acts and related rules or statutes aimed at protection of pure water in the state. (Water (protection and control of pollution) Act). **One of the aim of Kuttanad Package (Report of MSSRF)** is to allow the free flow of water throughout the area.

**Crucial remedies –** This is not a unique one. The entire nation is facing such grave crisis. in order to tackle this scourged situation the entire nation itself should come forward with the spirit of self righteousness. Initiative from the part of the government:

1. Stringent enforcement of the law and monitoring with the help of civil society.
2. Judiciary should have more involvement, as the guardian of guaranteed rights of the citizens with direct involvement, if needed.
3. Rules should be revised, if needed, by giving importance to eco-friendly life style.
4. Unused check dams, if there, to be removed for smooth flow of water.
5. Rigorous guidelines should be given to the operation of tourism.
6. Thannermukkom and Thottappally barriers are to be opened frequently for allowing the flow of salt water which may squeeze worms in the back water.
7. House sewage disposal system is to be installed in every house in surrounding areas.
8. Aid to be provided in constructing rainwater harvesting system in every house or in public sector.
9. Empowering the people to monitor the quality of their own water resources with the help of water testing kit.
10. So called development initiatives and tourism are to be restricted with respect to natural resources.

**Initiatives by the civil society**

1. **Human Right Organisations** should have the full freedom and responsibility to notice the matter before the concerned authority and should monitor the follow up action in constant manner. (For. example, Regarding increasing usage of chemical fertiliser, pesticides in agriculture, dumping sewages etc.).
2. Residents associations, Grama Sabha etc. also should have the same responsibility.
3. Awareness classes and follow up supervision can also be made by them.

## Individual Initiative

Marshalling the spirit of self-righteousness and self-relevance both in personal and social life. It is the high time to make aware about the principle of Dharma, enshrined in our culture, for the protection of all sorts of rights of every body in every phases of life. It is the **Dharma** of every individual (as social being) to wake up to the alarming situation of Mother Earth and take up the responsibility towards Her. As already pointed out, initiatives from every corner are to be made with the full spirit. Each and every one of us should be practiced our thoughts to worship the 'panchabhoota as God, *i.e.* Truth. In order to uphold the above said principles (**Sanatana Dharma**) first we need a value-based curriculum, with the implementation of acts, laws, packages etc. This kind of attitudinal change should be essential among all individuals and societies. We, the present generation should have the responsibility to take care of our nature by taking into consideration the even living condition of the future generation instead of keeping financial and other material conditions for them.

*"Pridhivyam thrini ratnani Jalam,annam, subhashitam*
*Mooddhe pashanakhandeshu Rathnasamja vidheeyathe"*

—*(Chanakya Darsanam)*

The world has three priceless diamonds (germs) water, food, and wise words.

Yet fools point to stones and say "those are diamonds".

# SECTION-III

# CLIMATE CHANGE AND HUMAN RIGHTS

13

# Climate Change and Right to Health: Need for Legal Measures

*Dr. K. C. Sunny*

One of the important features of climate change that is witnessed by most regions of the world is the variety of negative effects. Its effect on enjoyment of socio economic rights are unpredictable since some of the negative aspects of climate change are: (1) more extreme weather, (2) destabilisation of local climates, (3) sea level rise, (4) acidification of the oceans, (5) damaged ecosystems and loss of species, (6) drop in ecological productivity, (7) economic costs and (8) decline of agriculture. All these factors have its impact on right to health. There may be health problems generated as the result of malnutrition.

How climate change will impact food availability is a serious question. Food production in some areas is expected to face an overall net decline, though some regions in mid to high altitudes could see increases. The following factors of climate change have direct impact on food security :

- extreme weather events such as severe storms, floods, droughts
- sudden temperature changes at crucial stages in plant growth
- increase in weeds and new weeds
- increase in pests and pest resistance
- changes in water resources available for irrigation
- increase in ground level ozone, which is toxic to plants.

The food scarcity may have its impact on right to nutritious food which is an aspect of right to health. Under nutrition causes various health problems[1], but one can usually reverse them by eating a diet full of the nutrients your body needs[2]. Proper healing of wounds requires various nutrients such as protein, carbohydrates and vitamins. Collagen is a protein necessary to repair the skin, and it is proved that the strength of the collagen your body makes determines the success of the healing process. Vitamin C is also necessary for collagen formation, and inadequate intake results in wounds that form easily and heal slowly. Your body uses carbohydrates to make the energy it needs to heal properly; without an appropriate amount, the healing process may be delayed.

Lack of adequate caloric intake for an extended period results in extreme fatigue. The body needs a minimum amount of nutrition and calories to complete its basic life processes each day, including breathing, your heart beating and digesting food. This is your basal metabolic rate, and Discovery Health refers to it as the amount of calories you need if you remain in bed all day. You need additional calories for voluntary activities such as walking, cleaning, exercising and working. The decreased muscle mass and extreme fat loss that come from under nutrition can make even slight activity difficult. Fatigue eventually interferes with all aspects of daily life. If you feel fatigue resulting from inadequate caloric intake, slowly increase calories with healthy foods until your energy returns.

Studies reveal that prolonged under nutrition can lead to failure of the heart, liver or respiratory systems[3]. Failure to consume any calories for eight to 12 weeks can be fatal. If under nutrition is reversed in time and you maintain healthy habits, you can usually lead a healthy life. It's vital to determine the cause of under nutrition before the organs are affected because it's much more difficult to counteract this severe damage.

There are other factors of climate change which have its impact on right to health. According to the Fourth Assessment Report (2007) of the **Intergovernmental Panel on Climate Change** (IPCC), the observed effects include[4]:

1. The global average surface temperature has increased by approximately 0.65°C over the last 50 years.
2. Eleven of the last 12 years (1995–2006) rank among the 12 warmest years since records began in the 1850s.
3. The rates of warming and of sea level rise have accelerated in recent decades.
4. Many areas, particularly mid- to high-latitude countries, have experienced increases in precipitation and there has been a general increase in the frequency of extreme rainfall.
5. In some regions, such as parts of Asia and Africa, the frequency and intensity of droughts have increased in recent decades.

6. The frequency of the most intense tropical cyclones has increased in some areas, such as the North Atlantic, since the 1970s.

Our personal health may seem to relate mostly to style of life, heredity background, occupation and profession, local environmental exposures, and health-care access, but sustained population health requires the life supporting "services" of the biosphere. Existence of living species depend on supplies of food and water, freedom from excess infectious disease, and the physical safety and comfort conferred by climatic stability. The world's climate system is crucial to this life support. Climate is likely to affect all these conditions and hence have a powerful impact on human health and well-being[5]. In its Third Assessment Report, the United Nation's IPCC concluded that "climate change is projected to increase threats to human health." Climate change can affect human health directly (e.g., impacts of thermal stress, death/injury in floods and storms) and indirectly through changes in the ranges of disease vectors (e.g., mosquitoes), water-borne pathogens, water quality, air quality, and food availability and quality. Global climate change is, therefore, a newer challenge to ongoing efforts to protect human health[6].

It has been established through research that there is a close link between local climate and the occurrence or severity of some diseases and other threats to human health. It is estimated that climate change contributes to 150,000 deaths and 5 million illnesses each year, and the World Health Organisation estimates that a quarter of the world's disease burden is due to the contamination of air, water, soil and food.

In the last quarter of the 20th century, the average atmospheric temperature rose by about one degree Fahrenheit. By 2000, that increase was responsible for the annual loss of about 160,000 lives and the loss of five and a half million years of healthy life, according to estimates by the World Health Organisation. *The toll is expected to double to about 300,000 lives and 11 million years of healthy life by 2020.* Over the period of 1995-2004, a total of 2,500 million people were affected by disasters, with losses of 890,000 dead and costs of US$ 570 billion. Most disasters (75 per cent) are related to weather extremes that climate change is expected to exacerbate.

A massive increase in the frequency of occurrence of natural disasters such as floods, earthquakes, tsunamis, forest fires have been observed in last decades and have a direct impact on human health. Approximately 600,000 deaths occurred worldwide as a result of weather-related natural disasters in the 1990s; some 95 per cent of these were in poor countries. According to the Oxfam report (November 2007), the average number of natural disasters per year during early 1980s was about 120. Now, the number has increased to nearly 500.

The impact of climate change is very serious in India. While Himachal Pradesh and Uttaranchal experienced a cold wave, other parts in the country were subjected to heat wave. In 1998, the heat wave in Orissa was recorded as one of the worst, claiming more than 2000 lives[7].1998 was the warmest year globally. Andhra Pradesh reeled under heat wave in 2003, killing 1421 people, which is an all-time high in the history of Andhra Pradesh. Effects of heat wave were also observed in Uttar Pradesh, Haryana, Punjab, Rajasthan, Gujarat, Bihar, and Orissa in 2003. In June 2005, Orissa recorded the highest temperature of 46.3°C in Bhubaneswar of the last 33 years, which is ten degree above normal, leading to a heat wave. This is not limited to India only. In July 1995, a heat wave in Chicago, USA, caused 514 heat-related deaths (12 per 100,000 population) and 3300 excess emergency admissions. The record high temperatures in Western Europe in the summer of 2003 were associated with a spike of an estimated 70,000 more deaths than the equivalent periods in previous years. Most of the excess deaths during times of thermal extreme are in persons with pre-existing disease, especially cardiovascular and respiratory disease. The very old, the very young, and the frail are the most susceptible[8]. Extremes in maximum and minimum temperatures are also expected to increase. Therefore, it is anticipated that there will be an increase in the number of deaths due to greater frequency and severity of heat waves.

For tackling the health problems generated as the result of climate change certain legal measures are essential.

1. Necessary steps should be taken to ensure food security. For that purpose existing legal provisions relating to land utilisation, water resource management, production, supply and distribution of food grains, use of fertilisers and pesticides shall be reviewed.
2. Right to health shall be guaranteed as a fundamental right and all legal provisions relating to health care should be reviewed in tune with the concept of right to health.

The National Food Security Bill is a right move in this direction. The draft bill is expected to give the government a better idea on how much grain India will have left over for exports after maintaining comfortable buffer stocks in a rural economy heavily dependent on the annual monsoon rains. On the flip side, the bill will weigh on efforts to meet a fiscal deficit target of 4.6 per cent in 2012 by nearly doubling India's annual food subsidies to about $23 billion or two per cent of GDP. It could also perpetually lock the government into costly subsidies to ensure steady supplies of rice, wheat and coarse grain from domestic production or imports. Few key facts about the bill introduced in Parliament later this year are:

- Food and nutritional security, in human life cycle approach, by ensuring access to adequate quantity of quality food at affordable prices.
- Every person belonging to priority households to receive seven kg of foodgrain every month from the state government under the Targeted Public Distribution System (TPDS) at price not exceeding rupees three per kg for rice, rupees two for wheat and rupee one for coarse grains.
- General households to get not less than three kg foodgrain per person per month at subsidised price not exceeding 50 per cent of the minimum support price for wheat and coarse grain and not exceed 50 per cent of derived minimum support price for rice.
- Entitlement at subsidised price to extend up to 75 per cent of rural population and up to 50 per cent of the urban population with not less than 46 per cent of the rural and 28 per cent of the urban population being designated as priority households.
- Every pregnant woman and lactating mother entitled to meal, free of charge, during pregnancy and six months after child birth through the local anganwadis so as to meet the nutritional standards.
- Children up to age of 14 years entitled to free of charge meal through local anganwadis and one mid-day meal everyday in all government-aided schools.
- Provide meals through anganwadis to children who suffer malnutrition. Destitute people to get at least one meal every day. The homeless to get affordable meals at community kitchens.
- Eligible people to receive food security allowance in case of non-supply of the entitled quantities of foodgrain or meals within the time and manner prescribed by the central government.
- The central government to prescribe the guidelines for identification of priority, general households and exclusion criteria for the purpose of their entitlement.

- Identification of priority households and general households by the state government or such other agency as may be decided by the central government.
- Progressively undertake necessary reforms in the TPDS by the central and state governments.
- Eldest woman, not less than 18 years of age, to be treated as head of family for purpose of issuing ration cards.
- Obligation on the central and state governments to put in place an internal grievance redressal mechanism.
- Food commission to be constituted by every state government.
- Penalty on any public servant or authority found guilty by the state or national food commission.

One can expect that the Bill will be passed by the Parliament without any delay. The measures to reform the legal provisions relating to land utilisation, water resource management, production supply and distribution of food grains, use of fertilisers and pesticides shall be taken without any delay.

**Right to health** is not included directly in as a **fundamental right** in the Indian Constitution. However, the Constitution directs the state to take measures to improve the condition of health care of the people. Part IV of the Indian Constitution which is **Directive Principle of State Policy** (DPSP) imposed certain duties on States in this regard. If we analyse those provisions then we find that some provisions of them has directly or indirectly related with public health.

Article 38 of Indian Constitution imposes liability on State that states will secure a social order for the promotion of welfare of the people but without public health we cannot achieve it. It means without public health welfare of people is impossible. Article 39(e) related with workers to protect their health. Article 41 imposed duty on State to public assistance basically for those who are sick and disable. Article 42 makes provision to protect the health of infant and mother by maternity benefit.

The Directive Principle of State Policy under the Article 47 considers it the primary duty of the state to improve public health, securing of justice, human condition of works, extension of sickness, old age, disablement and maternity benefits and also contemplated. Further, State's duty includes prohibition of consumption of intoxicating drinking and drugs are injurious to health. Article 48A ensures that State shall Endeavour to protect and impose the pollution free environment for good health. Article 47 makes improvement of public health a primary duty of State.

Hence, the court should enforce this duty against a defaulting authority on pain of penalty prescribe by law, regardless of the financial resources of such authority[9].

Under Article 47, the State shall regard the raising of the level of nutrition and standard of living of its people and improvement of public health as among its primary duties. The Food Corporation of India being an agency of the State must conform to the letter and spirit of Article 47 to improve public health it should not allow sub-standard food grains to reach the public market[10]. The State under Article 47 has to protect poverty stricken people who are consumer of sub-standard food from injurious effects.

Some other provisions relating to health fall in DPSP. The State shall in particular, direct its policy towards securing health of workers. State organised village panchayats and gave such powers and authority for to function as units of self-government. This **Directive Principle** has now been translated into action through the 73rd Amendment Act 1992 whereby part IX of the Constitution titled "The Panchayats" was inserted. The Panchayat system has significant implications for the health sector. There will be discussed in relation to relevant Articles 243-243A to 243O contained in Part IX.

Article 41 provides right to assistance in case of sickness and disablement. It deals with "The state shall within the limits of its economic capacity and development, make effective provisions for securing the right to work, to education and to public assistance in case of unemployment, old age, sickness and disablement and in other cases of undeserved want". Their implications in relation to health are obvious. Article 42 give the power to State for make provision for securing just and humane conditions of work and for maternity relief and for the protection of environment same as given by Article 48A and same obligation impose to Indian citizen by Article 51A.(g).

Not only the State also Panchayat, Municipalities liable to improve and protect public health. Article 243G says "State that the legislature of a state may endow the panchayats with necessary power and authority in relation to matters listed in the Eleventh Schedule". The entries in this schedule having direct relevance to health are as follows:

*11-Drinking*

*23-Health and sanitation including hospitals, primary health centres and dispensaries.*

*24-Family welfare*

*25-Women and child development*

*26-Social welfare including welfare of the handicapped and mentally retarded.*

Article 243-W finds place in part IXA of the Constitution titled "The Municipalities:

*5-Water supply for domestic, industrial and commercial purpose.*

*6-Public health, sanitation conservancy and solid waste management.*

*9-Safeguarding the interest of weaker sections of society, including the handicapped and mentally retarded.*

*16-Vital statistics including registration of births and deaths.*

*17-Regulation of slaughter-houses and tanneries.*

The DPSP are only the directives to the State. These are non-justifiable. No person can claim for non-fulfilling these directives. But the Supreme Court has brought the right to health under the preview of right to life under Article 21which states that "No person shall be deprived of his life or personal liberty except according to procedure established by law." According to the Supreme Court right to live means something more than mere animal existence and includes the right to live consistently with human dignity and decency.

In 1995, the Supreme Court held that right to health and medical care is a fundamental right covered by Article 21 since health is essential for making the life of workmen meaningful and purposeful and compatible with personal dignity. The state has an obligation under Article 21 to safeguard the right to life of every person, preservation of human life being of paramount importance. The Supreme Court has in the case of *Parmanand Katra vs Union of India*[11], held that whether the patient be an innocent person or be a criminal liable to punishment under the law, it is the obligation of those who are in charge of the health of the community to preserve life so that innocent may be protected and the guilty.

In *Consumer Education and Research Center v. UOI*[12] the Court explicitly held that the right to health was an integral factor of a meaningful right to life. The court held that the right to health and medical care is a fundamental right under Article 21. Supreme Court, in *Paschim Banga Khet Mazdoor Samity & ors v. State of West Bengal & ors*[13], while widening the scope of Art 21 and the government's responsibility to provide medical aid to every person in the country, held that in a welfare state, the primary duty of the government is to secure the welfare of the people. Providing adequate medical facilities for the people is an obligation undertaken by the government in a welfare state. The government discharges this obligation by providing medical care to the persons seeking to avail of those facilities. So the following facilities be provided at the public health centres where the patient can be given basic treatment and his condition stabilized[14].

1. Hospitals at the district and subdivisional level should be upgraded so that serious cases be treated there.
2. Facilities for given specialist treatment should be increased and having regard to the growing needs, it must be made available at the district and subdivisional level hospitals.
3. In order to ensure availability of bed in any emergency at State level hospitals, there should be a centralized communication system so that the patient can be sent immediately to the hospital where bed is available in respect of the treatment, which is required.
4. Proper arrangement of ambulance should be made for transport of a patient from the public health centre to the State hospital.
5. Ambulance should be adequately provided with necessary equipments and medical personnel.

The Supreme Court in its landmark judgment in *Paramanand Katara v Union of India*[15] ruled that every doctor whether at a Government hospital or otherwise has the professional obligation to extend his services with due expertise for protecting life. No law or state action can intervene to avoid delay, the discharge of the paramount obligation cast upon members of the medical profession. The obligation being total, absolute, and paramount, laws of procedure whether in statutes or otherwise which would interfere with the discharge of this obligation cannot be sustained, and must, therefore, give way. In ***CESC Ltd. vs. Subash Chandra Bose***[16] the Supreme Court relied on international instruments and concluded that right to health is a fundamental right. It went further and observed that health is not merely absence of sickness: "The term health implies more than an absence of sickness. Medical care and health facilities not only protect against sickness but also ensure stable manpower for economic development".

While considering the issue of protection of environment in ***Virender Gaur v. State of Haryana***[17], the Supreme Court held that environmental, ecological, air and water pollution, etc., should be regarded as amounting to violation of right to health guaranteed by Article 21 of the Constitution. It is right to state that hygienic environment is an integral facet of the right to healthy life and it would not be possible to live with human dignity without a humane and healthy environment.

However at present there is no law intending to realize the above rights identified by the Supreme Court. The change in climate may make the health problems more acute. So the enactment of a comprehensive health care law, in tune with the mandate of the Constitution and directives of the Supreme Court is needed.

## References

1. Pelletier DL, Frongillo EA Jr, Schroeder DG, Habicht JP (1995) The effects of malnutrition on child mortality in developing countries, *Bull World Health Organ* 73: 443–448.
2. Hadley C, Tegegn A, Tessema F, Cowan JA, Asefa M, et al. (2008) Food insecurity, stressful life events and symptoms of anxiety and depression in east Africa: evidence from the Gilgel Gibe growth and development study. *J Epidemiol Community Health* 62: 980–986.
3. Sandra M. Nicol, Diane L. Carroll, Carol M. Homeyer, Colleen M. Zamagni, The identification of malnutrition in heart failure patients *European Journal of Cardiovascular Nursing*, 1:39-147.
4. Fourth Assessment Report. Geneva: IPCC; 2007. Intergovernmental Panel on Climate Change. Climate Change 2007: Synthesis Report. 3. Third Assessment Report. Vol. 1. Cambridge: Cambridge University Press; 2001. Intergovernmental Panel on Climate Change. Climate Change 2001.
5. Ravindranath NH, Sathaye J. *Climate Change and Developing Countries*. Dordrecht, Netherlands: Kluwer Academic Publishers; 2002.
6. Orissa state Disaster Mitigation Authority. Available from: http://v3.osdma.org/. (accessed on 20 June, 2008).
7. World Health Organisation. Summary. Geneva: WHO; 2003. Climate Change and Human Health: Risks and Responses.
8. See *Ratlam Municipal Council v. Vardichand*, AIR 1980 SC 1622.
9. See *Tapan Kumar v. FCI*, (1996) 6 SSC 101.
10. AIR 1989 SC 2039.
11. AIR 1995 SC 636.
12. (1996) 4 SCC 37.
13. *Ibid* pp. 47-48.
14. AIR 1989 SC 2039.
15. AIR 1992 SC 573, 585.
16. 1995 (2) SCC 577.

# 14

# Climate Change and Human Rights Religious and Ethical Dimensions of Our Ecological Responsibilities

*Gokul Das N.N.*

## Introduction

Our expanding knowledge of climate change has underlined the impact of anthropological thrust on atmosphere and has called for a concerted local, regional and international action. We have our Universal Ecological Responsibilities to be discharged through global thinking and local initiatives. It is not only a question of what we should do but also of what we should think, feel and meditate upon. This is the essence of the Eight Fold Path from the Right Views to Right Contemplation emphasised by **Gautama Buddha**. Enlightenment is a valid sense of knowledge of the Self, of the environment and of the whole universe so that we add to the well being of ourselves and of every other being. We should realise how we ought to live and why. Approaching the threat of climate change as an ecological problem or as an economic one is short sighted. Social, cultural, political and human rights implications and ethical dimensions of climate change should also be emphasised.

## Historical Background

Ours is a simmering planet. In 1827 Fourier postulated the theory that humans could affect the climate. In 1896 Arrhenius tried to show the relationship between burning of fossil fuels and global warming. In 1979 the first climate conference warned that nations of the world should urgently foresee and prevent man made changes in climate.[1]

An Advisory Group on **Green House Effect** was formed ten years after the first climate conference (12-23 February 1979) in Geneva. The conference was sponsored by the World Meteorological Organisation (WMO). This Advisory Group laid the ground work for the formation of Intergovernmental Panel on Climate Change (IPCC) by the WMO and the United Nations Environment Programme (UNEP). IPCC has three working groups. The Working Group on Science looks into the scientific aspects of climate change. The Working Group on Impact and Adaptation deals with the vulnerability of human and natural systems to climate change and options for adaptation. The Working Group on Mitigation is concerned with options for limiting green house gases and mitigating climate change. There is also a Task Force on National Green House Inventories. The working groups and task force have Technical Support Units also. Research is carried out within the framework of the World Climate Research Programme, the International Geosphere-Biosphere Programme and the International Human Dimensions of Global Environmental Change. Monitoring work is carried out within the frame work of the World Weather Watch, the Global Climate Observing System, the Global Terrestrial Observing System and the Global Ocean Observing System.[2]

The Fourth Assessment Report (AR4) of IPCC (2007) underlined that warming of the climate system is unequivocal. Most of the observed increase in globally averaged temperatures since the mid-20th century is very likely (>90 per cent) due to increase in anthropogenic greenhouse gas concentrations. The probability that this is caused by natural climatic processes alone is less than five per cent. World temperatures could rise by between 1.1 and 6.4°C during the 21st century. Sea levels will probably rise by 18 to 59 centimeters. There is a confidence level >90 per cent that there will be more frequent warm spells, heat waves, and heavy rainfall. There is a confidence level >66 per cent that there will be an increase in droughts, tropical cyclones, and extreme high tides. Global atmospheric concentrations of carbon dioxide, methane, and nitrous oxide have increased markedly as a result of human activities since 1750.[3] The IPCC is currently starting to outline its Fifth Assessment Report (AR5) which will be finalised in 2014.

## Climate Change Threatens Human Rights

Climate change directly threatens the fundamental human rights namely the Rights to Life, to Food, to Health, to Habitat and to Work. According to Kyung-wha Kang, the Deputy High Commissioner for Human Rights, global warming and extreme weather conditions have calamitous consequences for the human rights of millions of people.

Climate change may affect the very Right to Life. Countries have an obligation to prevent and address consequences that climate change may reap on human rights[4]. The major Human Rights Instruments were developed long before climate change was understood to be a looming threat to human security. However, the environmental dimension of these rights has been extensively elaborated by scientists, philanthropists, intellectuals, legal luminaries, human rights activists and moralists.

## Right to Life

According to Article 3 of the **Universal Declaration of Human Rights** (UDHR), every one has the **right to life**, liberty and security of person. Article 6 of the International Covenant on Civil and Political Rights (ICCPR) states that every human being has the inherent right to life. Right to life is not right to survival but right to live with dignity. Dignity is a term used in moral, ethical, and political discussions to signify that a being has an innate right for respect and ethical treatment. Many ethicists argue that the "right to life," where it exists, depends on conditions other than membership of the human species. According to Peter Singer, a notable proponent of this argument, the right to life is grounded on the ability to plan and anticipate one's future. This concept is extended to non-human species also.[5] Climate change threatens the right to life of all forms of life; destroys habitats by way of rising waves, tides and consequent erosion and extreme weather conditions including floods, and drought. Deterioration of habitat and health, diminishing access to safe drinking water and nutritious diet and increasing susceptibility to diseases may all result from climate change.

## Right to Food

The right to adequate food is recognised in several international human rights instruments; most comprehensively in the International **Covenant on Economic Social and Cultural Rights** (ICCPR). According to article 11(1), state parties recognize 'the right of everyone to an adequate standard of living for himself and his family, including adequate food, clothing and housing, and to the continuous improvement of living conditions', while article 11(2) recognise that more immediate and urgent steps may be needed to ensure 'the fundamental right to freedom from hunger and malnutrition'. The UN Special Rapporteur on the **Right to Food** has defined: "the right to adequate food is a human right, inherent in all people, to have regular, permanent and unrestricted access, either directly or by means of financial purchases, to quantitatively and qualitatively adequate and sufficient food corresponding to the cultural traditions of people to which the consumer belongs, and which ensures a physical and mental, individual and collective fulfilling and dignified life free of fear".[6]

Climate change will detrimentally affect the right to food. Regional food production is likely to decline because of increased temperatures and accelerating grain sterility. Shift in rainfall patterns renders productive land infertile. Accelerating erosion, desertification and reducing crop and livestock yields are other threats of climate change. Rising sea levels make coastal lands unusable, unstable and cause fish species to migrate away to distant seas or even disappear. This depletes fish catch and impoverishes fish workers, and threatens protein availability to the poor inhabiting costal areas in all continents. Also, an increase in the frequency of extreme weather events disrupt yield of crops.[7]

## The Right to Water

In 2002 the **UN Committee on Economic, Social and Cultural Rights** recognised that water itself is an independent right.[8] Availability of potable water is one of the most fundamental conditions for survival. As a result of climate change, the earth gets warmer. Heat waves and water shortages make access to safe drinking water most difficult and jeopardize hygiene and sanitation. Right to water is also articulated in the Article 24 (c) of the **Convention on the Rights of the Child** (CRC) and Article 14(2) (h) of the **Convention on the Elimination of Discrimination Against Women** (CEDAW). Lower and erratic rainfall and global warming will be exacerbated by the recession of the Himalayan glaciers, which flow in into the Ganges, Indus, Brahmaputra and other rivers.[9] Violent conflicts over water often called water wars between villagers, city dwellers, between ethnic groups and between nations are likely to become more severe and widespread.

## The Right to Health

According to Article 25 of the UDHR everyone has the right to a standard of living adequate for the health and well-being of himself and of his family. Article 12(a) of the ICESCR recognises the right of everyone to 'the enjoyment of the highest standard of physical and mental health'. Article 12 of the CEDAW contains provisions to eliminate discrimination against women in the field of health care and to ensure, on a basis of equality of men and women, access to health care services. The right to health is also referred to in a number of articles in the CRC. Article 24 stipulates that state parties must ensure that every child enjoys the 'highest attainable standard of health'.

Climate change poses significant risks to the right to health. A 2003 joint study by the World Health Organisation and the London School of Hygiene and Tropical Medicine states that global warming may already be responsible for more than 160,000 deaths a year from malaria and malnutrition; a number that could double by 2020.[10] Climate change may bring about a rainy warmer weather, providing a more hospitable environment for mosquitoes and other vectors and thus cause eruption of various vector borne diseases. A warm humid climate also increases incidence of respiratory diseases. Global warming leads to drought in some regions while causing unexpected heavy rainfall in other regions. Both these situations lead to increase in incidence of water borne diseases.

## Environmental Refugees

Disasters as a result of climate change such as droughts, floods, storms and hurricanes destroy human habitations. Rise in sea level will irreversibly submerge costal areas. This will create new influx of **environmental refugees**. The Climate Institute in Washington published in 1995 the first-ever rigorous assessment of the plight of a growing number of people displaced as a result of environmental problems such as drought, soil erosion, desertification and deforestation. With Norman Myers as Principal Investigator and assisted by Jennifer Kent, the study, Environmental Exodus: An Emergent Crisis in the Global Arena has drawn very favourable comment following its initial publication in July 1995. According to the study 3.3 million people will be affected by 2070 from flooding and inundation of settlements in low-lying areas in Indonesia. Jakarta, where excessive pumping of ground water has caused the land to subside alarmingly, is at particular risk, with the prospect of more than a one meter sea level rise by 2070. In India 7.1 million people are at risk. There will be a large-scale displacement in Bangladesh, Manila and other areas in the Philippines are likely to be submerged. In Vietnam where nearly 5,000 km of dikes need to be constructed or strengthened to save large populations living on river deltas.[11] Scholars predict that worldwide many more millions will be displaced because of rising sea levels, desertification, hurricanes, dried up aquifers, weather-induced flooding and other serious environmental changes.

## Persons in Costal Areas and Island Nations

According to U.N. Human Rights Council climate change could erode the rights of people living in small island states, coastal areas and parts of the world subjected to drought and floods. Maldives, Comoros, Tuvalu, Micronesia and other countries have called for "a detailed analytical study of the relationship between climate change and human rights," to be conducted by the Office of the U.N. High Commissioner for Human Rights. With fish as witnesses, the President of Maldives and his Cabinet wore scuba gear and used hand signals at an underwater meeting to highlight the threat climate change poses to the archipelago nation. The meeting, chaired by President Mohamed Nasheed, took place around a table about five meters underwater. At the meeting, the Cabinet signed a declaration calling for global cuts in carbon emissions.

## Indigenous Peoples

Reducing Emissions from Deforestation and Degradation in Developing Countries (REDD) is a recent addition to the climate change mitigation agenda of the United Nations. REDD has significant implications for indigenous peoples. Vast portions of the remaining standing forest in developing countries which are currently targeted for conservation and protection under REDD are home to indigenous peoples.

While it may be agreed that forest conservation is in everyone's interest, and certainly in the interest of indigenous communities which are vulnerable to both climate change and deforestation, schemes such as REDD could actually have negative consequences for indigenous peoples if their rights are not taken into account. Past experiences have shown that interests of indigenous peoples and forest conservation policies have not tended to fit on the same agenda. An estimated 60 million indigenous peoples are completely dependent on forests and are considered the most threatened by REDD. Therefore, indigenous leaders are among its most prominent critics. The International Indigenous Peoples' Forum on Climate Change declared that: '...REDD will steal our land. States and carbon traders will take control over our forests.'[12]

## Religious and Ethical Response to Climate Change

How should we respond to climate change? We have moral beliefs on the basis of which we understand what is right and wrong. This is true of environmental ethics also. A concern not only for other humans but other forms of life is the essence of bioethics. We are running up against the limits of our planet's capacity to absorb wastes produced by our affluent lifestyle. Indian thought always proclaimed that an ideal life is less reliant on high levels of material consumption. Those who consume more resources produce more pollutants including green house gases.

## Jainism and Buddhism

The atheist religion **Jainism** is called a religion of ecology or a faith in which ecology has turned into a religion. It has generated an environment-friendly value system and code of conduct. Because of the insistence on nonviolence Jains are always ready and willing to look positively and with enthusiasm upon environmental causes. Selflessness, mindfulness, compassion, and wisdom form the essence of the agnostic and rational religion of **Buddhism**. Peace is realized when we are mindful of each and every step. When we respect the environment, nature will be good to us. Every follower of the Buddha ought to plant a tree every few years and look after it until it is safely established. The universal observation of this rule would result in a high rate of genuine economic development independent of any foreign aid. Much of the economic decay of many other parts of the world is undoubtedly due to a heedless and shameful neglect of trees. The trees are like our parents. They provide us with everything; fruit for nourishment, fibre for clothing, twigs for fuel and timber and leaves for house building. They satisfy most of our needs and hence the Buddhist Emperor Ashoka (304 – 232 BC) created laws and engraved edicts for the protection of forests.

## Hinduism

**Hinduism has** always been an environmentally sensitive philosophy. Ecology is an inherent part of the spiritual world view in Hinduism. Vedic sages regarded Earth as sacred and inviolable. Nature or Earth has never been considered a hostile element to be conquered or dominated. In fact, man is forbidden from exploiting nature. He is taught to live in harmony with nature and recognise that divinity prevails in all elements, including plants and animals. Hindus are taught to be respectful towards mother earth and to use all her reserves judiciously. The rishis of the past have always had a great respect for nature. Theirs was not a superstitious primitive theology but a deep sense of respect for Nature. Their resourcefulness transcended time and is still universally applicable. In Hindu thought the degree of morality is inversely proportional to the obsession with self-interest. "Everything in the universe belongs to the Lord" *Isa Upanishad* proclaimed: "Therefore take only what you need, that is set aside for you. Do not take anything else, for you know to whom it belongs."[13] According to ***Srimad Bhagavatam*** (2.1.32-33) "The air is His breath; the trees are the hairs of His body; the oceans His waist; the hills and mountains are His bones; the rivers are the veins of the Cosmic Person and His movements are the passing of ages.[14] The best tribute ever paid to environment is found in Vedas. Sixty three mantras of *Atharva Veda* (12.1.1. to 12.1.63) pertain to Prithvi-sukta (Hymn to Earth), which glorifies Mother Earth. It proclaims that the earth is our mother and we are all her children.[15] In every act of ritualistic worship or devotion *(puja),* the priest implores mother earth and asks for her permission to undertake the puja upon her. Before beginning to plough the land the peasant seeks consent from the Mother Earth and begs for her pardon for he may hurt her for his livelihood. Every morning a Hindu is expected to request permission from *Prithvi Mata* (Mother Earth) to tread upon her. "O Goddess Earth, consort of Vishnu, the Lord of the Universe! You, whose garments are the oceans and whose ornaments are the hills and mountain ranges, please forgive me as I walk on you this day".[16] The **Vedas** extol water and pay homage to its forms (oceans, rivers, lakes) and virtues, unequivocally endorsing that it is to be utilised wisely. According to **Rig-Veda** (1.23): "Waters contain all disease dispelling medicaments useful for the upkeep of our body, so that we may live long to enjoy the bright sun. That there is ambrosia in waters, there is healing balm in them, and there are medicinal herbs, know this all, and by their proper use become wiser."[17] Trees and plants are fundamental to the Hindu faith and to the earth's survival. The *Devi Stotram* verifies this principle: "So long as this land will have mountains, forests and pastures that long will the Earth survive, sustaining you and the coming generations."[18] There are many specific teachings on environmental matters contained in ancient Hindu scriptures and ecological activists have drawn much inspiration from the text. *Rig Veda* tells not to cut trees, because they remove pollution."[19] Also, **Yajur Veda** warns not to disturb the sky and not to pollute the atmosphere."[20]

## Martyrdom of the Bishnois

**Bishnois** originally hailing from Thar, Rajasthan are now scattered in the states of Haryana, Punjab, Uttar Pradesh, Gujarat, and Madhya Pradesh. They are followers of Jambeshwar or Jamboji, a seer who lived between 1452 to 1537 CE. Along with devotion to God, and compassion to fellow animals, protection of nature figured in his teachings which led to symbiosis of Bishnois with nature. Bishnoi settlements are like oasis in Thar Desert with green-belts, birds, bucks and chinkaras which roam about fearlessly. Traditionally rainwater was collected carefully in underground wells. **Bishnois** are an exemplary community in environment protection.

**Khejarli or Khejadli** is a village in Jodhpur district of Rajasthan, 26 km south-east of the city of Jodhpur. The name of the town is derived from Khejri (*Prosopis cineraria*) trees, which were in abundance in the village. Giridhar Bhandari, a minister with Maharaja Abhay Singh, the Ruler of Marwar (Jodhpur) wanted to fell the sacred green Khejri trees to burn lime for the construction of his new palace. Since there was a lot of greenery in the Bishnoi villages even in the middle of Thar Desert, the king ordered his men to get the woods from Khejri trees. On the tenth day (a black Tuesday) of the month of Bhaadra according to Indian Lunar Calendar, (September) in 1730 A.D they came to cut down trees. In this village 363 Bishnois led by Amrita Devi sacrificed their lives while protecting green Khejri trees considered sacred by the community, by hugging them. This incident is the first event of Chipko Movement in the recorded history.[21, 22]

## Gandhi is a Role Model

**Gandhi's** entire life was an ecological treatise. According to him the mother earth provides everything for our need but not for our greed and any act of consuming more than our essential needs is nothing short of theft. No wonder, moralists, nonviolent activists, feminists, journalists, social reformers, trade union leaders, peasants, prohibitionists, nature-cure lovers, and environmentalists draw inspiration from Gandhi's saintly life and writings. **Gandhi** harked back to the ancient Indian tradition where the ideal is ahimsa or nonviolence. In judging what is good or bad, the Gandhian approach is more comprehensive and consists of three criteria: motive, means and consequences. Economics which departs from or is opposed to ethics should be renounced. According to Gandhi whatever we take, we are snatching from the mouth of others. Therefore, whenever we acquire anything we should judge whether it is really needed. Our wants shall be as few as possible.

## Zoroastrianism

**Zoroastrianism** claims to be the world's oldest revealed religion and also one of the world's first proponents of ecology, through caring for the elements and the earth. As the only conscious creation by God, it is humanity's ultimate task to care for the universe. The faith endorses the caring of the Seven Creations namely, the sky, water, earth, plants, animals, humans and fire, as part of a symbiotic relationship. The sacredness of the creations demands a greater awareness on the part of

Zoroastrians, for at the end of time humanity must give to Ahura Mazda a world in its original perfect state. Maintenance of the purity of nature is the greatest virtue. Giving the dead body to wild animals is not just the last act of charity a Zoroastrian is expected to do. The dead body is by law of nature due to scavenger animals.

## Semitic Religions

Though more anthropocentric as compared to Indian Religions which are cosmic in outlook, Judaism, **Christianity** and **Islam** also do not in any way allow followers to destroy or harm life. God created Adam and placed him in the Garden of Eden "to work it and conserve it."[23]. God led Adam around all of the trees in the Garden of Eden. God told him, 'See how beautiful and praiseworthy all of my works are. Everything I have created has been created for your sake. Think of this and do not corrupt the world; for if you corrupt it, there will be no one to set it right after you.'[24] Through the archetypal commandment to build a protective parapet around our house, the Torah commands us to take careful precautions to save life.[25] God has set the balance so that you may not exceed in the balance. Weigh with justice and do not fall short in the balance.[26] The accountability principle that governs relation of humans with the natural world is understood from this verse: "**Corruption** has flourished on land and sea as a result of people's actions and He will make them taste the consequences of some of their own actions so that they may turn back"[27]. The word "**corruption**" has been interpreted by many scholars to include **environmental degradation**.

## Climate Ethics, Climate Justice and the Eight Fold Path

The first tenet of the Eight Fold Path is Right Views or Right Understanding (samyag-drihsti / sammā-ditthi). Climate has become a highly political issue involving large economic interests. Right Views also envisages Climate Ethics. It is the new and growing area of research that focuses on the ethical dimensions of climate change and embraces the concept of Climate Justice. Climate justice links human rights and development to safeguard the rights of the most vulnerable groups sharing the burdens and benefits of climate change and its resolution equitably and fairly. All the peoples of the world, not just the rich and powerful, have the right to development. The importance of the concept of climate justice is most relevant in the present sociopolitical and economic scenario where twenty per cent of humans consume eighty per cent of the resources and give out the major chunk of green house gases and other pollutants.

Those who have benefited and still benefit from emissions, have according to the Right View an obligation to share benefits with those who are suffering from the effects of these emissions, mainly the vulnerable people in developing countries. Poor people in low income countries should have access to low-carbon technologies so that they can also progress without causing any damage to environment.

Development that meets the needs of the present without compromising the ability of future generations to meet their own needs is otherwise called sustainable development as revealed in Our Common Future[28]. The essential needs of the world's poor should be given overriding priority. Sustainable development ties concern for the carrying capacity of natural ecosystems with the sociopolitical challenges facing humanity. Sustainable development alone can deliver justice for all.

Do we want to be part of the problem or part of the solution? If we are not part of the solution we are the problem. What is our intention? This question should be borne in mind in accordance with the Right Aspiration or the Right Intent (samyak-samkalpa /sammā sankappa), the second tenet of the Eight Fold Path. International network of groups and individuals committed to Climate Justice should play their role expeditiously to prevent catastrophic changes in climate. The network namely Climate Justice Action (CJA) for instance promotes and strengthens the rights and voices of the indigenous and other affected peoples in confronting the climate crisis. They stand for reparations and the repayment of ecological debt to the South by industrialised North. They highlight the critical role of biodiversity in weathering the climate crisis and defend the existence of all species. They expose the roles of market-based "solutions" as well as corporate domination of climate negotiations. A total systemic transformation of our society is the need of the hour and that is what the Right Intent means. Real and just solutions to the climate crisis can be achieved if we sharpen our understanding of the crisis and address, the basic social, ecological, political and economic causes of the climate crisis.[29]

Right Speech (samyag-vāc / sammā-vācā), the third tenet means speaking in ways that are trustworthy, harmonious, comforting and worth taking to heart. All activists should bear in mind that they disseminate the most valuable and scientific information about climate change politely, objectively, explicitly, judiciously and compassionately. To quote Aristotle, anyone can become angry and that is easy; but to be angry with the right person, at the right time, for the right purpose and in the right way is not within everyone's power. To be angry at the affluent nations or to blame Indian cattle wealth and marshy paddy fields for methane emission is of no use. To quote **Buddha**, holding on to anger is like grasping a hot coal with the intent of throwing it at someone else; the angry person is the one who gets burned. However, the rights of the poor and the vulnerable should be defended because that forms the Right Speech.

The fourth tenet of the **Eight Fold Path** is the Right Behaviour or the Right Action (samyak-karmānta / sammā-kammanta). It is not simply abstaining from the five evils. Our behaviour and action should inspire others. The moral strength of a person goes on increasing when the genuine concern is backed by suitable action. We all have a part to play in mitigating the challenge of climate change. How can we make a difference? No doubt, the way every individual acts in the present moment does shape the future of the world. Burning fossil fuels such as natural gas, coal, oil and gasoline raises the level of carbon dioxide, the major contributor to the greenhouse effect and global warming. We can help to reduce the demand for fossil fuels, which in turn reduces global warming, by using energy more wisely. Bearing in mind the three R's of ecology namely Reduce, Reuse and Recycle, we can play our role in accordance with the Right Action to reduce waste by choosing reusable products instead of disposables. Buying products with minimal packaging will help reduce waste. If the rich could decrease their household garbage by ten per cent, 1,200 pounds of carbon dioxide can be reduced annually. And whenever we can, we should recycle paper, plastic, newspaper, glass and metal cans. If there isn't a recycling programme at the workplace or community do what is possible for starting one. By recycling half of the household waste, a middle class family can reduce 2,400 pounds of carbon dioxide annually. Avoiding air conditioning reduces more than 25 per cent of energy consumed. Switching off refrigerator in our house between 6 PM to 9 PM will not destroy anything stored but will help us save one-eighth of energy used by the refrigerator. Buying energy-efficient products is another step in the good direction. Wherever practical, regular light bulbs may be replaced with compact fluorescent light (CFL) bulbs. CFLs also last ten times longer than incandescent bulbs, use two-thirds less energy, and give off 70 per cent less heat. If every family and show room and trade centre replaced one regular light bulb with a CFL, it would eliminate millions of pounds of greenhouse gases emitted during generation. Less driving means fewer emissions. Let us use mass transit system to go to work or school. Let us make sure that each motor vehicle is running efficiently. For example, keeping tyres properly inflated can improve mileage by more than three per cent. Every gallon of petrol we save keeps 20 pounds of carbon dioxide from being let out to the atmosphere. Also, let us save fuel by using hot water only when necessary. Installation of more and more devices which can utilise alternative sources of energy such as sunlight, wind, waves and geothermal energy sources is possible if there is an international political will. Planting a sapling is another Right Action; trees and other plants absorb carbon dioxide and give off oxygen during photosynthesis. Trees are an integral part of the natural atmospheric exchange cycle on Earth, but there are too few of them to fully counter the increases in carbon dioxide emissions by human activities and natural causes.[30]

Right Livelihood (samyag-ājīva / sammā-ājīva) is the next important tenet. Is the type of study, work, or home duties that we undertake consistent with a future which must generate a cleaner environment and with clean, green or sustainable energy? The dictum, Polluter Should Pay, also means that if the rich cannot mend their ways by adopting Right Livelihood, they have the moral responsibility to bear the brunt. The **Greenhouse Development Rights** (GDRs) Framework, developed by Stockholm Environment Institute and Ecoequity, a small activist think tank, presents a burden-sharing framework based on a straightforward accounting of national responsibility and capacity that requires those who consume and emit more than a specified "development threshold" to carry the global cost of an emergency climate programme. Thus, the relatively wealthy population of the world who has produced higher levels of emissions can thereby protect the right to development of the world's poor. The GDRs framework could provide the basis of a solution to the burden-sharing problem at the heart of the climate negotiating impasse.

Based on the global development threshold, and national emissions history and income distribution data, it is possible to calculate any country's responsibility and capacity. A nation's responsibility is defined as the contribution it has made to climate change, and is specified in the GDRs standard case as its cumulative emissions since 1990. A nation's capacity is defined as the national income not demanded by the necessities of everyday life. Thus, any income above the development threshold is available to be "taxed" for investment in climate mitigation and adaptation. This can be interpreted as total income, excluding income below the development threshold. These measures of responsibility and capacity can be combined to determine a country's obligation for shouldering the climate challenge, which is represented as a Responsibility and Capacity Index (RCI). This calculation is done for all countries. In the 2010 standard case, the United States, with its exceptionally large population of individuals with incomes above the $7,500 development threshold (capacity) and the world's largest share of cumulative emissions since 1990 (responsibility), has the largest single share (32 per cent) of global RCI. The EU follows with 25 per cent of the global RCI. China, despite being relatively poor, is home to a significant number of people still living above the development threshold, and has a notable 6.6 per cent share of global RCI, which puts it close behind Japan with its 7.4 per cent. India is also large but far poorer, placing it far behind with a 0.8 per cent share. [31]

Right effort or Right Endeavour (samyag-vyāyāma / sammā-vāyāma) means that individuals as well as nations should make persisting efforts not only to abandon all the wrongs but also should take up right deeds. They should be good and useful to themselves and others. This tenet is a very important guideline to all. Threats posed by climate change demand Right Effort from all, more so from the rich. In mitigating climate change local initiatives involving right effort will contribute a lot. Right Effort begins with right understanding of the situation and involves right planning, implementation and monitoring. Right effort will not allow waste of time and hence efforts to reduce emission of green house gases should be pursued without delay.

**Aravalli Afforestation Project** launched in 1992 is an excellent example of Right Effort. Objectives of the project that cover ten districts of Rajasthan includes (*i*) checking desertification and restoration of the ecological status of the Aravallis by intensive reforestation to meet the needs of fuel wood, fodder grass, timber, fruit and minor forest produce, (*ii*) checking of soil erosion and thereby improving infiltration of water and hydrological balance, (*iii*) providing employment to the rural / tribal population and thereby developing their socio-economic condition and (*iv*) strengthening of the habitat for the animal population in the wild life sanctuaries. Aravalli Afforestation Project has a financial outlay was of Rs. 176.69 crores. The project during its implementation has generated employment potential to the extent of 469.21 million man-days of which more than 70 per cent beneficiaries belong to weaker and vulnerable sections of society. In fact, this project has been the biggest effort ever undertaken with people's participation to check desertification in the state. The direct beneficiaries have been the poor people living in and around the Aravalli hills. Overseas Economic Cooperation Fund (OECF) has rated this project as the model forestry project for India.[32]

**India's National Action Plan on Climate Change** (NAPCC) released on 30 June 2008 is also a Right Effort. The document is intended to provide a concrete road map detailing how India plans to move forward in combating climate change. The Plan, while recognises the immense threat posed by climate change starts by marrying climate change to development concerns in no uncertain terms. The Eight Point Mission includes National Solar Mission, National Mission for Enhanced Energy Efficiency, National Mission on Sustainable Habitat, National Water Mission, National Mission for Sustaining the Himalayan Ecosystem, National Mission for a Green India, National Mission for Sustainable Agriculture and National Mission on Strategic Knowledge for Climate Change; of course an eight point programme.[33]

**Ecotourism** is again a Right Effort. The International Ecotourism Society (TIES) has defined ecotourism as "Responsible travel to natural areas that conserves the environment and improves the well-being of local people." It involves responsible travel to fragile and pristine areas with the purpose of educating the traveller and providing funds for ecological conservation. It directly benefits the economic development and political empowerment of local communities and foster respect for different cultures and for human rights. **Ecotourism** is regarded as a genuine endeavour by environmentalists, so that future generations may experience destinations relatively untouched by humans.[34]

**Green Banking** is another equally important project that may be considered as a Right Effort. With the solar-powered ATMs banks can save energy besides reducing carbon emissions. It can also save power by replacing diesel generators with solar panels. In a bid to reduce the carbon footprint, Romesh Sobti, MD & CEO of IndusInd Bank, who describes "**green banking**" as his mission, has also introduced thin computing (which reduces the need for many personal computers), e-archiving, e-learning, **e-waste management**, paperless fax, energy conservation, CNG cars and supporting finance programmes with incentives to go green. IndusInd Bank is just one of the several leading Indian banks with similar plans. "There is already a group of leading banks in India that recognise the importance of their role and the commercial advantage this will give them," says Emily Farnworth, senior advisor on the finance sector to The Climate Group, which acts as secretariat to signatories of the Climate Principles.The State Bank of India (SBI), as part of its green banking policy, plans to set up captive windmills to generate 15 MW of power in Tamil Nadu, Maharashtra and Gujarat. A new study by Pricewaterhouse Coopers (PwC) commissioned by the

Indian Banks' Association (IBA) and The Climate Group confirms that India's leading banks are recognising and seizing opportunities in an emerging low-carbon economy.[35]

Green Production, Clean Technology and Clean Tech Law are other important areas. Cleaner production is a preventive, company-specific environmental protection initiative. It is intended to minimise waste and emissions and maximise product output. By analysing the flow of materials and energy, any industry can identify options to minimise waste and emissions. Improvements in organisation and technology would help reduce excessive use of materials and energy, avoid waste, reduce gaseous emissions and also ensure tranquility through noise-clean technology. Clean Technology hopes for Zero Emissions Techniques and Systems (ZETS). Clean Tech Law contemplates a diverse set of legal and policy issues related to the development and commercialisation of clean technology. Clean tech law could also address issues and conflicts surrounding the placement of such technologies.[36]

Right thought or Right Mindfulness (samyak-smriti / sammā-sati), the seventh tenet involves precision and clarity. We should be mindful of the tiniest details of our experience to develop farsightedness. Right Mindfulness easily assimilates the multidimensional aspects of mitigating climate change: greenhouse development rights (GDRs), environmentalism, eco-feminism, the land ethic, the biophilia hypothesis, deep ecology etc.

**Environmentalism** is a broad philosophy and social movement regarding concerns for environmental conservation and improvement of the health of the environment, particularly as the measure for this health seeks to incorporate the concerns of non-human elements. At its crux, environmentalism is an attempt to balance relations between humanity and their broader organismic and biogeochemical milieu in such a way that all the components are accorded a proper degree of respect.

As early as sixth century BCE since its beginning Buddhism had emphasised Gender Equality. **Buddha** admitted women into Sangha. In this context Buddhist teachings can appreciate the essence of Ecofeminism, the social and political movement which points to the existence of considerable common ground between environmentalism and feminism. Argument of Ecofeminists that important experiential, theoretical, and linguistic parallels exist between the oppression and subordination of women and nature is within the fundamentals of Buddhist view of nature.[37]

The Land Ethic is a perspective on environmental ethics first championed by Aldo Leopold (1887–1948) in his book A Sand County Almanac (1949). He wrote that there was a need for a "new ethic", "ethic dealing with man's relation to land and to the animals and plants which grow upon it." Leopold argues that the next step in the evolution of ethics is the expansion of ethics to include nonhuman members of the biotic community, collectively referred to as "the land." He states the basic principle of his land ethic as, "A thing is right when it tends to preserve the integrity, stability, and beauty of the biotic community. It is wrong when it tends otherwise." He explains further: "The land ethic simply enlarges the boundaries of the community to include soils, waters, plants, and animals, or collectively, the land. Land Ethic changes the role of Homo sapiens from conqueror of the land-community to plain member and citizen of it. It implies respect for his fellow-members, and also respect for the community as such."[38]

The **biophilia hypothesis** suggests that there is an instinctive bond between human beings and other living systems. Edward O. Wilson introduced and popularised the hypothesis in his book entitled *Biophilia*. The term "biophilia" literally means "love of life or living systems." It was first used by Erich Fromm to describe a psychological orientation of being attracted to all that is alive and vital.[39] Wilson uses the term in the same sense when he suggests that biophilia describes "the connections that human beings subconsciously seek with the rest of life." He proposed the possibility that the deep affiliations humans have with nature are rooted in our biology. Unlike phobias, which are the aversions and fears that people have of things in the natural world, philias are the attractions and positive feelings that people have toward certain habitats, activities, and objects in their natural surroundings.[40]

**Deep ecology** is a contemporary ecological philosophy that recognises an inherent worth of other beings, aside from their utility. The philosophy emphasises the interdependence of organisms within ecosystems and that of different ecosystems with one another within the biosphere. It provides a foundation for the environmental, ecological and green movements and fosters a new system of environmental ethics.

**Deep ecology's** core principle is the belief that, like humanity, the living environment as a whole has the same right to live and flourish. Deep ecology describes itself as "deep" because it persists in asking deeper questions concerning "why" and "how". Thus, it is concerned with the fundamental philosophical questions about the impacts of human life as one part of the ecosphere, rather than with a narrow view of ecology as a branch of biological science. It aims to avoid anthropocentric environmentalism, which is concerned with conservation of the environment only for exploitation by and for human purposes. Deep ecology seeks a more holistic view of the world. It emphasises that different components of the ecosystem (including humans) should function as parts of a whole. Arne Naess offers a set of eight principles for uniting Deep Ecologists:

1. The flourishing of human and non-human living beings has intrinsic worth. The worth of non-human beings is independent of their usefulness for human purposes.
2. Richness and diversity of life forms on earth including forms of human cultures have intrinsic worth.
3. Humans have no right to reduce this richness and diversity except to satisfy vital needs.
4. The flourishing of human life and cultures is compatible with a substantially smaller human population.
5. The present human interference with the non-human world is excessive, and the situation is worsening.
6. The foregoing points indicate that changes are necessary in the dominant way humans have behaved until now in their relation to the earth as a whole. The changes will in a fundamental manner, affect political, social, technological, economic and ideological structures.
7. The ideological change in the rich countries will mainly be that of increased appreciation of life quality rather than high material standard of living, in this way preparing the way for a global state of ecologically sustainable development.
8. Those who subscribe to the foregoing points have an obligation directly or indirectly, to try to implement the necessary changes by nonviolent means.[41]

Right Contemplation or Right Meditation or Right Concentration (samyak-samādhi / sammā-samādhi) is the last tenet of the eight fold path. Samadhi is used to overcome the five hindrances in order to enter into jhana. Jhana is an instrument used for developing wisdom by cultivating insight and using it to examine true nature of phenomena with direct cognition. This leads to cutting off the defilements, realising the dhamma and, finally, self-awakening. During the practice of right concentration, the practitioner will need to investigate and verify their right view and passes through different levels of knowledge or jhana and thus right knowledge will arise.[42] This is the best way we reach our inner stillness and use this to focus our hearts and minds so that we can be most effective in addressing global warming and its implications. Just as right contemplation relieves us of the five hindrances, we also get relieved from the anthropocentric vision of the universe. The Aristotelian concept that animals are not rational and hence are resources for man and that men are superior to women should give way to nobler thoughts. We are not on earth to 'rule over the fish of the sea and the birds of the air and over every living creature that moves on the ground.' Our dictum '*sarveshu pranishu samyamah*' as Buddha revealed it, means be disciplined and compassionate to all those that breathe.

## Conclusion

A way of life that does not ensure equity is not worth living. If we are to safeguard the world we need a new world order as envisaged in Buddhist Thought. Essentially, according to Buddhist teachings, the ethical and moral principles are governed by examining whether a certain way of thinking, action or speech is likely to be harmful to one's self or to others and thereby avoiding such actions which are likely to be harmful. Buddhism talks of a skilled mind. A mind that is skilful avoids actions that are likely to cause suffering or remorse to humans as well as nonhuman beings. This embraces climate justice. Faith alone never stops problems; understanding knowledge-wisdom always does. Lord Buddha himself said that belief in Buddha may be dangerous if people do not use their minds. A good life is one inspired by compassion and guided by knowledge.

**Buddhism** stands for equity. Spokes of Dharma Chakra are all of equal length. This means equality of justice for all – humans as well as nonhuman beings. All the spokes start from hub of the wheel. The hub represents the rational and compassionate mind where the Right Views evolve. In other words, the hub of the wheel represents the individual conscience. In the national and global contexts, the hub represents the political think tank, moralists and the intelligentsia who should guide the policy makers and statesmen so that justice for all including nonhuman beings is delivered at grass root levels. The Chinese proverb announces: if a man cheats the earth, the earth will cheat man. We must leave this earth - the atmosphere, the hydrosphere and the biosphere - in a better condition than it is at present.

## References

1. Gupta, Joyeeta. *Our Simmering Planet. What to do about Global Warming* Zed Books, New York, Books For Change India 2001, p. 12.
2. *Ibid.*
3. International Alert, A Climate of Conflict: the links between climate change, peace and war (November 2007) at p. 3.
4. Laura MacInnis 'Climate change threatens human rights of millions: UN' Reuters 19 February 2008.
5. Singer, Peter. *Practical ethics*, Cambridge University Press (1993), 2nd revised ed.
6. Jean Ziegler, *The Right to Food* (Report by the Special Rapporteur on the right to food to the Commission on Human Rights 57th session, 2001) UN Doc E/CN.4/2001/53 at p. 2.
7. Alan Dupont and Graeme Pearman, *Heating up the Planet: climate change and security* (Lowy Institute Paper 12, 2006) at pp. 30-31.
8. UN Committee on Economic, Social and Cultural Rights, *General comment No. 15 - the Right to Water* (2002) UN Doc E/C.12/2002/11.
9. Dupont and Pearman, *Heating up the Planet*, note 21, at p. 34.
10. Shaoni Bhattacharya, 'Global warming kills 160,000 a year', *New Scientist*, 1 October 2003.
11. Norman Myers' Assessment: "Environmental Exodus: An Emergent Crisis in the Global Arena" (1995).
12. A press release brought here on the request of Earth Peoples. September 24, 2008.
13. Isa Upanishad.
14. Srimad Bhagavatam (2.1.32-33).
15. Mata bhumih putro aham prithivyaha from Atharva Veda (12.1.12)
16. Samudravasane prithvi, parvathastanamandale/Vishnupatni namasthubhyam padasparsm kshamasvame.
17. Rig-Veda (1.23).
18. Devi Stotram.
19. *Rig Veda,* 6:48:17.
20. *Yajur Veda,* 5:43.
21. Vandana Shiva, *The Women of Chipko Staying Alive: Women, Ecology, And Development*, Zed Books, 1988. p. 67.
22. Roger S. Gottlieb, *Bishops: Defenders of the Environment This Sacred Earth: Religion, Nature, Environment*, Routledge, 1996. p. 159.
23. Genesis 2:15.
24. Ecclesiates Rabbah 7:13.
25. Deuteronomy 22:8.
26. Quran: 55:7-9.
27. Quran: 30:41.

28. The United Nation's Brundtland Commission published the report, *Our Common Future* 1987.
29. http://www.climate-justice-action.org/about/about-cja/
30. Larry West, Top 10 Things You Can Do to Reduce Global Warming About.com Guide.
31. Kartha, S.; Kemp-Benedict, E ; Athanasiou, T, Baer, P. *The Greenhouse Development Rights (GDRs) Framework*, Revised Ed. SEI, 2010.
32. http://rajforest.nic.in/aravalli_afforestation_project.
33. http://www.energymanagertraining.com/NAPCC/main
34. TIES, 1990.
35. www.indiaenvironmentportal.org.in/files/green%20banking.pdf
36. Yacooub, Ali; Johannes Fresner (2006). Half is Enough - An Introduction to Cleaner Production. Beirut, Lebanon: LCPC.
37. Ruether, Rosemary Radford (1993). "Ecofeminism: Symbolic and Social Connections of the Oppression of Women and the Domination of Nature."
38. A.Leopold, "A Sand County Almanac", Oxford University Press, New York, 1949.
39. Fromm, Erich (1964). *The Heart of Man*. Harper & Row.
40. Wilson, Edward O. (1984). *Biophilia*. Cambridge: Harvard University Press.
41. David Rothenberg, Is it too Painful to Think? Conversations with Arne Naess Mineapolis: University of Mineapoli Press from Guha, R, Environmentalism Aglobal History OUP.
42. Sangharakshita, 'The Buddha's Noble Eightfold Path', Windhorse Publications, 2007.

# 15

# CLIMATE CHANGE: ISSUES AND CHALLENGES

*Dr Joseph Sebastian Thekedam*

## Introduction

**Climate change** is one of the biggest issues facing the world today. It is not a new phenomenon in the Earth's history. **Climate change** refers to a significant variation in either the mean state of the climate or in its variability, persisting for an extended period, typically decades or longer. Studies indicate that during the last 100 years the rise in temperature is up to 1.3 degree Fahrenheit or about 0.72 degree Celsius and the present decade recorded the warmest years during the past century. Summer 2002 and 2003 were declared as warmest years during the current century on record by National Oceanic and Atmospheric Administration (NOAA), especially in the Asian sub-continent and in Europe. The tremendous loss of habitat and biodiversity due to climate change making it the most critical challenge not only for human beings but all living species too. Some of the serious implications of climate changes in the globe are so severe that there are strong views from different corners that the growth of modern world has actually led us towards dooms day. This seminar paper makes an enumerative presentation of the causes and consequences. of climate change and care needed to ward off these consequences and to protect Mother Earth.

## Causes of Climate Change

The causes of **climate change** can be put into categories of natural and manmade factors. Natural factors are cosmic happenings, oceanic happenings and terrestrial formulations. They regulate themselves. Man made factors which causes climate changes are considered here. The humans and their actions in the form of production, consumption and technological pursuits cause greatly to global warming because they have the carbon footprints.

(*a*) ***Population Size:*** A large global population means a large demand for everything. The world's population is currently growing by nearly 80 million people per year. Demographers at the United Nations projected that this growth would continue and world population would be in the region of 7.8 billion to 10.8 billion by 2050. The population bomb is behind several other bombs like Climate Bomb, Food insecurity Bomb and so on. Relentless population growth leads to environmental collapse with the supply lines of crucial irreplaceable resources like water and land get exhausted.

(*b*) ***Life Style of People:*** Life style of population can be characterised in terms of water footprint, carbon footprint and ecological footprint and so on. The water footprint is defined as the total volume of fresh water that is used to produce the goods and services consumed by the individual or community. The ecological footprint is a measure of human demand on the Earth's ecosystem. It represents the amount of biologically productive land and sea area needed to regenerate the resources humans consume and to absorb and render harmless the corresponding waste. The rise in all these harmful footprints have global warming consequences because they either tell production and its patterns or consumption levels and their patterns are at an unsustainable stage.

(*c*) ***Urbanisation:*** Urbanisation leads to concrete jungles leading to excessive real-estate build-up with attending rise in demand for energy and hence global warming.

(*d*) ***GDP and Global Warming:*** The size of GDP and the underlying technology of Economic activity have global warming implications. Structural changes in the production system involving more energy intensive products lead to global warming.

(*e*) ***Consumerism:*** **Consumerism** is economically manifested in the chronic purchasing of new goods and services, with little attention to their true need, durability, product origin or the environmental consequences of manufacture and disposal. Consumerism has adverse impacts on the environment. Some of the biggest sources of the latest environmental problems come from the act of consumption and its leftovers. More and more natural resources are exploited, processed and sold for the commodities that are consumed by the people. Big factories that produce commodities also often leave wastes that pollute air, land, and water. There are many examples of cases where the big factories do not pay careful attention to their waste disposal management. In Bhopal, more than 2,500 people died in 1984 because of the leaking of Union Carbide gas pipe. In Love Canal, Niagara Falls, Hooker Chemical carelessly dumped more than 20,000 tonnes of dangerous chemical substance. This substance causes many serious problems for the people there (Estes, 2005). The leftovers of the commodities consumed by the people also often become waste that pollutes the environment. Maybe the most obvious examples of the waste left by the people is the greenhouse gases that create greenhouse effects and which in turn will increase the temperature of the Earth. People waste so much of these gases in cars, motorcycles, and factories.

The consumption of many types of resources gives rise to environmental degradation. Consumption of forest resources can lead to environmental problems as well as the loss of critical habitat and species. In many parts of Africa and Asia, fuel wood consumption exceeds forest growth, contributing to forest degradation. Commercial tree plantations—which are increasing in number—can supply wood on a sustainable basis and prevent erosion, but do not support the same level of biodiversity as natural forests. Fossil fuel use results in land degradation. Metal mining degrades vast amounts of land and effects air pollution, disposal of chemicals used in mining, and dispersion of toxic trace metals found in many ores. Overuse of wells, ponds, and rivers for water needs of industries contaminates water supplies. Technological progresses also have a negative impact on the environment, for example, the technology chosen to package and deliver most of the consumer goods using plastic causing great damage to the environment.

(*f*) ***Consumption of Energy:*** The present life style of people is more energy consumptive like increased transportation, that too airways.

(g) ***Land Cover Change:*** Land use refers to application of land for activities such as agriculture, forestry and building construction. It alters the land surface processes including biogeochemistry, hydrology, biodiversity etc. Extensive clearing (deforestation) and intervention in Earth's surface have occurred since industrialisation. Land cover change increases the release of carbon dioxide to the atmosphere by disturbance of terrestrial soils and vegetation, due to deforestation, disturbance by tillage for cultivation and so on. Land cover change is also behind major changes in terrestrial emissions of other greenhouse gases, especially methane. There is also greedy conversion of farm lands into real-estate property or industrial property leaving vast tract of land without its green cover.

## Consequences

The consequences of climate change are the following:

| | |
|---|---|
| **Food Insecurity** | Melting glaciers will increase flood risk. It might harm plants and animals that live in the sea. These could affect food production. |
| | Crop yields will decline, particularly in Africa. Yields in the tropics might fall disastrously because temperatures there are already high that many crop plants cannot tolerate. |
| **Shrinking Land** | Rising Sea levels could leave 200 million people permanently displaced. |
| | High sea levels would submerge some coastal cities, small island nations and other inhabited regions. |
| | Many coastal areas would experience flooding, erosion, loss of wetlands, and an entry of sea water into fresh water areas. |
| **Eco System** | Up to 40 per cent of species could face extinction. |
| | High water temperatures can cause a damaging process called **'coral bleaching'** caused by expulsion of the algae that give them their colour and nourishment.The corals die unless the water temperature cools. |
| | Added warmth also helps spread diseases that affect sea creatures |

| | |
|---|---|
| **Weather Extremes** | Severe heat waves, hurricanes, draughts and other erratic events. |
| | Northern Hemisphere cover will decrease further, but the Atlantic ice sheet will increase. |
| | Sea level will rise by between 9 and 88 cm. |
| | Global mean temperature will increase by between 1.4 and 5.8 degree Celsius. |
| **Economy** | Mildly extreme weather could reduce global GDP by up to one per cent. |
| | A two to three degree Celsius rise in temperatures could reduce global economic output by three per cent. |
| | If temperatures rise by five degree Celsius, up to ten per cent of Global GDP could be lost. The poorest countries would lose more than ten per cent of their output. |
| | In the worst case scenario global consumption per head would fall 20 per cent |
| **Diseases** | Tropical diseases, such as malaria and dengue, might spread to larger regions. |
| | Longer lasting and more intense heat waves could cause more deaths and illnesses. |

India is projected to get severely affected by Climate change. The surface temperatures in India are going up at the rate of 0.4 degree Celsius per hundred years, during the post monsoon and winter season. Some studies predict that the mean winter temperatures will increase by as much as 3.2 degree Celsius in the 2050s due to greenhouse gases and summer temperatures by 2.2 degree Celsius in the 2050s. India is to experience a decline in summer rainfall by the 2050s. It may be noted that the summer rainfall accounts for almost 70 per cent of the total annual rainfall over India. Climate changes can cause large water resource problems, particularly in arid and semi-arid regions such as northwest India impacting adversely agriculture, drinking water and on generation of hydro electric power. Bovine animals may not be reared. Seven million people are projected to be displaced. Certain important coastal metros may face the wrath of sea-level rise induced by a two degree Celsius rise in temperature in about 100 years. Climate change is likely to hit the poorer sections of society the harder. As India is said to become the most populous in the world by 2045, the economic, social and ecological price of climate change is to be massive.

## Care for Climate

The core of most proposals made at Copenhagen (2009 United Nations Climate Change Conference) for combating climate change is the reduction of greenhouse gas emissions through reducing energy waste and switching to cleaner energy sources. Energy conservation methods include increasing the fuel efficiency of vehicles (often through hybrid, plug-in hybrid, and electric cars and improving conventional automobiles), individual-lifestyle changes and changing business practices. Newly developed technologies and currently available technologies including renewable energy (such as solar power, tidal and ocean energy, geothermal power, and wind power) and more controversially nuclear power and the use of carbon sinks, carbon credits, and taxation are aimed more precisely at countering continued greenhouse gas emissions. The ever increasing global population and the planned growth of national GDPs based on current technologies are counter-productive to most of these proposals.

## Energy Efficiency

**Efficient energy** use is the goal of efforts to reduce the amount of energy required to provide products and services. For example, insulating a home allows a building to use less heating and cooling energy to achieve and maintain a comfortable temperature. Installing fluorescent lights or natural skylights reduces the amount of energy required to attain the same level of illumination compared to using traditional incandescent light bulbs. Compact fluorescent lights use two-thirds less energy and may last six to ten times longer than incandescent lights.

## Energy Conservation

**Energy conservation** is broader than energy efficiency in that it encompasses using less energy to achieve a lesser energy service, for example through behavioural change, as well as encompassing energy efficiency. Examples of conservation without efficiency improvements would be heating a room less in winter, driving less, or working in a less brightly lit room. As with other definitions, the boundary between efficient energy use and energy conservation can be fuzzy, but both are important in environmental and economic terms. This is especially the case when actions are directed at the saving of fossil fuels.

## Transport

Modern energy efficient technologies, such as plug-in hybrid electric vehicles, and development of new technologies, such as hydrogen cars, may reduce the consumption of petroleum and emissions of carbon dioxide. A shift from air transport and truck transport to electric rail transport would reduce emissions significantly. Increased use of biofuels (such as ethanol fuel and biodiesel that can be used in today's diesel and gasoline engines) could also reduce emissions if produced environmentally efficiently, especially in conjunction with regular hybrids and plug-in hybrids. For electric vehicles, the reduction of carbon emissions will improve further if the way the required electricity is generated is low-carbon (from renewable energy sources). Increased use of public transport can also reduce greenhouse gas emissions per passenger kilometer.

## Urban Planning

Approaches such as New Urbanism and Transit-oriented development seek to reduce distances travelled, especially by private vehicles, encourage public transit and make walking and cycling more attractive options. This is achieved through medium-density, mixed-use planning and the concentration of housing within walking distance of town centres and transport nodes.

**Building design.** New buildings can be constructed using passive solar building design, low-energy building, or zero-energy building techniques, using renewable heat sources. Existing buildings can be made more efficient through the use of insulation, high-efficiency appliances (particularly hot water heaters and furnaces), double- or triple-glazed gas-filled windows, external window shades, and building orientation and sitting. Renewable heat sources such as shallow geothermal and passive solar energy reduce the amount of greenhouse gasses emitted. In addition to designing buildings which are more energy efficient to heat, it is possible to design buildings that are more energy efficient to cool by using lighter-coloured, more reflective materials in the development of urban areas (*e.g.* by painting roofs white) and planting trees. This saves energy because it cools buildings and reduces the urban heat island effect thus reducing the use of air conditioning.

## Eliminating Waste Methane

Methane is a significantly more powerful greenhouse gas than carbon dioxide. Burning one molecule of methane generates one molecule of carbon dioxide. Accordingly, burning methane which would otherwise be released into the atmosphere (such as at oil wells, landfills, coal mines, waste treatment plants, etc.) provides a net greenhouse gas emissions benefit. However, reducing the amount of waste methane produced in the first place has an even greater beneficial impact, as might other approaches to productive use of otherwise-wasted methane.

## Societal Controls

Another method is to make carbon a new currency by introducing tradable "Personal Carbon Credits". The idea being it will encourage and motivate individuals to reduce their 'carbon footprint' by the way they live. Each citizen will receive a free annual quota of carbon that they can use to travel, buy food, and go about their business. It has been suggested that by using this concept it could actually solve two problems; pollution and poverty, old age pensioners will actually be better off because they fly less often, so they can cash in their quota at the end of the year to pay heating bills, etc.

## Population

Various organisations promote population control as a means for mitigating global warming. Proposed measures include improving access to family planning and reproductive health care and information, public education about the consequences of continued population growth, and improving access of women to education and economic opportunities.

## Reforestation

It is an important measure for combating climate change.

## Additional Measures

Everyone has a role to play in combating climate change. Here is a list of things that everyone can easily do to fight against climate change.

### *SWITCH OFF*

- Don't forget to switch off the lights when you don't need them.
- Don't leave your TV, stereo or computer on standby. On average, a TV set uses 45 per cent of its energy in standby mode.
- Also, don't leave your mobile phone charging when the battery is full. If you do, 95 per cent of the electricity is wasted – only five per cent is used to actually charge your phone.

- Use energy-saving light bulbs – they last longer and use five times less electricity than conventional bulbs.
- When you choose new household appliances (fridges, washing machines, etc.), consider the energy saving label – that shows that they are energy efficient.
- If you turn off the tap while brushing your teeth, you savc several litres of water.

### *TURN DOWN*

- When you make a hot drink, just boil the amount of water you need.
- When you air your room, leave the window wide open for a few minutes and then close it again, rather than letting the heat escape over a long period.
- Defrost your fridge regularly. You can save up to 30 per cent of the energy used.
- Don't set your fridge at the highest cooling setting. When the temperature of your fridge is lower than 5°C, you will only consume more energy; your food will not keep fresh longer.
- Don't put hot or warm food in the fridge. Let it cool down first and place it in the fridge afterwards.

### *RECYCLE*

- When shopping, use a reusable bag instead of a disposable plastic one.
- Bring used glass to the bottle bank and sort paper, cardboard and cans from the rest of your waste. Recycling aluminium cans consumes ten times less energy than producing new ones. Factories use far less energy making paper from old newspapers than from wood pulp.
- If you have a garden, compost your biodegradable waste.
- Choose products that come with little packaging, and buy refills when you can.
- Take your lunch in a reusable lunch box instead of aluminium foil or paper bags.

### *WALK*

- For short distances, for example a few kilometers, avoid taking the car. Walk or cycle instead!
- When you travel further, consider taking a bus or a train.

- Also avoid air travel if you can – airplanes emit a huge amount of $CO_2$ into the atmosphere. Flying is the world's fastest growing source of $CO_2$ emissions.
- If you are about to buy a car, buy a small and fuel efficient model.

## *ADDITIONAL ACTIVITIES*

- Plant a tree in your garden or neighbourhood! Five trees soak up around one tonne of $CO_2$ throughout their life time.
- Look for goods with the Eco-label in shops and supermarkets.
- Use as little paper as possible: photocopy on both sides. Use email.
- Consume locally produced, seasonal food. Not only is it healthier, it is also better for the environment!
- Eat less meat. Producing meat is $CO_2$-intensive.

## CONCLUSION

Climate change is one of the multifaceted problems facing mankind today. It has several aspects and inter-linkages namely, science and technology, economy and trade, diplomacy and politics – that makes it not just another issue in this complicated world of proliferating issues, but the mother of all issues. It should be addressed by all countries with a shared perspective, free from narrow and myopic considerations. However the efforts so far in the direction of meeting the challenges of climate change have been sporadic and incoherent. So we urgently need a new economic paradigm, which is global, inclusive, cooperative, environmentally sensitive and above all scientific.

### References

1. Affisco, J.F., Nasri, F. and Paknejad, M.J. (1996). Environmental versus Quality Standards-an Overview and Comparison *International Journal of Quality Science*, Vol. 2, No. 1, pp. 5-23.
2. Alberti, M., Caini, L., Calabrese, A. and Rossi, D. (2000). Evaluation of the Costs and Benefits of an Environmental Management System, *International Journal of Production Research,* Vol. 38, No. 17, pp. 4455-4466.
3. Andrew Hoffman, (2004). Winning the Greenhouse Gas Game, *Harvard Business Review*, April, p. 20.
4. Baranzini A, Goldemgerg J. Speck S. (2000). A future of Carbon Taxes, *Ecological Economics: 32,* pp. 395-412.

5. Borghesi, S. and Vercelli A., (2003). Sustainable Globalisation. *Ecological Economics*, 44, pp. 77-89.
6. Commoner, B., M. Corr, and P. J. Stamler (1974). The causes of pollution. *Environment* 13(3), 2-19.
7. Epstein, M. J. (2006). 'Improving Environmental Management with Full Environmental Cost Accounting *Environmental Quality Management,* Vol. 6, No. 1, pp. 11-22.
8. Fulekar M.M. (2004). Biomass - A Sustainable Energy Source, *Journal of Current Sciences,* Vol. 5. No. 2.
9. Garg A. and Shukla, P.R., (2002). *Emissions Inventory of India*, Tata McGraw-Hill, New Delhi.
10. Parikh Jyothi, K. and Parikh Kirit, (2002). *Climate Change: India's Perceptions, Positions, Policies and Responsibilities,* OECD 2002, pp. 1-30.
11. Pearce, D., Atkinson, G., (1993). Capital theory and the measurement of sustainable development: An indicator of weak sustainability. *Ecological Economics* 8 (2), pp.103-108.
12. Ramachandran, K.S., (2001). Impact of Climate Change in Asia, *Frontline,* Volume 18, Issue 07, March 31-April 13.
13. Ramkumar, K.S. (2010). Meet Challenges of Climate Change for the Sake of Future Generations, *Tribune Business News*, Washington, March 10.
14. Scruggs, L. A., (1998). Political economic inequality and the environment. *Ecological Economics* 26, pp. 259-275.
15. Shah, Anup, (2006). *Behind Consumption and Consumerism.* (Online) http:www.globalIssues.org/consumption.asp
16. Wikipedia Foundation Inc. (2007). Consumerism (online) http://en.wikipedia.org/wiki/ Consumerism.

# 16

# Academic Discourse on Climate Change in the Social Science: A Critique

**Sajin Philip**

*The purpose of this paper is to argue that the climate change discourse in the social science is anomalous to social science research methodology in the Philosophy of Science. This study provides some insights to the psychology of research and the practice of researchers in conceptualising the question of research. 'Climate change research' has failed to orient in terms of sustainable human progress because of their blind emphasis on adaptation. In this sense, 'climate change research' in the social science is non-humanistic and at odds with the social science research which is supposed to have the normative ground for the centrality of human beings. The 'climate change research' is the classic example of worst deduction and failed positivist research by calling a basket of natural adverse events as 'climate change'. So, 'Climate Change Research' fails its purpose of knowledge production and do not deserve to join the league of Social Science as a branch which enrich it.*

Climate change research marches ahead in its progress in the social science. The purpose of this paper is to argue that it is anomalous to social science research methodology in the Philosophy of Science. (Kuhn, 1977). The Kuhn's analysis of knowledge production in the history of science shows that climate change research does not contribute to the knowledge production and it is only the output of certain technicians who produced the burgeoning of integration of data using technology with huge funding. The delimiting of the study into vulnerability induced adaptation in times of natural calamities does not pay attention to the perpetuation of existing social and economic inequalities which makes the human being versus nature relationship rigid and that poses great threat towards the human progress. This kind of research which is politically motivated does not give insights to the betterment of the people and it serves only the interest of some others who are politically motivated. This study suggests the need for reshaping the '**Climate Change Research Programme**' in the broad framework of Human being-nature relationship to fit squarely into the social science knowledge production.

The subject matter of the social science hinges on the interaction between human beings and material world as well as across human relationship such as caste relation, gender relation, landlord tenant relation, labourer-capitalist relation etc. In a social science exercise of knowledge production, there is the norm that human beings should be the central of the focus of enquiry. The rise of 'Climate Change Research' starts in the wake of fear centred human imaginations of their extinction from earth while they experience the frequent occurrence of the natural catastrophes. The fear centred research is illogical and unreasonable because it loses logic in the making of science. Science gives room for refinement through continuous questioning and widening the knowledge. Thomas S Kuhn, disciple of Karl Popper, advocates that the scientific nature of the study comes from questioning and logical reasoning. One should be aware of preserving the quality of knowledge 'production' by distinguishing it from knowledge 'reproduction' which is similar to the transferring of wine from the old bottle to the new one. The rationale of the knowledge production is concerned of the logical reasoning which is supposed to find out the default and the limitations of the studies earlier done and to rectify it through another study. The scientific study which is an epitome of the knowledge production must expose its limitations for enabling the further study keeping all the procedures used for it open for logical scrutiny without having any inclination to the imposition of fundamentalist ideological bias within it.

There is also a distinction between science and analysis. Science stands above the analysis which is a mere arrangement of information. Current researchers misconceive that information is synonymous with knowledge. Without being taught and realised that information is only an input to the knowledge generation. Science is not a mere logical arrangement of data or information. Beyond that, it is an output of knowledge production, which links the existing knowledge and future knowledge through critical enquiry. In that sense, knowledge production which is involved in the creation of knowledge is radical that it distinguishes from 'analysis' which is not necessarily a new creative output as it in the knowledge. Scientific spirit enables one to challenge, and accommodate which means finding space for the existing knowledge with the objective of the better refinement and improvement. Acquisition of data is not a scientific endeavour and it becomes scientific when the data gives new understanding and insights, adding something or making contrary to the existing knowledge. At the same time, it has to open up for future research allowing the existing one to be destructed after the testing of logical reasoning with the new availability of evidence. It is to be reminded that the 'creative destruction' of the incompetent ideas and the 'creative innovation' for the new ones are part and parcel of the scientific progress.

## Examination of Climate Change Research

The disagreement with the **climate change research** starts from the notions and definitions of 'climate change' itself. **Climate change** is defined to the miscellaneous group of natural calamities such as floods, earthquakes, droughts, cyclones etc. The coinage of the word 'Climate change' and its ideological implications is traced to be of recent origin. The adverse natural events that are occurring since the time immemorial are characterised as distinct from 'climate change'. There seems to be a decoupling of the climate change from the adverse natural events which has been done for the purpose of highlighting the 'climate change' as the centre of analysis. The rising significance of the climate change lies in the portrayal of its recent beginning due to the global warming and melting of ice glaciers in the polars. The upcoming hue and cry in the area of 'climate change' seems as if it awaits the ushering of highly funded, mega showcased research output in the form of plethora of studies. The argument inherent in the 'climate change research programme' is that it is a recent phenomenon assumed great importance due to the high apprehensions on the global warming and other natural catastrophes with the use of the word '**climate change**' opposed to the earlier disposition of people's interaction with the adverse natural events that are commonly appeared in the literature. It conveniently ignores the frequent occurring of the adverse natural events since the existence of human beings and the debates regarding the human beings nature relationship.

Another change worth mentioning is about the direction of climate change. Any reference of 'change' in the science must have a goal with a identifiable and definite process with a clear path, factors associated with it, and actors involved in it who try to retain the status quo to be or change it in accordance with their aspirations. As it is mentioned above, a science is to be viewed when it allows the method of questioning to improve the existing knowledge and widen it. If climate change is supposed to understand analogous with the 'social change', it is not clear what is to be studied in climate change as process, factors and actors. The science behind the climate change is not revealed in the 'climate change research programme' in the social science as they directly clubbing the heterogeneous adverse natural events. It is because of each one is caused by distinct causal mechanism and the clubbing of different events into one basket for making simple the ideological explanation raises the methodological questions from the Philosophy of Science. From the materialistic point of view, it has to be explained within the chemical and physical sciences. Apart from this, it has also to be reminded that the connection between climate change and human beings become relevant only when material changes in the world as far as concerned with the so called 'climate change' should have some kind of interaction with the human beings if it is to be taken granted in the social science analysis. When the range of 'climate change' stretches out to the other material sciences, it is questionable on the basis that something which is to be understood and explained in other disciplines has taken it into the social science and linked it to the human action without being found the potential scope for its association to the human action. The successful link between any material changes and human action happens only when it recognises the role of human will power and aspirations in the transformation of the material world. Human beings are small creatures in relation to the extent of living and non-living activities in earth as well as universe. So it emphasises the scientific endeavour in social science to be meticulous in finding logical reasoning and empirical evidence to produce knowledge on the interaction between human beings and material world as well as interaction among human beings.

There is an introduction needed for bringing the natural disasters in connection with the human action. Thereby one can understand how the natural disasters can be brought into the ambit of social science in connection with the human action. Contrary to the natural disasters, the human disasters are directly caused by intended or unintended actions of the human beings. This distinction between 'Climate Change' and the individual natural disasters can be explained on the basis that occurrence of 'Climate Change' cannot be established without the knowledge on process and factors in the material change with the governing principles. The erratic and sporadic occurrence of disasters not directly related on a spatial basis always does not have any clear, identifiable pattern with reasoning. The basic fallacy associated with the climate change is the establishment of the argument that 'Climate Change' is considered as the basket of various natural calamities and disasters. The natural disasters are of different types caused by various reasons. In this context, it can be questioned that on what basis they can be clubbed into one basket of 'Climate Change'.

On the focus towards '**climate change**', it is being argued that it is erroneous because of its conceptual limitations and of its ignoring the centrality of human action. When the climates change research is fear induced, such enquiries cannot lead to the progress of knowledge because they escape from the knowledge development of the survival techniques for existence. The implication of climate change research is messaging the idea that people automatically adapt with that situation while the events of climate change happens and they continue their living. In this way, the advocating of the reduction of green house gases and focusing towards it indirectly through adaptation research is politically mediated one. The study on 'Climate Change and Adaptation' diverts the attention to the green house gas reductions by making implicit statement in the studies that there is no need to worry about people because they can adapt and can reach to the their earlier situation before they were. Here, the welfare of the people in the long run is ignored.

It is anthropocentric view that human beings can control everything and human wisdom can capture anything. The limitation of the human wisdom and knowledge puts limitation to the wideness of social science. The 'Climate Change' by their definition is a huge external shock to the living organisms on earth, which cannot be under the human control. The mitigation approach of climate change in reducing the green house gases faces several constraints from many sides and these attempts are basically politically vitiated. Again, it is a query that how the 'mitigation' tackles to the heterogeneity of adverse natural events caused by different reasons and what the scientific basis is emanated from the material sciences. The common man's view of changes in weather and his observations on nature is entirely different from the coinage of word 'climate change'. The use of 'Climate change' in the social science literature is the starting ladder for some positivist academicians who mainly give technical explanation from empirical information collected from the sites of adverse natural events. As the popular usage of climate change in the common man's vocabulary is different from the academician's use of the same word in the social science, it demands the methodological enquiry in order to correct and give proper orientation to this branch of knowledge.

The origin of critique of the '**Climate Change**' ideology traces to the worry about life which is not in control of human beings. It ignores the concerns of existence and thereby it lacks realism in scientific endeavour. The 'Climate Change' researchers are confused about the purpose of life and the interaction of 'life' with the changes in the physical world. There is a need of distinction between life and existence. Life of any being is in the hands of many factors which is uncontrollable for the human beings at many circumstances. But existence is within the hand of human will power and action. There needs policy level coordination and individual human enterprises. The fundamental philosophical understanding of the 'meaning' of life is to exist when there is life. There is no logic in bothering about the 'life' because that is not under the control of human being at each and every moment. Any living organism which is born is destined to be decayed. The life can be lengthened, but growth of the particular organism is increasing and the limit of growth at a certain point of any living organism culminates into the ultimate destruction of it. The purpose of this narration serves to show the futility of worrying for their life on earth. The relative significance of human life is negligible on this earth when we compared with the rise and demise of many living beings in the history of earth. It is illogical to think that all things happening on universe and earth particularly are not only connected to the life of human beings. The life of human beings is similar to the all living beings in the interdependent life system on the planet earth. The continuation of 'existence' in life is important and existence is the goal of any life form. But existence as a goal is relevant only upto the end of life. The point put forward is that giving importance to exist is vital than worrying about life. This is supported by another reason that struggle to exist is under the human action and the concerns of 'life' have limitations from the part of human action. The human life is governed by its own rules of materialistic world rather than human determinism. Human determinism may be possible to a great extent in the manipulation of life such as lengthening manifested in curing the chronic disease and extending death etc., but it fails at a point when the life peaks in accordance with the natural rule of law. The Climate Change Ideology ignores the concerns of existence and thereby it lacks realism in scientific endeavour. Ideology is antithetical to the notion of theory in science. (Fine, 1980) So it lacks the relevance of the 'Climate Change Research' in Social Science and hence, it became non-humanistic in approach.

## Adaptation Revisiting

In the climate change research programme, there is mentioned of the vulnerability and adaptation. Because of people are vulnerable, they adapt and hence, the adaptation is the antidote to the vulnerability. The vulnerability induced adaptation only sustains vulnerability and it maintains the status quo of the situation. In other words, adaptation is the social reproduction of the existing system when the external shock happens. The same vulnerable situation is reproduced as part of adaptation and they continue living without bothered about the similar past experiences of disasters. The academics of the 'climate change research' comfortably forget the possibility of vicious cycle of adaptation in times of 'climate change' incidents in the absence of a long run approach of avoiding the situation of perpetuation of vulnerability. The adaptation does not raise the standard of living of the people in the long run. Instead, it talks only the immediacy of reaching into the previous position of living from the state of deterioration due to the 'climate change' events. The problem here is that this kind of research is only about the maintenance of the status quo. In a place where natural calamities are frequent, people acquired a kind of resistance to overcome the situation and continue their living there. It only reckons their tolerance capacity and helplessness of the vulnerable people.

The study on adaptation and vulnerability does not focus on the progress of human beings in their existence in the lifetime. This study wants to indicate that the strategy of adaptation has a shortsighted approach. It tells that adaptation is the response towards a particular situation of disaster or risk. Adaptation is not concerned about their over all development in the long run for building up of the livelihood in order to rescue from the structural barriers in developing the sustainable forms of existence. This is what this study considers as the limitation of adaptation. Vulnerability is a structurally determined one. The external shock has an interaction with the vulnerability and it is to be checked that shock is absorbed or not. The nexus link between vulnerability and adaptation in times of natural catastrophe make the community or section of people to remain vulnerable. This analysis shows that vulnerability cannot be annihilated by adaptation. The external shock in the form of disasters can make the existing situation more vulnerable and deprived. Adaptation is understood as part of the compensatory strategies of the people in the short run to make up what they have lost in the disasters.

The long run decision making process requires the various forms of resources such as clear vision about the goal of existence in life, wide network, access to the communication system, and command over the knowledge, which is suited to the long run livelihood settlement. This is in the context to remind that some of the academicians are path followers rather than path breakers who has to be continuously 'reborn' as the 'scientific' (Kuhn, 1980) intellectuals who acquires the logical reasoning for checking the defaults and limitations in the already done research.

The delimiting of the study into vulnerability induced adaptation in times of natural calamities does not pay attention to the perpetuation of the existing social and economic inequalities which makes the human beings – nature relationship rigid and poses great threat towards the human progress. This kind of research does not give insights to the betterment of the people and it serves only the interest of some others who brings reductionism in the case of 'adaptation in climate change' creating the absence of comprehension on the holistic human progress in their life. At the same time, they are only worried about the phenomenon of 'Climate Change' that is defined as in the form of many natural disasters. The apprehension over the climate change arises on the backdrop of the disputes of reduction over the green house gases and global warming among countries. This is the reason that the fear induced 'climate change research' mainly focused on vulnerability and adaptation. It does not go into the holistic dimension of human action for existence in life as a coping livelihood strategy of people in the long run. Hence, it is non-humanistic and that is misleading to the social science research methodology of knowledge production.

## Reorientation of the Climate Change Research

When we dismiss the 'Climate Change' research in general, it reminds us to remain open minded for receiving reflections from the output produced in this area for igniting the future research. The people sensitise themselves by their experiences to the changes happening in the nature in the form of cyclones, earthquakes, drought, melting of ice glaciers etc. as 'climate change'. These experiences and observations based on what is happening around them have to bridge with the rules of science. The development of science, both material and social sciences is important for having the successful and long run human action from policy level, other people's organisation's level, community level and individual level. The mutual interaction between theory and practice is unavoidable. But the gap between theory and practice is often unfilled and this vacuum is filled with 'myth'[1] in disguise of the theory. The 'climate change research' fails to fill the scientific task of meaningful and logical interaction between theory and practice. This study is a critique of the 'climate change research' which addresses the adverse natural events in the name of 'climate change'. The argument in this study puts that the 'climate change' research lacks substance in theory and it is more ideological in content supporting the myths. The word 'climate change' used widely, thanks to the dominance of the myth against the logic which is the essence of science. The use of 'climate change' is wide and not specific, but at the same time, global warming and melting of ice glaciers are specific terms to deal with. The issues with respect to the so called sensitivitisation of climate change from the ground reality, the topic dealt by the climate change academicians in the positivist tradition for finding the natural tendencies and laws both in social and material science, other types of disaster management and applied sciences dealing with the improvement and sustainability of the livelihood options of the people in the natural-calamity prone areas has to be pooled together to evolve a continuous dialogue between theory and practice in a new branch of knowledge which can be termed as 'Human Natural Science'. The broad methodology of '**Human natural Science**' is in the tradition of human being-nature relationship with the materialistic interpretation of space and time with a clear normative base grounded in the human progress on the earth vying all kinds of myths. This proposed scientific tradition includes both subjective and objective experiences from the academics, activists and people who are the spectators or victims. There is also no need of being completely positivist and normative and they can be mixed to suit the interest of the particularity of various factors such as the particularities of the nature of study, people and area. We want the output of knowledge production which makes human life beautiful on this earth.

There is a need to rectify the defaults in the 'Climate Change' research package to reorient it in the broad framework of human beings-nature relationship. The individual natural event has to be looked into independently rather than taking the 'climate change' as a group. The behaviour and risk combating skills of people with respect to adverse events is the centre of attention of this Human Natural Science. It has to take insights from the behavioural science and psychosocial analysis. But this branch of knowledge has to develop with the focused relationship between natural events and human action for the sustainable human progress without the fear of extinction from the earth. It is on the conviction that we all will be dead. We need the knowledge and pragmatism in the short run for the existence in life and we need ideas, dreams and vision in the long run to go forward to the infinite future at the level of human thought. Each event has to be studied in detail and specific to understand its relation with human beings. The 'Human Natural Science' seeks the human beings as the central focus of any disaster or any natural event in their response to the existence of human beings in life. It also ventures to take from the livelihood strategies of the people's their traditional knowledge and modern disaster management. The vulnerability induced studies has to go beyond the level of adaptation initiating enquiry into the causal mechanism leading to the short run aggravation of the problem. The enquiry into the independent natural disasters has to be deducted from the theory of human progress on the development of livelihood combating various types of challenges on the materialistic basis of time and space in history.

In order to make the so called 'Climate Change' research programme more humanistic in its nature of study and to possess the characteristics of knowledge production, the response of the human beings to the adverse natural calamities and how human action evolves in response to the external shock which is not under their control has to be looked into. It can be focused on the lines of regional specific, event specific, or time specific of the existing living system with a special focus to the human being's interaction with the material world when the external shock happens. The basic analytical framework in which theories have to be formed in the so called 'climate change research area' must be in the relationship between human beings and nature. This alternative way of study does not have any connection with the coinage of the word 'Climate Change'. Unless the evolutionary process of 'Climate Change' is explained with its process, actors and guiding principles with its direction towards, differentially caused natural events putting into one basket needs more elaboration. The erratic and unrelated incidents happening across space and time may not have unique characteristics because some regions are susceptible to particular type of calamities, others have more probability and some others have remote chance of happening in some places within centuries.

In this context, it is better to reorient the 'climate change' research programme mainly in favour of what is happening to the living system of human beings as a result of the natural calamities and adverse-risk events. The major query is about the human settlement pattern and the nature and evolution of the livelihood system in the area where the calamity is affected. This form of study is visioned to tailor in the basic framework of the human beings-nature relationship. The socio-economic importance of certain values and norms which continues their rigid human beings-nature relationship has to be enquired in each disaster prone region. How far human action which is leading to the various natural disasters and risk events has to be analysed for understanding the relationship between human beings and nature. The emission of green house gases can create serious environmental and health problems. It can be contained with the human intervention. The question is here how far natural disasters and human action is linked scientifically. It is mentioned above that there is limitations in human capacity to control and influence the natural events. Even if it is accepted that the control of human beings on nature is limited, they are not supposed to be the silent receivers of the destiny given by nature. They can do many things to improve their existence in life. Because of the urge to exist, their creativity would flower and find out ways for openings. The fight against the 'nature' from both internal and external is the corner stone of success of human beings' existence. The human settlement pattern of certain region which is continuously affected by the adverse natural events is to be studied in order to unearth the origins and causes of the continuation of human settlement in a highly risk area. For example, some fishermen communities settle in some calamity hit areas. Because of their vulnerability, they continue their living there. This situation cannot be mirrored through the simple notion of adaptation. It shows that vulnerable people extremely depend on their physical and manual labour and natural resources. The availability of natural resources and the extreme dependence on the physical labour make them to live in the disaster prone areas. The incorporation of vulnerability comes into the focus of analysis when they face structural barriers in the spheres of caste, gender, income, social network etc. which stand as impediments to improve their social and economic well being through migrating or upgrading skills for living. The vulnerability prevents the improvement of their socio-economic life. It is on a simple reasoning that the endowments that people acquire determine the economic progress and so the vulnerable people continue to be vulnerable and end in absolute deprivation. The vicious nexus between vulnerability and disasters makes their life miserable. It is because that they are vulnerable, they became the victims of disasters.

Another focus of the study can be the livelihood system of the people in a particular area for unearthing its resilience to cope up with the situations using technology and modern knowledge of long term disaster management. Along with this, affordability and accessibility of the people residing in these study areas for the movement of relatively risk neutral areas and for shifting to the risk-hazard neutral occupational structure is also to be taken into the orbit of focus. The rigid attachment to the particular livelihood system because of their deprivation in their entitlements makes them vulnerable. Their closed ended livelihood system has forced them to live in these areas continuously enjoying and suffering all the 'comforts and discomforts' in the presence and absence of disasters and risk. This kind of study stands above rationale of the vulnerability induced adaptation research model in the sense that the research should focus towards the betterment of people in the future with the hope and positive vision inspired from the past but at the same time, not being hung in the past. The normative value behind 'research' is asserted here as one of motivating the people in their existence of their life for taking better choices and having 'creative action' through their widening of understanding and developing the cognition to relate them with the complexity of material world and with the experiences of themselves in the real world for the ultimate goal of moving forward to the end.

The recent trend in the social science is the imperialistic tendency of academic disciplines over others which is prevalent in the form of hijacking of the independent research areas by making vague and fluid alliance with the major banner of research such as 'climate change' or 'globalisation' etc. Anything under the sun is being linked into this broad general issue which is conceptually wide. What happens here is the possibility of failure of deduction in many of these studies. The research on climate change and adaptation poses serious scientific dilemmas in their endeavour to imperialise the social science with the ideological dogmas. The inevitability of adaptation in the 'climate change' research modes deserves attention whether it fails in the methodological exercise of deduction. This study points out the improper deduction and immature positivism in the 'climate change' model of adaptation. When it degenerates into the collection and presentation of data without having the requisites of scientific enquiry, the positivism loses its objectives of research. From the positivist point of view, the climate change research has to find out the theoretical foundation in the area of relation between human beings and material world on the lines of materialistic interpretation of time. Based on this, each study has to make framework and novel objectives to gather and fashion the collected information in such a way to give competent interpretations so as to make the objective reality more evident than a mere a spectator or analyst can do with these information. Using the method of classification of data in the analytic cognitive framework developed by the researcher from studying the character of data (Schumpeter, 1954) can be found out the stylised facts and tendencies over time. There are classical studies in the positivistic framework to understand the objective world. To extend it, we can say that the subjective experiences can also be regarded as objective data by the narrator and can be taken it in the form of positivist analysis. If the same reasoning applies, we can argue that there is normativity behind the positivist methodology of research. The positivistic or normative approach does not create any problem per se to the knowledge production. Even though the dualism exist in the real world, the understanding has to be in mind that the production of knowledge is beyond the division of binaries and we can feel a mutual harmony between positivism and normativism in the human cognition. No study is perfectly normative and positive in itself and most of the studies are mixed in various degrees. The role of human centrality in the social science knowledge production makes relevant it in the philosophy of science. The central focus of the social science is the existence of human beings and how they overcome with their will power and determination, the external shocks which is not purely under the control of human beings in cognisance with the structural imperatives.

There are numerous questions that can be generated in the broad framework of human beings-nature relationship. It points out the reasons for the underdevelopment of the human resources and the lack of physical equipments to improve their productivity. The social and economic geography of the location is important for the evolution of livelihood structure and settlement pattern. For some sections of the population, the livelihood structure is characterised by the predominant use of physical labour in engagement with the natural resources. The gains from the livelihood opportunity due to their reliance on the primitive technology have not enabled them to develop more sustainable forms of existence with the help of suitable building, proper infrastructure, and communication development and inter connectivity. The engineering and other applied science can improve a lot the situations to cope with any urgency in order to improve the standard of living of the people. The scientific studies has to focus on the reasons for the social challenges and apprehensions in the execution of appropriate technology suited to the each location in order to find out the social solution by giving insights and understanding to the parties involved in the problem.

The study on vulnerability in times of natural catastrophe has to be oriented in such a way that should seek the origin and nature of the barriers of human action in the structure of the society which sustains the vicious cycle of poverty and inequality. The structural barriers on human action influence the crucial decisions in the long run. It can be looked whether the deprivation of these vulnerable communities in the calamity hit areas is due to the patterns of livelihood structures and social structures of caste and other social divisions. It is to be reminded that vulnerability is not caused by any so called 'climate change'. It is another form of deprivation and incapability. But this article suggests that our analysis starts from the vulnerability of the human beings due to their incapability and less endowments in the form of assets, land, employment, symbolic icons of social status etc. The continuous lack of the economic growth into the disaster prone areas in the backdrop of particular structural specificities has to be unearthed rather than satisfying with the research output in the climate change model adaptation. But the struggles for existence against the natural calamities may lead to the structural change of them with the occupational shift and diversification. The productivity of the human beings in connection with the natural resources for their bare minimum of livelihood has to be improved continuously on par with any other section of people who share the fruits of economic development.

The **social science research** has to focus on why people cannot move forward for their social and economic progress. 'Climate change research' has failed to orient in terms of sustainable human progress because of their blind emphasis on adaptation which includes the natural way of risk averse behaviours and methods. They are not delineating the need for turning attention towards the origin and causes of perpetuation of social and economic deprivation and inequalities in times of adverse natural events. In this sense, 'climate change research' at the current level is non-humanistic and at odds with the social science research which is supposed to have the normative ground for the centrality of human beings.

## Concluding Remarks

The study reminds the imperative of revisiting the 'Climate Change and Adaptation' research because it sidelines the centrality of human beings in the social science research. It brings the physical phenomena like 'climate change' into social science, without being confirmed its process, factors and the governing principle in a logical unanimous manner in the natural science and physical science branches of knowledge. Besides, it fails in the case of effective logical deduction to the relation between natural adverse events and human action. The 'climate change research' is the classic example of worst deduction and failed positivist research by calling a basket of natural adverse events as 'climate change' and not going beyond the mere arrangement data in pursuit of huge funds rather than going to the level of making science through giving and taking insights as well as linking the existing knowledge and the future knowledge by filling the research gap. Hence, 'Climate Change Research' fails its purpose of knowledge production and do not deserve to join the league of Social Science as a branch which enrich it. The imperialistic designs of adaptation research incorporating everything into its ambit forget the beauty of the autonomy of the independent issue or area research. Another point mirrors that research is not for the sake of research and it has a grand goal of knowledge production in the human history for leading to the betterment of human welfare and the progress of human development with a cosmopolitan vision. The vulnerability research in the adaptation model in times of 'climate change' goes against this kind of ideal of research. The 'climate change' research is degenerated into the level of plethora of studies which have a disjunction from the spirit of progressive social change of the vulnerable sections of the people's vision in the long run. Therefore, it is imperative for India to pull up its socks and increase its renewable energy investment so that it does not lag behind the rest of the emerging economies in the world. Despite having a huge and flourishing Information Technology (IT) sector, very few innovations have been made on the front of renewable energy technology in the country. When there are no dearth of IT brains in the country, nothing should stop the Government from taking advantage of them and find long-term solutions. The policies framed by India tend to focus more on the low-hanging fruits and at some level, the loopholes in them could be exploited by the "growth-first stonewallers" to thwart the efforts of the "progressive realists" and the "progressive internationalists on.

# 17

# IMPACT OF CLIMATE CHANGE ON HUMAN HEALTH

*Muralidharan, P.T.*

Global climate change has become one of the most visible environmental concerns of the 21st century. Today, most climate change research has focused on environmental effects and not health effects. It is clear that climate change endangers human health, but there is need to improve the science and knowledge base of how it occurs. We have to focus on the long-term, and complex consequences of climate change on human health, a challenging research task.There is no doubt, however, that climate change is currently affecting public health through myriad environmental consequences, such as sea-level rise, changes in precipitation resulting in flooding and drought, heat waves, changes in intensity of hurricanes and storms, and degraded air quality, that are anticipated to continue into the foreseeable future.

The **World Health Organization** (WHO) estimated 166,000 deaths and about 5.5 million disability-adjusted life years (DALYs, a measure of overall disease burden) were attributable to climate change in 2000.Today, the majority of analyses on climate change and health have focused on diseases that predominantly affect people in the developing world, and therefore, are perceived as less relevant to more developed countries. However, as the recent pandemic of H1N1 virus has shown us, diseases do not respect international boundaries. Climate change can be a driver for disease migration, but even so, such diseases do not represent the broadest range of possible, or even lik‥y, human health effects of climate change, nor do they reflect the likely co-benefits of mitigation and adaptation to climate change, some of which may have their greatest impact in the developed world.

For over 170 years, scientists have studied the complicated relationship between the weather, climate, and human health. Since the first attempt at scientific consensus on climate change nearly four decades ago,scientists have been examining whether climate is indeed changing as a result of human activity. However, the complicated relationships between climate change, the environment, and human health have not represented high priorities for scientific research.

Such gaps impair our ability to identify optimal strategies for mitigation and adaptation that will prevent illness and death in current human populations while simultaneously protecting the environment and health of future generations.

The major impacts of climate change on human health are through changes to the human environment such as rising oceans, changing weather patterns, and decreased availability of fresh water. Mitigation of climate change refers to actions being taken to reduce greenhouse gas emissions and to enhance the sinks that trap or remove carbon from the atmosphere to reduce the extent of global climate change. Adaptation refers to actions being taken to lessen the impact on health and the environment due to changes that cannot be prevented through mitigation. Appropriate mitigation and adaptation strategies will positively affect both climate change and the environment, and thereby positively affect human health. In addition, some adaptation activities will directly improve human health through changes in our public health and health care infrastructure.

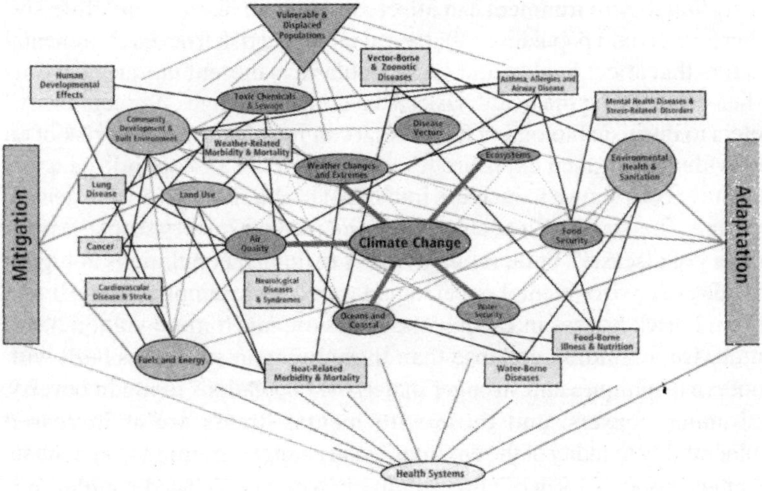


**Fig. 17.1.**

Categories of human health consequences of climate change:

1. Asthma, Respiratory Allergies, and Airway Diseases
2. Cancer
3. Cardiovascular Disease and Stroke
4. Foodborne Diseases and Nutrition
5. Heat-Related Morbidity and Mortality
6. Human Developmental Effects
7. Mental Health and Stress-Related Disorders
8. Neurological Diseases and Disorders
9. Vector borne and Zoonotic Diseases
10. Waterborne Diseases
11. Weather-Related Morbidity and Mortality.

## CROSSCUTTING ISSUES FOR CLIMATE CHANGE AND HEALTH

In the process of identifying and characterising research needs on the health implications of climate change for the 11 categories of consequences, it became evident that multiple crosscutting issues span all aspects of the research needs. In the sections below, we briefly summarise the major areas of overlap. Susceptible, Vulnerable, and Displaced Populations.

The World Health Organization defines "**environment**" as "all modifiable physical, chemical, and biological factors external to the human host, and all related behaviours that are critical to establishing and maintaining a healthy livable environment". Within this definition, it is likely that the environment can affect most human diseases and illnesses. There are certain populations that are at increased risk from environmental factors that affect health, and such populations present unique concerns when considering the health risks from climate change. "Susceptibility" refers to intrinsic biological factors that can increase the health risk of an individual at a given exposure level. Examples of susceptibility factors that have been shown to increase individual health risks are certain genetic variants, life-stage such as childhood, and medical history such as a prior history of disease. "Vulnerability" refers to human populations at higher risk due to environmental or personal factors. For example, people living in mud brick houses in earthquake zones are much more vulnerable to injury from building collapse than those living in structures built with modern techniques and stronger materials. Populations living in poverty, substance abusers, and those with mental illness are at increased vulnerability to many of the environmental changes resulting from climate change. Another form of vulnerability is seen in displaced populations, who have been shown to be at higher risk of a number of diseases, including diarrheal and vectorborne diseases resulting from exposure to poor sanitation, as well as mental health illnesses due to increased acute and chronic stress.

Populations with both susceptibility and vulnerability factors are referred to as "sensitive" populations. An example of a sensitive population would be certain members of the displaced population that evacuated New Orleans following Hurricane Katrina. Studies have shown that within this population, older people (susceptible) who were of low income (vulnerable) were the slowest to recover from the disaster. Virtually every human disease is likely to have both susceptible and vulnerable populations associated with it. One key aspect to mitigating the effects of climate change is a better understanding of diseases and the unique risks of various exposed or affected populations so that strategies may be developed that take such risks into account and are tailored to address them.

In the case of diseases linked to climate change, a number of populations are particularly at risk. Children, pregnant women, and the elderly are generally more susceptible, especially for heat-and weather-related illness and death, vectorborne and zoonotic diseases, and waterborne and foodborne illnesses.

Also, children and some minority groups are very susceptible to asthma and allergies that may be exacerbated by climate change. Genetic links and markers that help to identify and define susceptible populations exist for many climate-related diseases.

Poverty generally makes people more vulnerable to many of the health effects of climate change, largely due to inadequate access to health care. Poverty also increases the risk that a population displaced by extreme weather events or environmental degradation will not easily recover, and as a result, will suffer much higher disease risks.

The same is true for people who abuse drugs, those who suffer mental illness, and others who for various reasons are socially isolated For such populations, the effects of climate change such as temperature and weather extremes, disruptions in access to public services including health care and food assistance programmes, and increased stress are all magnified by their preexisting conditions or situations. Outdoor workers and people living in coastal and riverine zones also are likely to experience increased vulnerability to climate-induced environmental changes resulting from flooding and extreme weather events.Data to support a broad understanding of which populations will be most susceptible and vulnerable to diseases affected by climate change are generally lacking at this time; however, data are available that identify vulnerable populations for some diseases with environmental causes or triggers that are likely to be altered by climate change. For example, reducing vehicle emissions may mean that populations living near freeways, who are at higher risk of cardiovascular disease, asthma, and spontaneous abortion, may see a reduction in incidence of these effects.

Expanding research on these diseases to incorporate effects of climate change will help to identify vulnerable populations, and also to develop the strategies needed to adapt to climate changes and avoid excess health risks. These research efforts, if they are to be effective, must involve a broad spectrum of research scientists from epidemiologists and physicians to environmental engineers and community planners. Such efforts also will require a broad-based, multi-agency federal programme that builds on the strengths of each agency to develop an overall comprehensive research agenda.

## Public Health and Health Care Infrastructure

The term "**public health**" describes the science of preventing disease, prolonging life, and promoting health and its application to society, communities, and groups. In contrast, "health care" primarily focuses on the treatment of illness and the protection of mental and physical wellbeing in individuals through services provided by physicians and other health care professionals. Together, these two areas are tasked with the protection of the health of the people of the United States.

Public health agencies exist across the United States in most large cities, as well as at the county, state, and federal levels. Schools of public health and other training and research institutions add to the total public health infrastructure investment of the United States, which is very large and quite complex. The public health system will play a critical role in the prevention of human disease from climate change. As such, public health agencies should be deeply involved in researching, developing, and implementing adaptation strategies to climate change.

The health care delivery infrastructure in the United States is even more diverse and complicated than the public health infrastructure (though there are multiple overlaps between the two systems). From family doctors in small towns to complex university research hospitals in large cities, health care professionals are the primary source of medical treatment, prenatal and pediatric care, and individual health protection and promotion for people in the United States. But this infrastructure is also vulnerable to climate change in a number of very important ways. Disasters can severely hinder the delivery of health care, with long-term impacts. Changes in the numbers of patients and the spectrum of diseases with which they present could occur in some regions as the climate changes. The types of advice offered to patients with chronic conditions and the infrastructure to support them may need to be adapted to protect against climate-induced changes that may make these individuals more vulnerable. Currently there is limited research to guide these types of decisions.

The public health community is in the early stages of developing modeling skills and capacity in relation to climate change, particularly for combining climate models with ecological and other health outcome models for use in projecting disease dynamics under various climate scenarios. In order to understand these dynamics, a sustained surveillance infrastructure that integrates human and ecological health (terrestrial, marine, aquatic) is critical. While the public health community has developed considerable expertise in behavioural science and health education, this expertise has yet to be applied to the most trenchant issues related to climate change. Sea-level rise, coastal erosion, and population displacement will create challenges for public health infrastructure that has been constructed over a period of hundreds of years. Disruption of coastal routes and harbours by sea-level rise will present additional challenges to health care delivery and food distribution. It is doubtful that transportation infrastructure will be able to adapt quickly enough to large population shifts that may be made in response to changes in rainfall patterns. Displaced populations will need sewer and water resources in new locations. The sewer and water resources in coastal locations may be threatened directly by sea-level rise.

## Capacities and Skills Needed

Many of the existing skills used in public health and health care are well established and applicable to dealing with the health effects of climate change, but new skills will also be needed. Skills used in certain types of disease surveillance are well established. Less well established are the skills and methods needed to integrate current and future surveillance activities and retrospective datasets with weather and climate information. Understanding of how to conceptualize and conduct epidemiological analysis using weather and climate as exposures is also preliminary. Methods and skill in combining spatial epidemiology with ecological approaches are also lacking. There is a strong need for the ability to translate vulnerability mapping and health impact assessments (HIAs) into behavioural changes and effective public health actions.

A greater emphasis must be placed on developing and maintaining interdisciplinary and inter-institutional collaborations, as well as on ensuring that established resources and expertise of all of the relevant disciplines, including climatology, modeling, environmental science, risk assessment, public health, and communications and education, are applied to these pressing problems. Many additional disciplines including ecology, social science, economics, geography, behavioural psychology, and others will need to play a vital role in climate and health decision making.

## Communication and Education

Other areas where public health professionals may contribute robustly to efforts to address the impacts of climate change are in communication and education. Public health educators have a strong history of promoting health and wellness through educating individuals and communities about healthy behaviours and disease prevention or management. The same skills are critical to helping raise awareness of the potential impacts of climate change, and translating the scientific research and other technical data into credible and accessible information for the public to use in making informed decisions that will protect their health and the environment.

Recent studies show that the majority of those living in the United States now believe that climate change is a real and serious threat that is caused by human activity. However, research is still needed to determine how to effectively educate and organise the public to respond.This is complicated by recent research showing that various audiences within the American public respond to the issue of climate change each in their own distinct way. Research is needed that will aid climate change communicators and educators in adapting their messages and approaches to most appropriately and effectively reach and be assimilated by each individual audience.

In addition to the general public, other audiences—each with their own culture and means of acquiring information—also require effective communication on issues of climate change. Stakeholders such as natural resource managers, policy makers, infrastructure planners, health care providers, and others also need access to credible and timely climate change information to inform their decision-making.

Protecting human health is an issue that crosses institutional, scientific, and political boundaries. In the United States, no single institution at the local, regional, or federal level can fully protect public health without cooperation from other institutions. In addition, no single scientific field is capable of accomplishing all aspects of the research needed to understand the human health consequences of global climate change; such an endeavour will require a broad-based, trans-disciplinary research portfolio. And in our global society, the highly integrated activities of individuals around the world mean that no one country can be solely responsible for addressing the health impacts of global climate change. Through the process of developing this white paper, it rapidly became clear that identifying research needs; mobilising and creating the expertise, resources, tools, and technologies to address them; and translating these efforts into solutions that will enable human adaptation to our changing environment while protecting public health will require collaborations on an unprecedented scale. Such collaborations should build on the strengths and capacities of individual organisations in ways that maximise the efforts of the group toward these shared goals.

## Categories of Human Health Consequences of Climate Change

### Asthma, Respiratory Allergies, and Airway Diseases:

**Asthma is** the leading cause of chronic illness among children and is rapidly rising among children less than five years of age; however, the prevalence of asthma is highest among adults.

In recent decades, the world has seen a sharp rise in prevalence as well as severity of such respiratory diseases. Many respiratory allergic diseases are seasonal with climate sensitive components; climate change may increase the incidence and exacerbation of such allergic diseases.

Climate change will affect air quality through several pathways including production and allergen city of aeroallergens such as pollen and mold spores and increases in regional ambient concentrations of ozone, fine particles, and dust. Some of these pollutants can directly cause respiratory disease or exacerbate respiratory disease in susceptible individuals.

*Mitigation and Adaptation*

**Mitigation** and adaptation strategies have the potential to both positively and negatively affect human health. Reduction of vehicle miles travelled will reduce ozone precursors, thereby reducing the ozone associated with myriad respiratory health effects. Alternative transportation options such as walking and bicycling will reduce toxic emissions while providing positive benefits for health such as increasing cardiovascular fitness and contributing to weight loss.

*Research Needs*

Developing and validating real-time remote sensing and other *in situ* monitoring techniques to evaluate air quality, aeroallergens, aerosolized pathogens, dust burdens, and other climate-sensitive exposures directly linked to asthma and airway diseases.

Understanding and modeling the impact of climate change on air quality, aeroallergens, and aerosolised marine toxins, and the resulting effects on asthma and airway diseases including in vulnerable populations

Examining chemicals used in energy efficient technologies to ensure that they do not contribute to lung sensitisation, asthma, or other respiratory diseases.

Developing early warning systems for state and local governments and public and environmental health officials to anticipate and mitigate climate-related health impacts.

Identifying and mapping populations and communities at increased risk of climate-related respiratory disease, which will also help to identify populations at risk for other climate-related health impacts as many environmentally mediated diseases share common risk factors.

**Cancer**

Cancer refers to a group of diseases in which abnormal cells divide without control and are able to invade other tissues. There are more than 100 different types of cancer, and they are generally referred to by the organ or type of cell in which they arise (e.g., breast, prostate, colon). The main cause of lung cancer is smoking, especially cigarettes, but air pollution, including indoor air pollution and fine particulates also contributes to the burden of lung cancers.

Climate change is also expected to increase heavy precipitation and flooding events, which may increase the chance of toxic contamination leaks from storage facilities or runoff into water from land containing toxic pollutants. Very little is known about how such transfers will affect people's exposure to these chemicals—some of which are known carcinogens—and its ultimate impact on incidence of cancer.

One possible direct impact of climate change on cancer may be through increases in exposure to toxic chemicals that are known or suspected to cause cancer following heavy rainfall and by increased volatilisation of chemicals under conditions of increased temperature. In the case of heavy rainfall or flooding, there may be an increase in leaching of toxic chemicals and heavy metals from storage sites and increased contamination of water with runoff containing persistent chemicals that are already in the environment. Marine animals, including mammals, also may suffer direct effects of cancer linked to sustained or chronic exposure to chemical contaminants in the marine environment, and thereby serve as indicators of similar risks to humans. Climate impact studies on such model cancer populations may provide added dimensions to our understanding of the human impacts.

Another direct effect of climate change, depletion of stratospheric ozone, will result in increased ultraviolet (UV) radiation exposure. UV radiation exposure increases the risk of skin cancers and cataracts. The incidence of typically nonlethal basal cell and squamous cell skin cancers is directly correlated to the amount of exposure to UV radiation. This effect is compounded by several other variables including temperature and exposure to other compounds that can amplify the carcinogenic potential of UV radiation.

*Mitigation and Adaptation*

Decreases in greenhouse gas emissions are generally associated with decreases in cancers that occur due exposure to such pollutants. Several technologies currently being pursued to decrease greenhouse gas emissions may also help to reduce cancer incidence. For example, reducing greenhouse gas emissions from the transportation sector may be accomplished by reducing vehicle miles travelled through a variety of approaches such as high-density development, preservation of green space, and widespread use of mass transit.

**Nanotechnology** may be promising for mitigating climate change through its use in efficient hydrogen powered vehicles, enhanced and cheaper solar power technology, and the development of a new generation of batteries and super capacitors, yet little is known about potential links to cancer and other health outcomes.

Research is needed to understand if there are cancer implications from the use of electric vehicles, including the production and disposal of portable electric storage systems. Manufacturing of batteries for electric cars and photovoltaic (solar) power systems may have consequences including increased exposure to metals. The most common type of battery currently in use is the nickel-metal-hydride (NiMH) battery, with other types of batteries (lithium ion, lithium ion polymer, valve regulated lead acid, and nickel-cadmium) also under development for vehicle use. Increased use of NiMH batteries will necessarily require significant increases in nickel production and the impacts associated with nickel mining and refining. High-level nickel exposure is associated with increased cancer risk, respiratory disease, and birth defects; the same is true with certain other metals, especially cadmium and lead.

Increased production of solar cells also can lead to increased environmental risks. For example, cadmium-tellurium (CdTe) compounds in photovoltaic systems and the potential for increased cadmium emissions from mining, refining, and the manufacture, utilisation, and disposal of photovoltaic modules.

*Research Needs*

- Understanding the impact of increased heavy precipitation and flooding events on the risk of toxic contamination of the environment from storage facilities or runoff from land containing toxic chemicals, including the geographical areas, ecosystems, and populations most likely to be impacted and the health outcomes that could result.
- Understanding how climate changes such as changes in temperature and precipitation affect exposure to toxic chemicals including volatile and semi-volatile compounds and known or suspected human carcinogens.
- Elucidating the effects of ambient temperature on UV radiation-induced skin cancers, including the amplification of non-melanoma skin cancers.
- Evaluating the potential cancer risks through the entire life cycle of biofuel production, including risks from novel air pollutants and changes in agricultural practices that may increase exposures to pesticides, herbicides, and other environmental contaminants.
- Developing mechanisms to conserve and explore marine and terrestrial biodiversity in environments likely to yield cancer cures and treatments.

## Cardiovascular Disease and Stroke

**Cardiovascular disease** refers to a class of diseases that pertain to the heart or blood vessels.There is evidence of climate sensitivity for several cardiovascular diseases, with both extreme cold and extreme heat directly affecting the incidence of hospital admissions for chest pain, acute coronary syndrome, and stroke.

Weather conditions such as extreme heat serve as stressors in individuals with pre-existing cardiovascular disease, and can directly precipitate exacerbations.

There is also evidence that heat amplifies the adverse impacts of ozone and particulates on cardiovascular disease.

Cardiovascular mortality associated with heat has been declining over time, presumably the result of increased air conditioning use; mortality associated with extreme cold has remained constant.

Indirect impacts of weather, weather variability, and climate changes on cardiovascular disease are many and varied. Ozone, whose formation increases with temperature, increases cardiac effort and impairs pulmonary gas exchange.

Ozone concentrations modify the association between temperature and cardiovascular mortality, and are also associated with acute myocardial infarction

*Mitigation and Adaptation*

The likely impacts of climate change mitigation activities on risk of cardiovascular disease and stroke depend primarily on emissions-associated energy production activities, particularly in the transportation sector. Some mitigation activities related to energy production, such as the increased use of wind, wave, solar, and nuclear sources of power generation, are likely to reduce cardiovascular disease risks by reducing particulate and other air pollution emissions.

Mitigation activities such as increasing the density of urban development, enhancing public transportation options, and encouraging alternatives to single occupancy vehicle use are likely to benefit cardiovascular fitness, reducing the overall burden of cardiovascular disease.

*Research Needs*

- Enhancing research on the complex synergistic effect of temperature, weather variability, long-term climate change, and environmental exposures such as criteria air pollutants on the incidence of various cardiovascular disease outcomes.
- Targeting research on early warning systems and health communications aimed at groups particularly at risk for adverse cardiovascular outcomes related to climate change.
- Identifying and quantifying the co-benefits to cardiovascular health of reducing our reliance on fossil fuel-based energy and changing emission scenarios.

- Characterising both the potential health risks and benefits of novel fuels and other energy production activities being considered for large-scale adoption as part of a national mitigation strategy.

## Food Borne Diseases and Nutrition

Nutrition is the sum of the processes by which humans and other living organisms take in food and use it for growth and nourishment. Along with clean air, water, and shelter, nutritious food is a basic necessity of life. Failure to obtain sufficient calories and an adequate mixture of macronutrients (calories, fat, proteins, and carbohydrates), micronutrients (vitamins, minerals) and other bioactive components of food can result in illness and death.

Extreme weather events and changes in temperature and precipitation patterns can directly damage or destroy crops and other food supplies, as well as interrupt transport and distribution of food. This may happen seasonally, but is anticipated to become a more chronic problem under changing climate conditions.

In addition to being a source of essential nutrients, food can be a source of exposure for foodborne illness. Such illness results from ingesting food that is spoiled or contaminated with microbes, chemical residues such as pesticides, biotoxins, or other toxic substances.

The safety of agricultural crops and fisheries also may be threatened through contamination with metals, chemicals, and other toxicants that may be released into the environment as a result of extreme weather events, particularly flooding, drought, and wildfires, due to climate change.

### *Mitigation and Adaptation*

In the long term, mitigation and adaptation decisions affecting food and nutrition including, for example, the diversion of staple crops for biofuel feedstock, the increased need for agricultural chemicals due to climate-related increases in pests and changes in pest habitats, and planning needs for the maintenance of food supply infrastructure and transport in the wake of extreme weather events are important factors to be considered in a strategic research plan for climate change and health. The benefits of biofuels, genetically modified organisms, new pesticides, and alternative energy on nutrition and foodborne illness must also be considered. All of these technologies have great potential to help humans mitigate and adapt to climate change, and each should be carefully evaluated to ensure that the best are implemented.

*Research needs*

- Understanding and predicting potential ecosystem changes from climate change that may establish new foodborne pathogens, chemical contaminants, or biotoxins, as well as new pathways for human exposure.
- Assessing the impacts of climate change on outbreak incidence, geographic range, and growth cycles of insect pests and pathogens that can infect food crops and seafood, and cause human disease.
- Understanding the effects of changes in food safety due to climate change-related alterations in the accumulation and toxicity of foodborne contaminants, biotoxins, and pathogens.
- Understanding of changes in nutritional status associated with climate change that may increase individual susceptibility to the adverse health impacts of other environmental exposures such as chemicals and heavy metals.
- Improving surveillance of disease-causing agents (chemical contaminants, pathogens, toxins) in food animals, agricultural crops, and seafood, as well as monitoring of exposed human populations in order to improve estimates of disease related to contamination of the food supply.
- Identifying and characterising aspects of food production and distribution systems that will reduce risk of contamination and disease and ensure sustainability under climate change scenarios.
- Understanding the effect of ocean acidification from climate change-related increases in air pollution on seafood quality and availability.
- Developing and implementing models linking climate change and other environmental data (such as land use, land cover, hydrology) to crops and seafood to improve prediction and risk assessment.
- Developing and implementing early warning systems to manage agriculture and fisheries risks related to climate change, including improved communications with domestic and international food security agencies.

## Heat-Related Morbidity and Mortality

Global average temperatures are projected to increase between 1.8 and 4.0°C by end of this century. Climate change is expected to raise overall temperature distribution and contribute to an increase in the frequency of extreme heat events, or heat waves.Temperature, particularly temperature extremes, is associated with a wide range of health impacts.

The health outcomes of prolonged heat exposure include heat exhaustion, heat cramps, heat stroke, and death. Both increased average temperatures and increasingly frequent and severe extreme heat events produce increased risks of heat-related illness and death.

Public health actions and widespread physiologic and behavioural adaptations such as robust heat early warning systems and other health communications, increased air conditioning use, decreased time spent outdoors, and increased wearing of sun-shielding clothing it will be possible to reduce overall rates of illness and death, though some of these measures may result in negative health consequences as well.

*Research Needs*

- Both acute exposure to extreme heat events and long-term, chronic exposure to increased average temperatures, including how such exposure may alter human physiology (for example, by impacting the body's ability to metabolise and excrete harmful environmental toxicants).
- Identifying which temperature-related metrics are most strongly related to increased hospitalisation and mortality during heat waves.
- Quantifying the combined effects of exposure to heat waves and ambient air pollution on excessive illness and death.
- Conducting comparative analyses of heat-related death risks for application to national scale analyses.
- Determining attributes of communities, including regional and seasonal differences, that are more resilient or vulnerable to adverse health impacts from heat waves.

## Human Development

Many of the chemicals that we use to control pests and improve crop yields can impact human development. Climate change will alter rainfall and temperature in various parts of the planet. In some cases, climate change will lead to changes in agricultural practices for crop yields that might increase pesticide use and thereby increase human exposures. Some changes to the environment resulting from climate change could alter normal human development both in the womb and later in life.

Malnutrition and under nutrition in pregnant women are a global cause of low birth weight and other poor birth outcomes that are associated with later developmental deficits.

*Research Needs*

- Understanding the effects of climate change-induced stress on human reproduction and development, including chronic and acute heat stress, and traumatic stress as a result of extreme weather events.
- Understanding how malnutrition may alter human development, how climate change may exacerbate such alterations, and how to develop effective strategies to minimise these impacts in vulnerable populations.
- Understanding the impacts of changes in weather patterns and ecosystems on the incidence, exposure, and distribution of chemical contaminants and bio toxins known to cause developmental disorders.
- Understanding how weather events affect access to health care and the implications of this for normal human development.

## Mental Health and Stress-Related Disorders

Psychological impacts of climate change, ranging from mild stress responses to chronic stress or other mental health disorders, are generally indirect and have only recently been considered among the collection of health impacts of climate change. A variety of psychological impacts can be associated with extreme weather and other climate related events. Extreme weather events such as hurricanes, wildfires, and flooding, can create increased anxiety and emotional stress about the future. Prolonged heat and cold events can create chronic stress situations that may initiate or exacerbate health problems in populations already suffering from mental disease and stress-related disorders.

The most commonly cited figure of projected population displacement from climate change is 200 million people worldwide by 2050.Research is needed to better understand mental health impacts on such people as they relate to climate change and climate change-related migration.

*Mitigation and Adaptation*

There is a need to fully understand what gaps currently exist in mental health infrastructure, resources, and services; how these gaps may be exacerbated due to climate change; and the resulting impacts on mental health status, worldwide.

*Research Needs*

Immediate research needs on the mental health implications of climate change include:

- Understanding of how psychological stress acts synergistically with other forms of environmental exposures to cause adverse mental health effects.
- Understanding the critical social and economic determinants for mental health and overall community well-being that might be altered by climate change.
- Developing mental health promotion and communication programmes related to proposed climate change mitigation and adaptation strategies.

## Neurological Diseases and Disorders

Climate change may impact the prevalence of neurological diseases such as Alzheimer Disease (AD) and Parkinson Disease (PD) is occurring at earlier ages across the population. Factors affected by climate with particular implications for neurological functioning include malnutrition; exposure to hazardous chemicals, biotoxins, and metals in air, food, and water; and changes in pest management.

The most frequent human exposures are via consumption of seafood containing algal toxins, although some toxins may be present in freshwater sources of drinking water.

Health effects including amnesia, diarrhea, numbness, liver damage, skin and eye irritation, respiratory paralysis, and PD-and AD-like symptoms may be severe, chronic, and even lead to death.

*Mitigation and Adaptation*

Mitigation to climate change may reduce our reliance on fossil fuels. This reduction in fossil fuel use will reduce the release of a number of neurotoxicants including arsenic, mercury, and other metals into the environment. Simple actions that reduce the amount of energy needed, such as expanded use of compact fluorescent light bulbs, will reduce the amount of toxic metals emitted into the air by coal-fired power plants.

However, additional mercury releases into the environment might occur due to breakage of these fluorescent bulbs or improper disposal, resulting in human exposures and potential neurological effects.

*Research Needs*

More research is needed regarding the link between environmental exposures, the onset and severity of neurological diseases and disorders, and the relationship to climate change. Research needs include:

- Improving understanding of the mechanisms and pathways of acute and chronic exposures to harmful algal biotoxins and their impacts on fetal, postnatal, and adult development.
- Expanding research on the toxicity of chemicals known or suspected to cause neurological disorders, particularly pesticides, and on understanding how climate change may affect human exposure to such chemicals.
- Improving our understanding of the impact of increased heavy precipitation, ice melts, and flooding events on the risk of toxic contamination of the environment from storage-related issues or runoff, focusing on the likelihood of the event, the geographical areas and populations likely to be impacted, and the health outcomes that could result.
- Examining the neurological health benefits and costs of new climate change mitigation technologies, including research on the toxicity of new metals and metal compounds, including nanotechnologies, being used to improve battery performance for electric vehicles.

## Vector borne and Zoonotic Disease

Climate is one of several factors that influence the distribution of vectorborne and zoonotic diseases. Vector borne and zoonotic diseases (VBZD) are infectious diseases whose transmission cycles involve animal hosts or vectors. **Vectorborne diseases** are those in which organisms, typically blood-feeding arthropods (insects, ticks, or mites) carry the pathogen from one host to another, generally with amplification (increased virulence) in the vector (for example, malaria). Zoonoses are diseases that can be transmitted from animals to humans by either contact with animals or by vectors that can carry zoonotic pathogens from animals to humans (for example, avian flu).

*Research Needs*

Given the potential for significant increases in the burden of VBZD as a result of climate change, public health preparation is required, and research needs include:

- Understanding of VBZD transmission cycles and the impact of ecological management and disruption on VBZD transmission, including the impact of new and intensified selective pressures due to climate change.
- Developing methods to detect, quantify, characterise, and monitor potential VBZD transmission associated with changes in terrestrial, ocean, coastal, and Great Lakes environments.
- Developing and validating models of VBZD ecology that link established datasets of VBZD disease transmission, identify relevant climate-related patterns, and integrate downscaled climate projections of likely impacts.
- Understanding of secondary effects of climate change such as increased malnutrition, conflict, and population displacement on VBZD, and evaluation of the effectiveness of prevention strategies.

*Mitigation and Adaptation*

Changes to wetlands may affect mosquito burden in certain areas by altering breeding area size and potentially altering the incidence of malaria, dengue, or other mosquito-borne diseases. Climate change adaptation strategies include activities that provide early warning and reduce exposure to environmental hazards associated with climate change, and limit susceptibility in exposed populations.

*Waterborne Diseases*

There is a clear association between increases in precipitation and outbreaks of waterborne disease, both domestically and globally. Climate change is expected to produce more frequent and severe extreme precipitation events worldwide.

Water borne diseases are caused by a wide variety of pathogenic microorganisms, biotoxins, and toxic contaminants found in the water we drink, clean with, play in, and are exposed to through other less direct pathways such as cooling systems.

The World Health Organisation estimates that 4.8 per cent of the global burden of disease and 3.7 per cent of all mortality attributable to the environment is due to diarrheal disease.

Globally, the impact of waterborne diarrheal disease is high and expected to climb with climate change. Improving domestic surveillance is a high priority, as this would enhance epidemiologic characterisation of the drivers of epidemic disease. In particular, weather and climate-related drivers are not well understood.

*Research Needs*

- Understanding the likelihood and potential magnitude of waterborne disease outbreaks due to climate change including increases in the frequency and intensity of precipitation, temperature changes, extreme weather events, and storm surges.
- Researching the vulnerability of water systems to sewer overflow or flooding caused by extreme weather events, especially in water systems where there is already considerable water reuse; and examining the impacts of other water reuse and recycling strategies.
- Understanding how toxins, pathogens, and chemicals in land-based runoff and water overflow interact synergistically and with marine species, especially those important for human consumption, and the potential health risks of changing water quality.
- Developing or improving vaccines, antibiotics and other preventive strategies to prevent and reduce the health consequences of waterborne disease on a global basis.

## Weather-Related Morbidity and Mortality

Climate change is expected to increase the frequency and intensity of some extreme weather events, including floods, droughts, and heat waves. The health impacts of these extreme weather events can be severe, and include both direct impacts such as death and mental health. A changing climate coupled with changing demographics is expected to magnify the already significant adverse effects of extreme weather on public health.

*Mitigation and adaptation*

Climate change mitigation includes activities that reduce greenhouse gas emissions. Important sources include land use changes, transport, energy production, and buildings. Some proposed mitigation strategies to reduce the occurrence of extreme weather events could impact human health. A reduction in personal automobile usage is one way to lower carbon emissions. However, a greater reliance on pubic transportation could either improve or reduce the ability to quickly evacuate a city prior to a severe weather event, depending on how it is managed.

*Research Needs*

- Exploring the impact of extreme precipitation events on waterborne disease, particularly cholera, and on the ecology of vectorborne and zoonotic disease.
- Improving understanding of extreme weather events associated with naturally occurring climate phenomena such as El Niño, La Niña, and monsoons, and their impacts on human health.
- Assessing the ability of health care systems to respond to extreme weather events and provide uninterrupted access to and delivery of health care services under a variety of scenarios.
- Improving understanding of how to anticipate and address food security and nutrition issues after extreme weather events, domestically and globally.
- Improving understanding of how to anticipate and address water quality and availability concerns associated with extreme weather events, domestically and globally. Weather related research intersects with several other areas of climate change research. Examples include waterborne and vector-borne illness following floods and hurricane storm surges, as well as post-traumatic stress disorder and related mental effects that can result from personal tragedy and displacement after extreme weather events. Studies of marine ecosystems and associated health impacts also overlap with extreme weather studies. Research in health communications and early warning systems is clearly applicable to periods proceeding and following weather disasters, as well as disaster preparedness and critical infrastructure development and protection.

## Conclusion

- Humans have successfully adapted to environmental change over time, from evolving natural physiological responses to the use of science, technology, and knowledge to improve our lives and advance our health.

- Climate change will force humans to negotiate with their changing environment for short-term protection and long-term alleviation of health consequences.
- There is no doubt that we have the capacity to find ways to avoid many of the worst health effects of climate change.
- The research needs helping us to develop proper tools and make informed choices that will ultimately result in better health and better lives for citizens of the world.

## References

1. Christopher J. Portier, Phd (Coordinating Lead Author) *National Institute of Environmental Health Sciences,* Kimberly Thigpen Tart,. JD (Coordinating Editor) *National Institute ofEnvironmental Health Sciences.* A Human Health Perspective on Climate Change A Report Outlining the Research Needs on the Human Health Effects of Climate Change April 22, 2010, 2010 Published by *Environmental Health Perspectives* and the National Institute of Environmental Health Sciences.
2. USGCRP (2009). *Global Climate Change Impacts in the United States.* Karl, T.R., J.M. Melillo, and T.C. Peterson (eds.). United States Global Change Research Program. Cambridge University Press, New York, NY, USA.
3. CCSP (2008). *Analyses of the effects of global change on human health and welfare and human systems.* A Report by the U.S. Climate Change Science Programme and the Subcommittee on Global Change Research. Gamble, J.L. (ed.), K.L. Ebi, F.G. Sussman, T.J. Wilbanks, (Authors). U.S. Environmental Protection Agency, Washington, DC, USA.
4. EPA (2010). *Our Nation's Air: Status and Trends Through 2008* (PDF). U.S. Environmental Protection Agency. EPA -454/R-09-002.
5. NRC(2010). *Adapting to the Impacts of Climate Change.* National Research Council. The National Academies Press, Washington, DC, USA.
6. http://www.epa.gov/climatechange/impacts-adaptation/health.html
7. A.J. McMichael (2003). A. McMichael. ed. "Global Climate Change and Health: An Old Story Writ Large". *World Health Organization* (Geneva).

# 18

# Climate Change: Impact on the Other Half

Asha Ajith

Climate change and gender inequality are the two major issues of concern in the present era.

Addressing the threat of climate change has become a global priority. There is broad consensus that climate change is best addressed in the context of sustainable development. Unless it is effectively dealt with, climate change will have a dramatic impact on the environment and on economic and social development. Climate change is also likely to exacerbate both natural disasters and potentially conflicts over natural resources. The United Nations Climate Change Conference in Bali in December 2007 clearly signaled Member States' commitment to addressing climate change and delivered the Bali Action Plan – the crucial mandate to launch negotiations for the achievement of a comprehensive global agreement by the end of 2009.

The Bali Action Plan confirmed that effectively addressing climate change requires *mitigation* and *adaptation* action as well as *technology* and *financing*. Mitigation involves a process of curbing greenhouse gas emissions from human activities, for example, emissions from fossil fuels as well as deforestation, with a view to stabilising greenhouse gas concentration at a safe level. Adaptation involves a range of activities to reduce vulnerability and build resilience, for instance in key sectors such as water, agriculture and human settlements. New and improved technologies and financing initiatives at all levels, are also receiving attention as part of the collective efforts to address climate change.

The International Conference on Population and Development (1994), the **Beijing Declaration** and Platform for Action (1995), the World Summit on Sustainable Development (2002), and the 2005 World Summit recognised the essential role women play in sustainable development. In its recent follow-up to the Beijing Platform for Action, the General Assembly highlighted the need to "involve women actively in environmental decision-making at all levels; integrate gender concerns and perspectives in policies and programmes for sustainable development; and strengthen or establish mechanisms at the national, regional and international levels to assess the impacts of development and environmental policies on women".

At its 46th session in 2002, the Commission on the Status of Women took up climate change issues when it addressed environmental management and the mitigation of natural disasters. The agreed conclusions adopted by the Commission called for action to mainstream a gender perspective into ongoing research by, inter-alia, the academic sector on the impact of climate change, including the root causes, and to encourage the application of the results of this research in policies and programmes.

## Critical Issues

There are important gender perspectives in all aspects of climate change. Gender inequalities in access to resources, including credit, extension services, information and technology, must be taken into account in developing mitigation activities. Adaptation efforts should systematically and effectively address gender-specific impacts of climate change in the areas of energy, water, food security, agriculture and fisheries, biodiversity and ecosystem services, health, industry, human settlements, disaster management, and conflict and security.

Women make up a large number of the poor in communities that are highly dependent on local natural resources for their livelihood and are disproportionately vulnerable to and affected by climate change. Women's limited access to resources and decision-making processes increases their vulnerability to climate change. Women in rural areas in developing countries have the major responsibility for household water supply and energy for cooking and heating, as well as for food security, and are negatively affected by drought, uncertain rainfall and deforestation. Because of their roles, unequal access to resources and limited mobility, women in many contexts are disproportionately affected by natural disasters, such as floods, fires, and mudslides. It is important to identify gender-sensitive strategies for responding to the environmental and humanitarian crises caused by climate change.

Women are not only victims of climate change, but also effective agents of change in relation to both mitigation and adaptation. Women have a strong body of knowledge and expertise that can be used in climate change mitigation, disaster reduction and adaptation strategies. Women's responsibilities in households and communities as stewards of natural resources has positioned them well for livelihood strategies adapted to changing environmental realities. Women tend, however, to be underrepresented in decision-making on sustainable development, including on climate change, and this impedes their ability to contribute their unique and valuable perspectives and expertise on climate change.

Financing mechanisms must be flexible enough to reflect women's priorities and needs. The active participation of women in the development of funding criteria and allocation of resources for climate change initiatives is critical, particularly at local levels. Gender analysis of all budget lines and financial instruments for climate change is needed to ensure gender-sensitive investments in programmes for adaptation, mitigation, technology transfer and capacity building.

Technological developments related to climate change should take into account women's specific priorities and needs and make full use of their knowledge and expertise, including traditional practices. Women's involvement in the development of new technologies can ensure that they are user-friendly, effective and sustainable. Women should also have equal access to training, credit and skills-development programmes to ensure their full participation in climate change initiatives.

Governments should be encouraged to mainstream gender perspectives into their national policies, action plans and other measures on sustainable development and climate change, through carrying out systematic gender analysis, collecting and utilising sex-disaggregated data, establishing gender-sensitive indicators and benchmarks and developing practical tools to support increased attention to gender perspectives. Consultation with and participation of women in climate change initiatives must be ensured and the role of women's groups and networks strengthened.

The discourse on climate change does not pay adequate attention to women, either at the local project level or in international negotiations. Women are unable to voice their specific requirements even though the impact of climate change affects women and men differently. In several rural areas of the South, although women are responsible for feeding their families and are therefore more dependent on natural resources such as land, wood and water, their access to these resources is limited. They are also denied full access to loans, education and information.

Second, the potential of women as agents of change for climate mitigation and adaptation remains untapped: Their extensive theoretical and practical knowledge of the environment and resource conservation is not given due consideration. In terms of economic participation, they are not paid for the environmental services that they already provide (*e.g.*, reforestation). Their potential contribution to climate mitigation by being part of the economic cycle is not sufficiently exploited.

There are, however, several ways of promoting women's economic participation while also counteracting climate change. One approach in the field of climate mitigation is the promotion of renewable energies that help avoid greenhouse gas emissions. Not only are jobs created for women who can be engaged in the upkeep and maintenance of solar plants, but solar-powered lamps also extend the productive time available to street vendors. Additionally, pilot experiences in climate adaptation have shown that women, given their vast knowledge, are able to develop and disseminate innovative cultivation methods that are adapted to climate change. It goes without saying that the involvement of men in gender and climate related issues is of crucial importance. Nevertheless, the main focus of this discussion paper is on the advancement of women's economic empowerment because of its relevance as described above. The economic empowerment of women through climate mitigation and adaptation fosters economic growth and socioeconomic development, reduces poverty, keeps environmental problems in check, and increases the potential for adaptation, which is to the benefit of both women and men.

## Combining Climate Change with the Economic Empowerment of Women?

The discourse on climate policy is increasingly addressing the development dimension of climate change, not only because the effects of climate change can jeopardize the progress made by development, but also because mitigation and adaptation offer opportunities both to industrialised and developing countries. The latter, in particular, can benefit from the transfer of innovation, technology and funds within the scope of climate policy measures. Similarly, enhancing the economic empowerment of women is a catalyst for development, which helps boost a country's economic growth, promotes the socioeconomic development not only of women, but of the entire population, and helps reduce poverty. The opportunities for developing countries that lie in mitigation and adaptation are only rarely mentioned in the gender context in general and the empowerment of women in particular. Little has been done so far to address the gender-specific dimension of the climate problem. If the issue was considered at all in the discourse, the discussion has focused primarily on how women are particularly susceptible to climate change (women as victims). While this is a part of the connection between climate and gender, the potential of and for women with regard to climate protection is rarely addressed (women as stakeholders and actors of change).

United Nations Framework Convention on Climate Change (UNFCCC) describes it as follows: "In the context of climate change, a human intervention to reduce the sources or enhance the sinks of greenhouse gases. Examples include using fossil fuels more efficiently for industrial processes or electricity generation, switching to solar energy or wind power, improving the insulation of buildings, and expanding forests and other 'sinks' to remove greater amounts of carbon dioxide from the atmosphere." (UNFCCC 2010). Based on the IPCC definition, UNFCCC describes climate adaptation as "Adjustment in natural or human systems in response to actual or expected climatic stimuli or their effects, which moderates harm or exploits beneficial opportunities" (UNFCCC 2010). With reference to development policy, we should add "[...] that adaptation can take place at different levels of society and be influenced by various groups of vulnerable actors". Even less attention is paid to the potential that lies in the combination of climate mitigation/ adaptation and the economic empowerment of women. Yet mitigation or adaptation activities offer opportunities to advance the economic empowerment of women. In particular, this applies to work that is already being undertaken by women or activities in which women could assume a leading role.

In developing countries, for instance, women frequently play a major role in the reforestation and afforestation of cleared land and in forest conservation. Yet they have hardly ever benefited from these environmental services, say in the form of payments for environmental services (PES). Similarly, the Clean Development Mechanism (CDM) defined in the **Kyoto Protocol** is a tool to promote emission reductions in developing countries. Small-scale projects in which the level of emission stored is low (compared with large industrial projects) could be included in CDM; these would be projects in the agricultural sector, in food production, domestic energy generation, etc. (in other words, in areas in which the majority of those involved are women). This potential is, however, seldom tapped even though women could benefit from the transfer of technology, access to finances, etc., which would contribute to their empowerment, to greater equality, the socioeconomic development in a particular society, and to climate protection. In other words, there is the potential, albeit largely untapped, to facilitate the integration of women's economic empowerment in mitigation and adaptation measures and thus be able to achieve several objectives simultaneously.

## Climate Change and Gender–the Linkages

Development-policy issues, particularly gender equality aspects, have long been ignored by the climate discourse. Gender equality has been paid increasing attention only since the publication of the UNDP report and that of the Intergovernmental Panel on Climate Change (IPCC) in 2007 (Rodenberg 2009: 7ff.). This is surprising as the consequences of climate change are by no means gender-neutral. The gender dimension in climate change comprises primarily two aspects: women, particularly in developing countries, are more vulnerable than men to the consequences of climate change (higher vulnerability); second, men and women play different roles in dealing with climate change, whereby women are major actors in several areas of mitigation and adaptation (agents of change).

## Gender-specific Impact

As a rule, poor social groups bear the brunt of climate change not only because they are more dependent on natural resources, but also because they lack the requisite capacity to adapt to climate change. About two-thirds of the world's population living in poverty is women, which underlines their greater vulnerability to the changing climate. The differential impact of climate change on women and men is due to social norms, traditional roles and different power structures. CDM is one of the **Kyoto Protocol's** three flexible mechanisms (Article 12) to meet the emission-reduction commitments of industrialised countries. The financing of emission-reduction projects in developing countries is a cost-efficient option for the donor country to meet its Kyoto commitments. The partner country, for its part, benefits from the additional funds, the transfer of modern technologies and know-how [Oberthür/Ott {2000}, 203]. CDM is intended to facilitate not only climate mitigation but also sustainable development (Article 12.2, Kyoto Protocol). It enables developing countries to participate in carbon trading, as they can sell the emission credits generated by CDM projects to industrialised countries. The problem is, however, that this increases the overall volume of emissions for industrialised countries. Nevertheless, the significance of CDM, particularly with regard to expanding environmentally friendly capacities in recipient countries, is not to be underestimated.

Women are usually responsible for providing the family with its basic nutrition, yet they rarely have access to and control over the resources required to fulfil this task when cultivation conditions deteriorate. Hence climate-induced crop failure also puts the food security of the entire population at risk (Denton 2002: 14). More than anything else, however, women lack land rights, ownership rights for the means of production, technology, finances, information and training, *e.g.*, in climate adaptation and disaster prevention (see Rodenberg 2009: 11). Studies have shown that women and children are 14 times more likely to lose their lives in a natural disaster (Araujo et al. 2007:1). This is also explained by socio-cultural stereotypes: warnings of disasters announced in public places that are often inaccessible to women (and which often do not reach them) are only one example (Rodenberg 2009: 30). In the aftermath of natural disasters, the lack of ownership titles poses an enormous problem to women, as they are denied the right to buy a new plot of land should they have to resettle (Rodenberg 2009: 27). Moreover, after a disaster, women face a heavier workload involving clean-up work, subsistence activities and nursing the sick (Rodenberg 2009: 30). Consequently, not only are they left with virtually no time for income-generating activities, but they also run the risk of being exhausted and overworked (BRIDGE 2008: 3). Given that women are frequently discriminated against in the distribution of resources such as food or medicine, as it is the risk of them falling ill is higher than that of men and, because of economic or cultural constraints, they are often denied access to medical facilities (BRIDGE 2008: 3). Climate change also increases the frequency of heat waves and other adverse weather conditions, resulting in a higher incidence of disease; rising temperatures encourage the spread of infectious diseases such as malaria or dengue fever (Rodenberg 2009: 29). Moreover, the likelihood of a woman's health deteriorating increases because of the discrimination against women referred to above. In post-disaster situations, there is also a greater danger of women becoming victims of sexual violence (Rodenberg 2009: 13). Climate change and its impact on the income security for the family increases the potential for domestic violence, as it shatters the image of the man as bread-winner, which can cause psychological stress.

## Gender-specific Adaptation

With regard to climate adaptation, it should be noted that women often do not have much of a say in decisions taken by the family or the community and are therefore unable to diversify cultivation, for example (see Rodenberg 2009: 3). Furthermore, it is usually women who are responsible for collecting water and fuel (*e.g.*, firewood) for the household. The scarcity of these resources induced by climate change increases a woman's workload and time poverty, burdened as she already is by the many roles she has to play. She is consequently left with no time for income-generating activities, education, training or participation in community decision making processes. In overall terms, climate change intensifies the existing economic and social gender disparities.

Apart from the differential vulnerability, the sexes also play different roles in dealing with climate change. It is generally recognised that women are major actors in mitigation and adaptation measures (see IUCN 2007; Rodenberg 2009; UNDP 2009; UNFPA/WEDO 2009) and their role in adaptation measures in developing countries is often highlighted. Women play a particularly significant role in ensuring a family's food security. They shoulder the responsibility for this activity, have extensive knowledge about their natural surroundings, and are at the forefront in the conservation and selection of seeds of different crops (IUCN/ UNDP/ GGCA 2009: 122). In many areas women are already adapting to the fallout of climate change and are fully aware of where their own needs and those of their families lie (BRIDGE 2008: 12). Greater decision-making powers for women at the family and community level with regard to agricultural cultivation and the farming of new and more resistant crops could increase agricultural production, leading to greater food security, the production and marketing of surpluses, and ultimately to a source of income.

## Gender-specific Mitigation

The role of women in mitigation measures should not be underestimated. Developing countries have the potential to reduce or store greenhouse gases, particularly in areas in which women are already active. Thus, providing energy for the household is usually a woman's job and she often resorts to the energy-inefficient open burning of biomass, *e.g.*, firewood. The use of efficient energy systems at the household level (*e.g.*, special cooking stoves and ovens) could reduce emissions and harness the potential of women as actors for mitigation measures. Women worldwide are also involved in natural resource and forest conservation. The forests supply women with vital products and are used not just to gather firewood, but also to obtain other raw materials, food or medicinal plants to provide for their families and to boost their income (IUCN/ UNDP/GGCA 2009: 155). The conservation and care of forests coupled with reforestation and afforestation for which women are responsible helps avoid the emissions caused by deforestation and leads to greater sequestration of greenhouse gases from the atmosphere. Women, therefore contribute directly to climate mitigation. Given their significant role in mitigation and adaptation efforts, it is imperative that women be involved in the relevant measures.

## Access to Education, Training and Upgrading

In the context of climate, measures designed for training and continuing education could be particularly significant in the following areas:

- Awareness of the causes and consequences of climate change in order to sensitise women to the dangers of climate change and to the possible requirements/mechanisms of adaptation.
- Awareness of existing mitigation and adaptation programmes in which women can be involved and from which they can benefit.
- Training programmes on adaptation measures with a special focus on the needs of women (*e.g.*, alternative cultivation methods and more resistant crops in agriculture, more efficient domestic and agricultural use of available water resources, alternative sources of domestic energy).
- Training programmes on the use of (new) technologies (*e.g.*, means of agricultural production, energy-efficient cooking stoves and ovens, renewable energy systems, information and communication technologies).
- Awareness of existing rights and laying claim to these rights in different spheres of life (*e.g.*, land ownership or land use rights, ownership rights for means of production).

**Access to and control over productive resources**, including **access to land and ownership rights** presupposes the existence of a relevant legal framework; in the context of the climate and gender problem, this means, above all:

- To own land and be able to use it according to one's own needs and wishes in order to be active in climate mitigation and adaptation.
- To procure, own and be able to use the means of production, particularly new technologies, and the related technical know-how.
- To obtain, own, and be able to deploy financial capital for one's own undertakings in order to have investments available for the adoption or development of climate-related work.

**Access to services means first and foremost**

- To have access to (medical) care and child-care services in order to ease the burden on women, reduce time poverty, and gain more time for income-generating activities.
- To have access to the (agricultural) extension services required, for example, to expand agricultural production or nature and resource conservation work.
- To be able to formalise one's own enterprise, which involves neither a great deal of time nor money.

**Access to markets (land, labour, financial and product markets) in this context implies**

- To be able to acquire (additional) land or sell it.
- To be able to use one's own labour in the formal and informal labour markets.
- To have access to loans and funds and, in the context of climate, (indirect) access to international climate finance mechanisms (*e.g.*, climate funds or CDM).
- To be able to access product markets to sell one's own products and so have access to the information required about market prices and trading options.

Drawing benefit from the deployment of **public funds**, particularly for infrastructure, and enjoying access to **public services** means:

- Being equipped with the necessary technical and social infrastructure that helps reduce working time and fosters economic activity; this implies primarily.
- Safe and affordable public transport.
- Medical care and child-care facilities in the locality.
- Electricity and water connections.
- Access to information and communication technologies (ICT) to develop one's own capacity and business potential.

Enforcing claims for **unpaid (reproductive) work** and being able to benefit from the **re-distribution and remuneration** for such work means:

- Being remunerated for reproductive work or not being solely responsible for such work and so having more time available.
- Being able to obtain benefits and/or remuneration from environmental services that are to the benefit of the community or society as a whole.

And finally the **ability to generate income by using one's own labour** should be understood as follows:

- To be able to undertake work or income-generating activities outside the house.
- To have control over the income earned and be able to determine how it should be used.

**Approaches to the economic empowerment of women through climate mitigation and adaptation.**

**Greenhouse gas reduction: natural resource conservation, agroforestry, energy.**

As described at the outset, while climate change and its consequences may pose challenges, there are also opportunities to be found in adaptation and mitigation. In several developing countries, the people (chiefly women) are already engaged in traditional work that does not cause greenhouse gas emissions or captures emissions that have been released. Several commitments to enhance the economic empowerment of women have also been made by donors and partners at international, transnational and national levels. These are two key arguments that support the integration of the economic empowerment of women into climate mitigation and adaptation measures.

## Natural Resource Conservation

Women worldwide are at the forefront of the **conservation** of forests, the reforestation and afforestation of cleared land and the conservation of **natural resources** in general.

However, they have rarely been paid for these **environmental services**. Yet with instruments such as CDM, emissions trading, as well as numerous bilateral and multilateral climate funds, recourse could be made to resources (climate finance) for compensation and support for these services. Mechanisms such as Reducing Emissions from Deforestation and Degradation (REDD) are potentially suited to ensure that women are paid for forest conservation.

The REDD approach, which is meant to be an integral part of the follow-up agreement to the Kyoto Protocol that expires in 2012, attempts to assign an economic value to the carbon stored in forests. Developing countries are offered (financial) incentives to preserve their forests and so reduce emissions, and to invest in low-carbon, sustainable development (UN-REDD Programme 2010). At the 13th Conference of the Parties to the United Nations Framework Convention on Climate Change in Bali, the industrialised countries committed themselves to co-finance climate mitigation and forest conservation in developing and newly industrialised countries (Spencer/Bals 2009: 17). A decision adopted by COP 13 encouraged industrialised countries to mobilise resources to help reduce emissions released by deforestation in developing countries.

(UNFCCC COP 13 2007). However, it is still not clear whether the requisite measures should be financed through a fund and/or emissions trading. Nevertheless, it is clear that when planning and implementing REDD projects in developing countries, it is essential to involve the local communities that often live in and from the forest and know a great deal about forest conservation and natural resource management, to ensure the ecological and social success of REDD (see IBRD 2010, UNREDD Programme 2010). As primarily women use forest resources and play a role in forest conservation, there are paid employment opportunities for them within the framework of (internationally funded) REDD projects.

### Agroforestry

As part of the reforestation and afforestation efforts, women can also plant trees that not only sequester emissions, but also produce a crop (agroforestry), which may provide them with a source of income. Such projects could be tied to emissions trading, and reduced emissions resulting from afforestation could be traded in the form of certificates. This could be used to fund further measures and related services in such projects. Complementary training programmes that focus on the processing and marketing of these products would further enhance the economic benefits for women. In many developing countries, women are traditionally excluded from the commercial production of agricultural produce (cultivation of cash crops) (see GTZ programme on Promoting Gender Equality and Women's Rights 2008, UNCCD, USAID 2005), and agroforestry could help address this problem.

### Energy

As is the case with the cultivation of agricultural products for the market, the **energy sector** is also largely viewed as a 'male' sector in which women are assigned a minor role (Carlsson 2007: 9). However, in most developing countries, domestic energy, *e.g.*, for cooking, heating or lighting, is still obtained from the energy-inefficient and toxic burning of biomass, such as wood, charcoal or agricultural waste, which is traditionally women's work (Carlsson 2007: 9). Even when households are connected to an electricity network, the power available is usually used only for smaller electrical gadgets and for lighting; it is not used as a substitute for biomass, particularly not in rural areas (Carlsson 2007: 11). Women therefore, continue to spend enormous amounts of time on procuring the biomass they require and they need larger amounts of fuel as they burn it inefficiently. Not only does this give them even less of an opportunity to pursue alternative, income-generating activities, but, as it is virtually impossible for them to meet this need sustainably, the practice exacerbates deforestation, land degradation and desertification (GTZ HERA 2007: 5).

The use of energy-efficient stoves and ovens (promoted by GTZ HERA, for instance) could help reduce unhealthy emissions and improve the situation described, not least because these stoves and ovens reduce the quantity of biomass required while cutting down on cooking time. It is also conceivable that projects promoting such stoves and ovens are tied to emissions trading. The sale of emission certificates could help expand their production and increase their distribution besides bringing down prices and enabling a larger number of people to have access to cleaner, safer, time- and cost-saving energy (GTZ HERA 2009: 6).

Besides energy-efficient ovens, it is particularly important for the rural population to be connected to the electrical grid, with electricity ideally generated by renewable energy. The production factor that is most readily available to the poor, and therefore above all to women, is the use of their own labour (UN 2009: vii). Hence the bulk of a woman's income generating activities is labour-based, which is why greater attention should be paid to the issue of energy supply as it is directly responsible for reducing the human workload involved in production (Ramani 2002: 8). In other words, power is required to run electricity-based means of production that would increase a woman's productivity while reducing her workload.

Another option for the use of solar energy would be to install domestic solar power systems; as an emission-reducing development measure, they could also be linked to CDM. Similar measures would contribute to efforts to adapt to depleting sources of energy. A climate-friendly path of development can also be supported within the framework of small-scale projects, particularly in areas for which women are traditionally responsible (*e.g.*, food security, water and energy for the household).

## Adapted Agricultural Production

In the context of **agricultural production,** in which most of the women work to ensure food security for the family (IUCN/UNDP/GGCA

2009: 118), this refers primarily to the use of cultivation and irrigation methods that allow for crop security even in the case of natural resource depletion or unforeseen weather events. In irrigation, it is important to adapt type, time, and use (IUCN/UNDP/GGCA 2009: 129). Ideally, one can switch from traditional irrigation methods to efficient, technified irrigation systems. As regards cultivation methods, it is advisable to select crops that can flourish despite floods or heat waves or those with a short growth cycle which can, for example, be harvested before the flooding season or can be planted during the (short) rainy season. Moreover, it would be possible to grow different crops on one and the same field in order to optimise the use of soil and irrigation and perhaps to counter the onset of erosion. Locally produced organic fertiliser could also be used that would not only fertilise the soil, but would also prevent disease or ensure crop survival in times of drought or frost. All in all, these adaptation measures could actually increase production, as with the existing resources the highest possible yields could be attained. However, complementary training and agricultural extension services are required to teach women about the economical use of scarce resources and about processing and marketing methods for agricultural products. The latter includes converting raw materials into derivates that usually fetch higher prices and reduce dependence on raw material prices.

## Soil and Water Conservation

Besides adapting production methods, it is also important to **conserve soil and water sources** as the basis of agricultural production. Here, too, women across the world are involved as central players and therefore could make a significant contribution towards meeting adaptation requirements (IUCN/UNDP/GGCA 2009: 118). Soil degradation and the unused water runoff could, for instance, be reduced by planting the area or by constructing infiltration ditches (WEDO/ABANTU for Development/ ActionAid/ENDA 2008: 31). According to a case study from Senegal, women are keen to address the problem of erosion mainly because erosion reduces their agricultural productivity and makes it more difficult for them to access water (WEDO/ABANTU for Development/ActionAid/ ENDA 2008: 31). Both are fundamental requirements if production is to be increased and is to generate income. In addition to soil and water sources, ecological systems in the wider sense must be rehabilitated to conserve soil, water sources and habitat and therefore also to maintain the basis for life and livelihoods. As repeatedly mentioned, women today are already often engaged in work that addresses the rehabilitation of eco-systems

However, it is clear that reductions in ozone levels will lead to higher levels of ultra violet-B [UV-B] reaching the Earth's surface. The sun's output of UV-B does not change; rather, less ozone means less protection, and hence more UV-B reaches the Earth. In Antarctica, studies have shown that the amount of UV-B measured at the surface can double during the annual ozone hole. A United Nations Environmental Programme (UNEP)[3] assessment estimates that for every one per cent decrease in ozone, biologically damaging ultraviolet radiation will increase 1.3 per cent. Another study recently confirmed the relationship between reduced ozone and increased UV-B levels in Canada during the past several years.

## Equity and Inequality

Concerns about equity and inequality also arise from the effect of various policy responses designed to deal with climate change. As policies are introduced to mitigate the effects of climate change, one of the major challenges for policymakers will be the equity implications of their policies. A major concern is that the impact of climate change and associated policy responses on vulnerable geographical areas of the globe and disadvantaged sections of society could be disproportionate, that is, those nations and individuals least responsible for global warming may become the most at risk. Recent reports on climate change are therefore, increasingly focusing on the need for social policy responses to mitigate these effects.

Those nations least responsible for the ill-effects of climate change are often least able to mitigate the impact of these issues without assistance. The United Nations Development Programme (UNDP) latest development report *Fighting climate change—human solidarity in a divided world* forecast that the impact of climate change on the world's poor will have long term consequences.

Failure will consign the poorest 40 per cent of the world's population—some 2.6 billion people—to a future of diminished opportunity. It will exacerbate deep inequalities within countries. And it will undermine efforts to build a more inclusive pattern of globalisation, reinforcing the vast disparities between the 'haves' and the 'have nots'.

The inequity of climate change is increasingly of interest to scientists and social policy researchers who highlights the potential negative impact of some mitigation strategies.[4] In addition, not only is the health burden from climate change itself greatest among the world's poor, but some of the major mitigation approaches to reduce the degree of warming may produce negative side effects disproportionately among the poor. Should they bear the brunt of adverse effects caused by industrialised nations? The potential inequity of the situation looms large and is already a major part of the international negotiations toward solutions to combat global climate change.

Evaluations of impacts from increased ultraviolet radiation at a given location must consider the time of year and the latitude. Ultraviolet radiation naturally varies with time of year, latitude, and altitude.[5] For example, four times as much ultraviolet radiation reaches the earth's surface at Philadelphia at 10 AM in the summer than in the winter. Southern latitudes receive more ultraviolet radiation than northern latitudes.

Scientists believe that Global Warming will lead to a weaker Ozone layer, because as the surface temperature rises, the stratosphere (the Ozone layer being found in the upper part) will get colder, making the natural repairing of the Ozone slower.

NASA, for example, reports that by 2030, "climate change may surpass chlorofluorocarbons (CFCs) as the main driver of overall ozone loss."

The ozone layer is a layer in Earth's atmosphere which contains relatively high concentrations of ozone ($O_3$). This layer absorbs 97–99 per cent of the Sun's high frequency ultraviolet light, which is damaging to life on Earth. It is mainly located in the lower portion of the stratosphere from approximately 13 km to 40 km above Earth, though the thickness varies seasonally and geographically.

The Ozone layer protects all life on Earth from the harmful effects of the Sun's rays. It has been depleting for many years now. Scientists have said that currently over Antarctica **the Ozone hole** is three times the size[6] of the United States and growing. Also, September 9 to 10, 2000, the ozone hole stretched over a populated city for the first time. It was in Punta Arenas, a southern Chile city of about 120,000 people, exposing residents to very high levels of ultraviolet radiation. Also, according to scientists, more than 60 per cent of the ozone layer blanketing the Arctic Circle was lost in the 1999/2000 winter.

## Facts and Findings

The ozone depletion has also been correlated with higher levels of cancer in humans and animals.

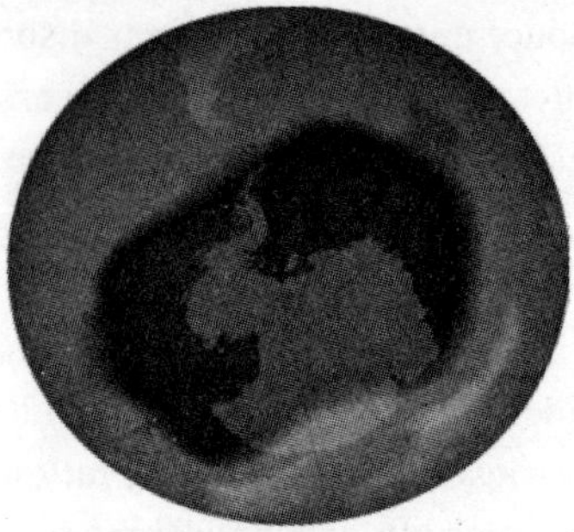

### Ozone Depletion

From September 21-30, 2006 the average area of the ozone hole was the largest ever observed, at 10.6 million square miles (27.5 million square kilometers).[7] This image, from September 24, the Antarctic ozone hole was equal to the record single-day largest area of 11.4 million square miles (29.5 million square kilometers), reached on Sept. 9, 2000. Satellite instruments monitor the ozone layer, and we use their data to create the images that depict the amount of ozone. The blue and purple colours are, where there is the least ozone, and the greens, yellows, and reds are, where there is more ozone.

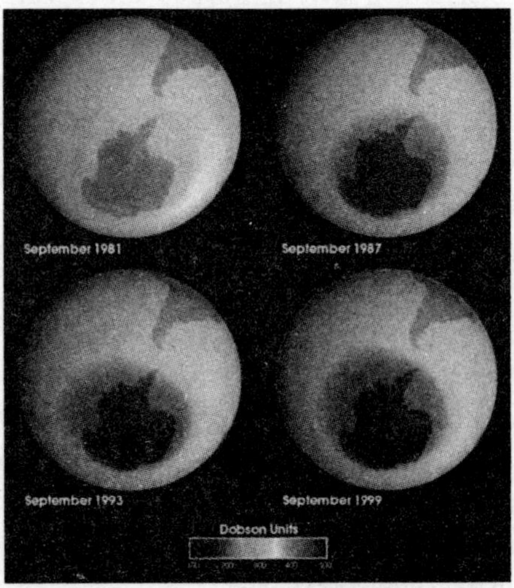

Chlorofluorocarbons (CFCs), chemicals found mainly in spray aerosols heavily used by industrialised nations for much of the past 50 years, are the primary culprits in ozone layer breakdown. When CFCs reach the upper atmosphere, they are exposed to ultraviolet rays, which cause them to break down into substances that include chlorine. The chlorine reacts with the oxygen atoms in ozone and rips apart the ozone molecule. One atom of chlorine can destroy more than a hundred thousand ozone molecules.[8]

The **ozone layer above** the Antarctic has been particularly impacted by pollution since the mid-1980s. This region's low temperatures speed up the conversion of CFCs to chlorine. In the southern spring and summer, when the sun shines for long periods of the day, chlorine reacts with ultraviolet rays, destroying ozone on a massive scale, up to 65 per cent. This is what some people erroneously refer to as the "ozone hole." In other regions, the ozone layer has deteriorated by about 20 per cent. About 90 per cent of CFCs currently in the atmosphere were emitted by industrialised countries in the Northern Hemisphere, including the United States and Europe. These countries banned CFCs by 1996, and the amount of chlorine in the atmosphere is falling now. But scientists estimate it will take another 50 years for chlorine levels to return to their natural levels.

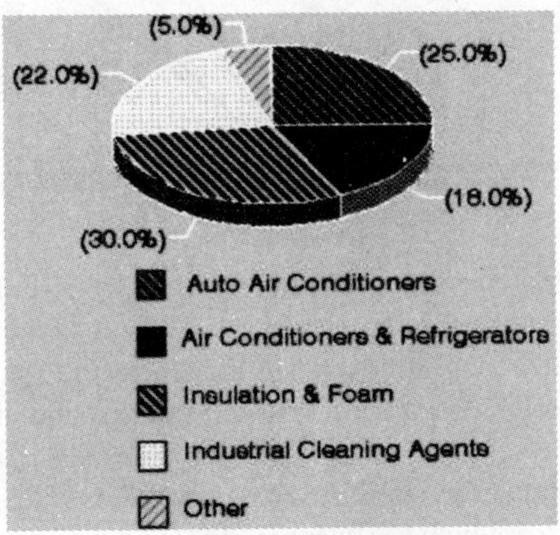


Use of CFC's. Information from the US Environmental Protection Agency.[8]

## The Development of the Ozone Hole 2001

High levels of molecular chlorine ($Cl_2$) can be produced in the stratosphere at the poles during the winter. In the spring, the Sun reappears and levels of solar ultra-violet radiation increase. This ultra-violet radiation breaks down the $Cl_2$ into chlorine radicals, these then destroy ozone and an ozone hole forms. As a result, we see the ozone hole at the same time each year and ozone levels don't recover until the ice clouds thaw and the chlorine radicals are removed by other reactions.

The **ozone depletion** process begins when CFCs and other ozone-depleting substances (ODS) are emitted into the atmosphere. Winds efficiently mix the troposphere and evenly distribute the gases. CFCs are extremely stable, and they do not dissolve in rain. After a period of several years, ODS molecules reach the stratosphere, about 10 kilometers above the Earth's surface.

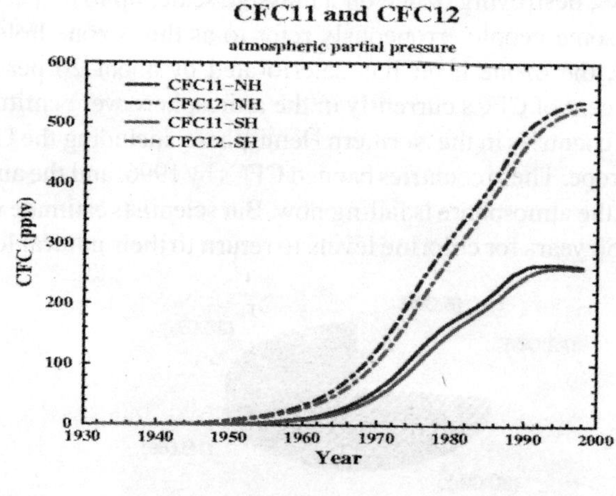


CFCs were banned globally by the Montreal Protocol[9] on substances that deplete the Ozone layer-1987 (and further amendments). As they have such long atmospheric lifetimes (the longest lived have lifetimes of the order of 100 years) it will take around another 50 years until all the CFC's released so far have been destroyed in the stratosphere and ozone concentrations stabilise. Maximum CFC concentrations in the stratosphere were predicted to occur in 2000 and the ozone hole has been rather constant in size over the past few years. However, there are exceptions to this trend. In 2002 no significant ozone hole was seen. The reason why was simple: it was too warm and the polar vortex did not form as usual. Once again, an example that atmospheric processes sometimes ignore any prediction! But in 2003 the hole was back to its previous size[10], the second largest ever observed.

It is not enough to know how much ozone is in the air. We need to know where it is! That's one reason NASA has developed the Tropospheric Emission Spectrometer, or TES.

## Conclusion

Even minor problems of ozone depletion can have major effects. Every time even a small amount of the ozone layer is lost, more ultraviolet light from the sun can reach the Earth. Every time one per cent of the ozone layer is depleted, two per cent more UV-B is able to reach the surface of the planet. UV-B increase is one of the most harmful consequences of ozone depletion because it can cause skin cancer. The increased cancer levels caused by exposure to this ultraviolet light could be enormous. The EPA [11] estimates that 60 million Americans born by the year 2075 will get skin cancer because of ozone depletion. About one million of these people will die. In addition to cancer, some research shows that a decreased ozone layer will increase rates of malaria and other infectious diseases. According to the EPA, 17 million more cases of cataracts can also be expected. The environment will also be negatively affected by ozone depletion. The life cycles of plants will change, disrupting the food chain. Effects on animals will also be severe, and are very difficult to foresee. The main source of the halogen atoms in the stratosphere is photo dissociation of man-made halocarbon refrigerants (CFCs, freons, halons). These compounds are transported into the stratosphere after being emitted at the surface.[8] Both types of ozone depletion were observed to increase as emissions of halo-carbons increased, halons, and other ozone-depleting chemicals such as carbon tetrachloride and trichloroethane. It is suspected that a variety of biological consequences such as increases in skin cancer, cataracts, damage to plants, and reduction of plankton populations in the ocean's photic zone may result from the increased UV exposure due to ozone depletion.

Any persistent drop in the amount of protective ozone resident in the stratosphere will increase the amount of solar ultraviolet radiation that reaches the surface of the Earth, at the risk of direct and deleterious effects on human health: that much is known with certainty. Likely effects include permanent clouding of the lens of the eye, which is particularly sensitive to the U-VB exposure: a reduction of seven per cent in the amount of stratospheric ozone (the maximum expected in summer for middle latitudes by the end of the century) could increase the incidence of cataracts in sun-exposed people by three to four per cent. Even more liable to damage is the sun-exposed skin, in the form of increased skin cancer. A total reduction of seven per cent in ozone in summertime would probably increase the incidence of non- melanoma skin cancer by about 16 per cent. The incidence of more deadly melanoma could also rise. Chronic exposure to the increased UV-B that would accompany any persistent loss in ozone would also affect the natural immune system, with an increased potential for infection and disease.

## References


1. *United Nations Development Programme*, Brasilia, 27 November, 2007.
2. Kevin Watkins, *Director of the Human Development Report Office*, 2000.
3. http://hdr.undp.org/en/media/hdr, *Human Development Report 2007–08*, UNDP, 2008, p. 8.
4. Jonathan Patz, *Global Health-Environmental Health*, University of Wisconsin in Madison, 22 July. 2009.
5. Zure, Pamela, "Looming Ban on Production of CFCs, Halons Spurs Switch to Substitutes", *Chemical and Engineering News*, **71**(46), 1993, p. 1218.
6. Michael Kurylo, *NASA*, Friday, 8 September, 2000, 11:30 GMT 12:30 UK.
7. Paul Newman, NASA's Goddard Space Flight Center, www.universetoday.com/820/biggest-ozone-hole-ever/, October 19, 2006.
8. The U.S. Environmental Protection Agency, *www.epa.gov/startospheric ozone*, March, 1994.
9. *The Montreal Protocol on Substances That Deplete the Ozone Layer*, September 16, 1987.
10. Lambert Kuijpers and Walter Brunne, *The Montreal Protocol on Substances That Deplete the Ozone Layer*, May, 2003.
11. *www.fueleconomy.gov*–U.S. *Environmental Protection Agency [EPA]*-Office of Transportation and Air Quality, 21 Dec 2011.

20

# 'Greening the Minds' Through Curriculum-for Sustainable Development

*Sreekala. K.L*

With the increasing urgency of environmental issues – from climate change and energy shortages to waste disposal and water conservation – the more we can educate today's younger generations, the better. The enhanced pace of developmental activities and rapid urbanisation have resulted in stress and degradation of natural resources and in turn the quality of life. All the major natural resources in the country are in grave danger today. A society cannot survive if its natural resources are rendered unfit for use by its people. The only hope of overcoming this dangerous situation if by making the youth aware that they need to proactively begin to protect the environment they exists. It is need of the hour to inculcate the needed attitudes and values related to Mother Earth in our learners with the essential elements of moral philosophy.

Developing a '**responsive environmental behaviour**' is one of the most important tasks of education, in this global era. This behaviour is defined as 'the whole actions of an individual within the society that makes into account, in a conscious way, the perennial and harmonious relationship between these actions and environment'. But these efforts could not bring about the needed attitudinal changes in learners or equip them to face the environmental challenges and help them in making the right decisions. So we need to impart education such that it helps to develop responsible environmental behaviour leading to an improved environment. It needed, instilling proactive action in curriculum/syllabus change - change in pedagogy, evaluation, teacher training and implementation strategies, monitoring and networking.

The focus in curriculum must be on reducing consumption with a view to achieve sustainability. The content should be holistic, including all essential components, necessary to inculcate the needed knowledge, attitudes, skills and values related to **environmental consciousness**. We have to make our learners realise that they are part of this universe, which is crowded with problems and issues therefore they have to be part of the solution also. Mere theoretical input will make nature studies a boring option; instead it should be introduced as a voluntary, extra curricular activity to arouse the interest and awareness of students in **'green'** issues. Teacher's role in developing environmental responsive behaviour is an important aspect. The interdisciplinary skills they learn today will be the planet saving skills of tomorrow. It is high time for children to develop a connection with the outside world through both learning and experience. Here comes the concept of **'greening the minds'**...Greening the minds doesn't means doing big things. It is as simple as opening the eyes of a child to the flora and fauna just near the school campus or near home. Instill a connectedness to nature and environment – it is very essential to make sense of the world around them. To teach students about global issues about climate change and **endangered species make** learners familiarise with the local issues related to recycling, air pollution etc.

'Greening the Minds' means ensuring that students are capable of taking on the 21st century challenges of global warming and climate change, social inequities, unhealthy lifestyles, lifestyle diseases, and the urgent need to switch to a renewable energy-based economy. 'Greening the minds' also means being open to Nature as teacher, the outdoors as classrooms and sustaining life for all future generations as the most important learning objective in our curriculum. Because of the present severe environmental issues like global warming and climate changes, we now live in a world heading for the collapse of human civilisation. But we have to face it. The present curriculum is outdated and irrelevant. So there is need to revise the curriculum urgently to meet the dangerous global situation. Students have a right to know the present state of the planet. Our learners need to develop related knowledge, skills and attitudes towards environmental issues. For inculcating this in learners, we need to integrate Nature, Ecological principles, Environmental issues and Sustainable development along with ethics, global warming, and renewable energy resources into the existing curriculum from the grassroot level itself. Research shows that how vital it is for children to spend time in a natural world. Parents and school must give their students the opportunity to play and learn in nature. Educating for sustainability offers innumerable opportunities for integrating ecological literacy and environmental ethics into the curriculum. This integration mould students in a holistic way, that we value the Earth and their future. All these aspects can be successfully incorporated in the curriculum through promoting different eco-friendly strategies. Some of them are listed below:

1. **Fostering Naturalistic Intelligence in Learners.** Professor Howard Gardner added **Naturalistic Intelligence** as eighth intelligence, in his theory of Multiple Intelligences. According to him, people possessing this intelligence are keenly aware of changes in environment even at subtle levels. Often this is due to their highly developed levels of sensory perception. Their heightened senses may help them notice similarities, differences, and changes in their surroundings more rapidly than others. Developing the naturalist intelligence is no different than teaching other subjects. Teachers must provide the opportunity for this intelligence to grow in classrooms. By observing outside we can see those same patterns of mathematics blocks in nature and understand connections. The quality of life on this planet requires that our children have experience with nature. So as teachers we must provide the best educational learning opportunities for fostering the naturalistic intelligence.
2. **Inculcating Eco-Psychological concepts in the Curriculum.** Eco-psychology refers to a variety of endeavours bring together the methods and understandings of ecology and psychology in order to promote healthy **Human–Earth relationships**. The theoretical base of eco-psychology sees the earth as a living system. Human beings, their psyches as well as their cultures are integral and crucial parts of that system. The practice of eco-psychology is based on the recognition that the needs of the earth and the needs of the human individual are interdependent and that human sanity include sustainable and mutually enhancing relations with the natural world. The understanding of what constitutes healthy human earth relationships is the heart of **eco-psychology**. Hence, eco-psychology points out the strong relationship between 'vision of the self' and 'vision of the world' and leads us to see and to use personal growth as a practical tool to develop a deeper environmental consciousness. Eco-psychology holds that there is a synergetic interplay between planetary and personal well-being. 'Synergy' here means, the needs of the planet are

the needs of the person and the rights of the person are the rights of the planet. Considering the present situation of our Planet Earth, it is high time to raise the 'ecological ego' in our students. Secondary level is the best stage for inculcation of ecological environ-mental consciousness because raising environmental consciousness means implementing a way of thinking in a youngster's life. As teachers, we are responsible for teaching our students to live each day of their lives with a consciousness towards environment.

3. **Enhancing Outdoor Education in Educational Institutions.** Outdoor Education usually refers to organised learning that takes place outdoors. Outdoor education draws upon the philosophy, theory and practices of experiential education and environmental education. Local and global environments are undergoing transformations at a rapid pace and at a scale that is unparalleled at any time in human history. Students need to understand the consequences of human actions on environments. Outdoor education provides an opportunity for integrating personal experience and formal learning. **Outdoor education** programmes also contributes to personal growth and social awareness and develops skills for life and the world of work. Outdoor education introduces active learning to the environment in a way which develops understanding, appreciation and respect. It fosters sensitivity to the environment, helps young people to see themselves in a global context and helps to develop citizens with awareness to the need for sustainable use of the world's natural resources. Moreover, challenging outdoor experiences promote the development of communication, problem solving and decision making skills which are much needed in this era. Young people horizons are broadened, new challenges came to be relished, and perseverance and determination are reinforced. Values and attitudes developed in a context of shared endeavour help to form a sound basis for responsible citizenship.
4. **Instilling Experiential Learning Strategies.** The basic theory of **Experiential learning** is anchored in the work of John Dewey: the interaction of knowledge and skills with experience is key to learning. Students learn best not by reading the Great Books in a closed room but by opening the doors and windows of experience. Experiential learning is a teaching methodology that uses meaningful practical experience to better understand

course content and enhance the learning of abstract concepts. Through direct involvement with people and issues, students learn to apply their knowledge to real life situations. These experiences are integrated into the students' academic curriculum through the Reflective discussions, a means which provides an academic forum for students to analyse, discuss and write about what they observed and practiced in the field. Through the field experience, students learn about different social and professional cultures by working directly within these communities. As active participants, students will also share their knowledge, ideas and perspectives with members of the on-site community and their classmates. Similarly, many educational research studies have been focused on the theoretical underpinnings of experiential learning, especially Kolb's research on experiential learning theory published in 1984. The term experiential learning is a broad term, generally used by educators to describe a series of pragmatic activities sequenced in such a way that it is thought to enhance the educational experience for the student learner. Experiential learning, on the other hand offered "meaningfulness, connection, interest and purpose in the place of memorisation, abstraction, remoteness and isolation". (Hopkins, 1994). When learning occurs through experience, the students became independent, responsible, self-motivated problem solvers and critical thinkers who were excited about learning. The greatest impact was the building of self-confidence, the students were not afraid to voice their thoughts and opinions to share ideas and help each other.

5. **Integrating Environmental Education in Syllabus. Environmental education** integrates the study of interactions among physical, chemical/biological components of the environment. It is an interdisciplinary academic field which systematically studies human interaction with the environment. The field encompasses study in basic principles of ecology, and environmental science as well as associated subjects like environmental sociology, environmental justice, pollution control and natural resource management.

   Our nation's future relies on a well-educated public to be wise stewards of the very environment that sustains us, our families and communities and future generations. It is environmental education which can best help us as individuals make the complex conceptual connections between economic prosperity, environmental health and our own well being. A good environmental education programme promotes interest in and engagement with the natural world and encourages the next generation of learners who will protect our precious natural resources.

## Conclusion

Today's citizens are tomorrow's decision makers and citizens. So they need to learn and practice the skills necessary to protect, preserve and restore the environment. The above said strategies lead to the acquisition of knowledge, the development of analytical skills, and the beginning of nature conscious attitudes and ultimately a responsive behaviour. Environmental Literacy is the need of the hour. 'Greening Minds' is related to inculcation of **environmental literacy**. It is all about creating awareness where learners gain familiarity with local flora and fauna and ecological relationships in nature, where learners actually go out and develop a personal connection and sense of belonging to nature, about personal empowerment and a life long commitment to engage in environmentally-related activities.

The future of our students depends on us – on our willingness to open our classroom doors to the natural world, on our courage to seek out nature as teacher, on our understanding of the global climate change emergency, and on our compassion for our students and future generations of all species. By placing the students in rich learning environments beyond the classroom, educators can improve educational institutions by increasing learning. The time has arrived to step outside together to explore the community and environment.

## References

**Books:**

1. Vishwanath, H.N. (2006). *Models of Teaching in Environmental Education*. New Delhi: Discovery Publishing House.
2. Mishra, M.P. (2008). *Environmental Education*. New Delhi: S. Chand & Company Ltd.
3. Bonnes, Mirilia and Secchiaroli, Gianfranco. (1995). *Environmental Psychology*. New Delhi: Sage Publications.
4. Kumar, Bharati. (2005). *Environmental Education*. New Delhi: Dominant Publishers and Distributors.

5. Roy, Rajarshi. (2008). *Beyond Curriculum, Pedagogy and Teachers Training for Environmental Education*. New Delhi: Shipra Publishers.
6. Gardner, Howard. (1993). *Multiple Intelligences: The theory in practice*. USA: Basic Books.
7. Gardner, Howard. (1983). *Frames of Mind*. New York; Basic Books.
8. Glock, Jenna, Meyer, Maggie, and Wertz, Susan. *Discovering the Naturalist Intelligence: Science in the school yard*. (1999). Zephyr Press.
9. Adams, D. and Hamm, M. (1994). *New Designs for Teaching and Learning: Promoting active learning in tomorrow's schools*. San Francisco: Jossey-Bass Publishers.
10. Singh, M.S. (2007). *Environmental Education*. New Delhi; Tarun Offset Printers.
11. Bharucha, Erach. (2005). *Text Book of Environmental Studies*. Hyderabad; UGC, Universities Press.
12. Rajagopalan, R. (2005). *Environmental Studies – from Crisis to Cure*. New Delhi; Oxford University Press.
13. Rao, V.K. and Reddy, R.S. (2007). *Environmental Education*. New Delhi; Roshan Offset Printers.
14. Reddy, Purushothaman K & Reddy, Narasimha, D. (2007). *Environmental Education*. Hyderabad; Neelkamal Publishers Private Limited.

**Journals:**

1. Singh, Manmohan. (2003). School Education vis-à-vis Environmental Values. *Journal of Value Education*, Vol. 5, No. 1&2, Jan. and July 2005, NCERT. p. 56.
2. Dadhich, L.K., (2003). Emerging challenges in value based Environmental Education. *Journal of Value Education*, Vol. 3, No. 2, July 2003, NCERT.
3. Saxena, A.B. (2003). Promoting Environmental Values through New approaches in schools. *Journal of Value Education*, Vol. 3, No. 2, July 2003, NCERT.

**Websites:**

1. http://www.armstrong.co.uk/commflareu/en-gb/linoleum-architects-berger-roecker.html
2. http://EzineArticles.com/?expert=Victoria
3. http://eyesoncuccess.com/tag/environmental-awareness/
4. http://envis.mse.ac.in/Environmental%20Problems.asp
5. www.edu.earthday.org/about/what-is-a-green-school
6. http://edu.earthday.org/about/what-is-a-green-school

# 21

# The Human Rights Dimensions of Climate Change

*Dr. V. Asha*

Climate change is perhaps one of the biggest challenges facing the world today. Climate change is a change in the statistical distribution of weather over periods of time that range from decades to millions of years. It may cut across the whole earth. For a long time, governments have approached the problem of climate change as an ecological problem alone. Because of that the social and human rights implications of climate change have gained little attention. No doubt, climate change directly threatens fundamental human rights like right to life, to food, to a place to live and work and the like. There is a close link between climate change and human rights. According to the fifth report from the working group of Climate Change and Development, 2007, "the human drama of climate change will largely be played out in Asia, where over 60 per cent of the world's population, around four billion people lives."

The modern human rights system is based on international law. The **Universal Declaration of Human Rights (UDHR)** was adopted by the General Assembly of the United Nations on 10th December 1948. Truly it was one of the epoch making Declarations of the General Assembly. The fundamental Human Rights contained in the UDHR have been strengthened by subsequent human rights treaties like the **International Covenant on Civil and Political Rights (ICCPR)** and the **International Covenant on Economic, Social and Cultural Rights (ICESCR)**. However, the major human rights treaties were developed before climate change was understood to be a great threat to human security and human existence. Therefore, the interconnection between climate change and international human rights law system is to be developed yet.

The major question raised here is how climate change and human rights are interlinked and what are the major challenges to human rights due to the climate change. When one analyses the impact of climate change on human rights, Right to Life should be given priority. The Right to Life is protected in both the UDHR and the ICCPR. Article 3 of the UDHR provides, "every human being has the inherent right to life". This right shall be protected by law. No one shall be arbitrarily deprived of his life. "The right to the life of children also receives specific protection in Article 6 of **Convention on the Rights of the Child (CRC).**

Surely, climate change may affect human life both directly and indirectly. The impact may be sometimes immediate, sometimes gradual. The U.N. Deputy Commissioner for Human Rights Ky unge – Wh a Kang has rightly pointed out, "global warming and extreme weather conditions may have calamitous consequences for the human rights of millions of people........ Ultimately climate change may affect the very right to life of various individuals... (Countries) have an obligation to prevent and address some of the direct consequences that climate change may reap on human rights".

Secondly, The Right to Adequate Food is threatened by climate change. The right to adequate food is recognised in several international instruments, mainly in the ICESCR. It recognises the fundamental right to freedom from hunger and malnutrition.

Climate change will seriously affect the right to food in a significant manner. Regional food production is likely to reduce because of increased temperatures, shift in rainfall patterns may make the land infertile, may reduce crop and livestock yields, rising sea level making coastal land unusable and causing fish species to migrate and extreme weather conditions disrupt agriculture. The worst affected would be millions of small and marginal farmers and people who are already the most vulnerable.

The Inter governmental Panel on Climate Change Fourth Assessment Report 4(2007) (**IPCCAR4**) (reports that, "Future climate change is expected to put close to 50 million extra people at risk of hunger by 2020 to an additional 132 million, and 266 million by 2050 and 2080 respectively". Yet another dangerous situation is given by Nicholas Stern in the 'Stern Review on the Economics of Climate Change" published in 2006. He says "around 800 million people are currently at risk of hunger (–12 per cent of a world's population) and malnutrition causes around 4 million deaths annually almost half in Africa....." It is also estimated that in Australia up to 20 per cent more droughts are expected by 2030 and up to 80 per cent more droughts by 2070 in South Western Australia".

The third concern due to climate change is the Right to Water. Eventhough the right to water is not expressly articulated in the ICESCR, it is related to a number of rights like right to food and right to health. The right to water is specifically mentioned in the Article 24 of the Convention on the Right of Child (CPC) and Article 14 (2) of the Convention on the **Elimination of Discrimination against Women (CEDAW)**. The UN Committee on Economic, Social and Cultural Rights recognised that water itself is an independent right in 2002.

It is an undeniable fact that the right to safe drinking water is most important for human life. Water scarcity will be a great concern for the future generation. In the opinion of Samuel P. Huntington, the future wars will be for drinking water. The IPCCAR 4 states that drought affected areas will probably increase. Increased frequency and severity of floods and droughts will have implications for sustainable development due to global warming. People will feel the impact of climate change strongly through changes in the distribution of water around the world and its seasonal variability. The effects of rising temperatures against the background of growing population are likely to cause changes in the water status of billions of people.

The Right to Health is yet another right affected by climate change. The right to health is provided in the UDHR itself. Art 25 of the UDHR states that "everyone has the right to a standard adequate for the health and well being of himself and his family". Surely climate change poses significant risks to the right to health. A joint study by the WHO and London School of Hygiene and Tropical Medicine in 2003 reveals that global warming may already be responsible for more than 160000 deaths a year from malaria and malnutrition, a number would double by 2020. It will affect the intensity of a wide variety of diseases-vector borne, water borne and respiratory. In the Pacific region, changes in temperature and rainfall will make it harder to control dengue fever. Climate change will amplify the health disparities between rich and poor parts of the world. This seems to be a very serious problem.

Another concern due to climate change is the Rights of the Indigenous People:- The Rights of the Indigenous People to practise and revitalise their cultural practices, customs and institutions have been recognised under the 2007 Declaration on the Rights of the Indigenous People. There is close link between the indigenous culture and land. It is said that the indigenous people do not see the land as distinct from themselves. If they feel that the ecosystem has been changed, it is a mental anxiety to them. They may feel that they have lost control of their country. Moreover, climate change may threaten the very survival of their communities. One CSIRO report predicts that the economic and health status of remote indigenous communities is likely to worsen owing to climate change.

When we look at climate change through the lens of human rights, we can notice the human rights dimensions of climate change. Surely there will be more catastrophes in the future. Climate change seriously threatens the capacity of individuals and communities to realise their human rights. A well thought out human rights law is an urgent need. If we build human rights criteria into our future planning, we will better understand who is at risk and how we should act to protect them. It is high time for the international community to come together on a common platform to discuss and to devise means to cope with this phenomenon, which threatens the very survival of human beings across the globe. The nations of the world should come out of their narrow national outlook and to formulate action plans to minimise the incidence of climate change on basic human rights. It is the obligation of the world community to create a kind of international and social order that the farmers of the UDHR dreamed of. As pointed out by the UK Secretary of State for the Environment, "socially, climate change raises profound questions of justice and equity, between generations, between the developing and developed worlds, between rich and poor within each country. The challenge is to find an equitable distribution of responsibilities and rights". The most effective means of facilitating this is to adopt a "human rights based approach" based on international human rights standards to fight against the dangers of climate change upon fundamental human rights.

## References

1. Agarwal Anil and Sunita Narain – "Global Warming in an Unequal World" – A Case of Environmental Colonialism, Centre for Science and Environment, 1991.
2. Adamantia Pollis and Peter Schwab – "Human Rights: New Perspectives, New Realities" (Ed), Viva Books Pvt. Ltd, 2002, New Delhi.
3. "Climate Change and Human Rights: A Rough Guide" – 2008, International Council on Human Rights Policy, Versoix, Switzerland.
4. "Human Rights and Climate Change" – Human Rights and Equal Opportunity Commission (HREOC) – 2008.
5. IPCC – "Climate Change 2007, Impacts, Adaptation and Vulnerability" – Contribution of working group II to the Fourth Assessment Report of the IPCC, Cambridge University Press, 2007.

and observations, consistent with a strong connection to changes in the lower atmosphere. Recent changes in noctilucent cloud distributions, now observed on a global scale by the AIM satellite remove these words are thought to be symptomatic of cooling temperatures in the upper atmosphere. Rising greenhouse gas concentrations alter the ionosphere in a variety of ways and could be transmitted to the magnetosphere. These changes may have unforeseen consequences for space-related technologies and societal infrastructures.

## The CAWSES-India Programme

The CAWSES-India programme had begun in 2004 almost as soon as it was announced as the programme of SCOSTEP in 2004. CAWSES-India is fully supported by the Indian Space Research Organisation (ISRO). At the national level, the CAWSES programme has been extended with Phase-II activities with three major themes, namely, (1) Solar Influence on Climate, (2) Space Weather and Space Climate, and (3) Atmospheric Coupling Processes. CAWSES-India has essentially provided a platform wherein different scientists can come together and work on problems of common interests. Many results have emerged out under the auspices of this programme.

## Artificial Neural Network (ANN)

As part of the CAWSES-India programme, we are carrying out a project to design an ANN, to predict storm time horizontal (*H*) component of earth's magnetic field (output) for equatorial/low latitude stations of Indian sub-continent, using solar wind parameters (input). For this, training and testing will be carried out by giving proper choice of solar wind parameters as input and horizontal component measured at various stations of India, as output. The solar-magnetosphere coupling during storms and substorms leads to many processes with a wide range of space and time scales. But these processes are not modeled easily by first principle approaches.

The nonlinear dynamical approach provides an alternative and has been used to develop models of magnetospheric dynamics from observational time series data. These models will capture inherent dynamics of magnetosphere. Artificial Neural Network (ANN) works as model, which trained on the combinations of input and output variables, the connections are adjusted so that the network reproduces the system output as closely as possible. An important neural network theory is that, a two-layer network can reproduce any smooth input-to-output function, given a sufficient amount of low-noise data. ANNs are non-linear adaptive models, and their structural flexibility leads to higher accuracy than their linear counterparts. An advantage of the neural network technique is that a much diversified set of input data can be handled simultaneously. Any parameters that contribute information on the solar wind or on the magnetospheric state can be included in the input. Aim of this study is to develop an ANN, and functional relation between solar wind (input) and magnetosphere (output) systems, during geomagnetic storms of different categories (like weak or major storms occurred at low, moderate and high solar activity periods). Another objective of this project is to design an ANN, to predict storm time horizontal (*H*) component of earth's magnetic field (output) for equatorial/low latitude stations of Indian sub-continent, using solar wind parameters (input). For this, training and testing will be carried out by giving proper choice of solar wind parameters as input, and horizontal component measured at various stations of India, as output.

## Methodology

An artificial neural network is an assembly of interconnected nodes where the strength of the connection between any two nodes is determined by a modifiable weight. Each node is fed by the sum of the weighted outputs from all the nodes in the previous layer, and passes on the output to all the nodes in the following layer. An additional node, the bias node, is set to 1.0 and connected to all hidden and output nodes in the network. ANNs have the ability to map a space which is called input space to another one which is called output space. Neural networks are dynamic systems which contain many simple processing units. Each of these processing units is called neurons. A neuron is simple processing node which calculates the output O according to an input I. A multilayered ANN contains an input layer, a hidden layer, and an output layer. Training of an ANN is the process of initialising the weights W (which are the only free parameters in network and are also the connection between neurons) so that the error between the computed output and desired output for all samples is minimised (Maier and Dandy, 2001; Unnikrishnan, 2008; 2012).

## The ANN Model Development Process

(*a*) *Choice of variables*: The choice of input variables is generally based on apriori knowledge of causal variables in conjunction with inspections of time series plots of potential inputs and outputs. If the relationship to be modeled is less well understood, cross-correlation analysis or a stepwise modeling approach can be used.

(*b*) *Choice of Network Geometry*: Network geometry is generally defined by the number of hidden layer nodes and the number of nodes in each of these layers. The optimum number of hidden layer nodes, on the other hand, generally has to be found using a trial and error approach. However, there are some general guidelines which may be followed. Hecht-Nielsen (1987) suggests the following upper limit for the number of hidden layer nodes in order to ensure that ANNs are able to approximate any continuous function

$$N^H \leq (2N^I + 1) \qquad ...(1)$$

where $N^H$ is the number of hidden layer nodes and $N^I$ is the number of input nodes (= number of inputs). Based on this analysis, it is observed that ANN model with eight hidden neurons has reasonably good performance (Figs. 1 and 2). The optimum choice of input parameters are IMF Bz, V, nPa, and IEF to reproduce the storm time Dst values (Figs. 3).

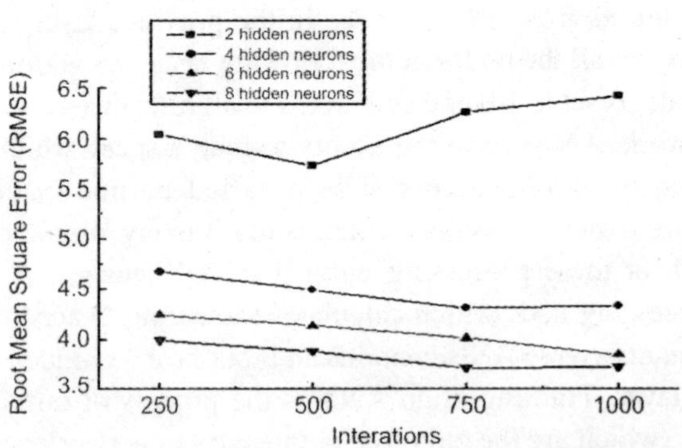


**Fig. 1:** Variation of RMSE with hidden neurons and iterations.

It is observed that if the number of hidden neurons is eight, and iteration is 750, RMSE would be the least.

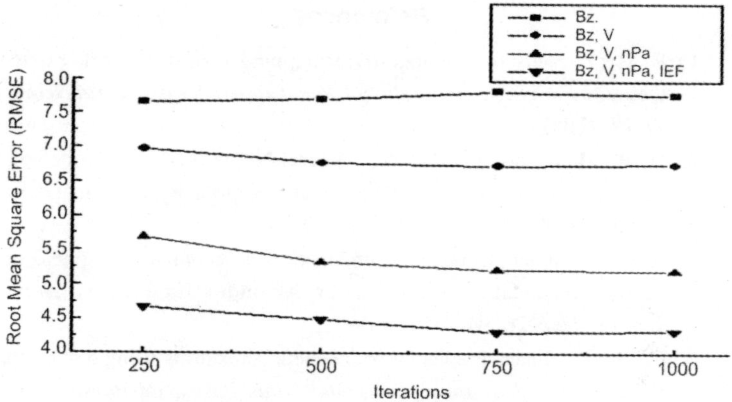


**Fig. 2:** Variation of RMSE with different choice of input parameters and iterations.

It is observed if Bz, V, nPa, and IEF are used as input and iteration is 750, RMSE would be the least.

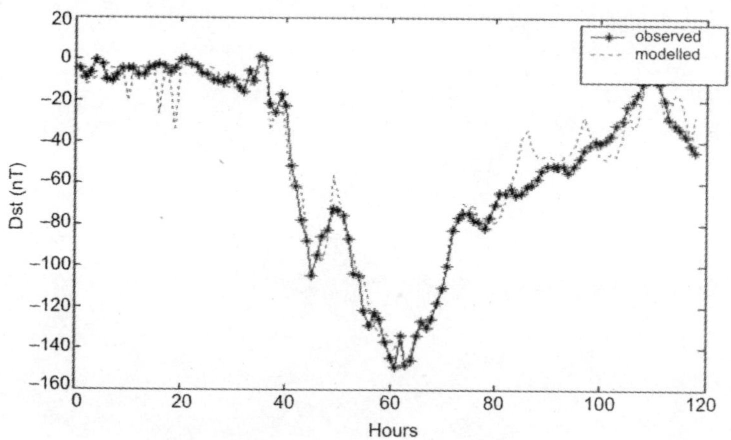


**Fig. 3:** Dst values generated by ANN model are reasonably in agreement with observed Dst values, which underlines the efficiency of the model developed by this study.

**Acknowledgements:** K. Unnikrishnan is thankful to ISRO, Government of India, for providing financial support to carry out this work, under CAWSES, Phase -2, Theme-2 project.

## References

1. R. Hecht-Nielsen, Kolmogorov'a mapping neural network exietence theorem, *First IEEE International Joint Conference on Neural Networks, 11-14,* (1987).
2. H. R. Maier, and G.C. Dandy, Neural Network Based Modelling of Environmental Variables: A Systematic Approach, Mathematical and Computer Modelling 33, 669-682, (2001).
3. K. Unnikrishnan, Comparison of chaotic aspects of magnetosphere under various physical conditions using AE index time series, *Annales Geophysicae*, 26, 941-953, 2008.
4. K. Unnikrishnan, Prediction of magnetic substorms using a state space model, *Journal of Atmospheric and Solar Terrestrial Physics*, 75–76, 22–30, 2012.

# SECTION-IV

# CLIMATE CHANGE AND FOOD SECURITY

23

# Agricultural Production and Climate Change in Kerala

Akhila P. Nair

## Introduction

Kerala, the state located in the Southern tip of India is bordered by Arabian Sea and the extensive network of azure backwaters, rivers and streams, boasts of an agrarian economy. The abundance of water due to the 34 lakes and other small streamlets, innumerable backwaters and waterbodies and 49 rain fed rivers flowing over the terrain of the state and also the adequate annual rainfall of 118 inches received by this state probably facilitates agriculture to a great extent and hence the economy of the state is dominated by agriculture.

Agriculture in Kerala is characterised by a diversity of crops in which many are garden crops grown as inter crops in a given area. While most of the crops are grown all over the state regional specialisation exists in the case of some crops. The major crops cultivated in the state can be broadly classified into three. They are food grains, plantation crops, and garden crops. The major food grains are rice, jowar, ragi and pulses. Rubber, tea, coffee and cardamom are the prominent plantation crops and coconut, cashew, arecanut, pepper, tapioca, banana, tobacco, sugarcane and ginger are the main garden crops.

## Food Grains

Among the food grains, paddy occupies the predominant position accounting for nearly 96 per cent of the area under food grains and 12 per cent of the gross cropped area in the state. Among the districts, Palakkad, Ernakulam, Thrissur, Alappuzha and Malappuram are the major rice-growing regions. These districts account for nearly 73 per cent of the total area under rice cultivation in the state.

The production of food grains is depicted in Table 1 shows the production of rice showed an increasing trend during the period between 1960-1961 to 1975-1976. From the mid - seventies onwards, the production was continuously declined; and the production of all other food grains were falling with slight variations. This trend is similar in 2010.

**Table 1. Production of Food Grains ( in million Tonnes)**

| *Year* | *Rice* | *Jowar* | *Ragi* | *Pulses* | *Other cereals* |
|---|---|---|---|---|---|
| 1960-1961 | 1067530 | 640 | 8010 | 17550 | 2910 |
| 1965-1966 | 997490 | 450 | 7030 | 16900 | 3120 |
| 1970-1971 | 1298010 | 840 | 4880 | 13050 | 3170 |
| 1975-1976 | 1364867 | – | – | – | – |
| 1980-1981 | 1271962 | – | 1139 | 22479 | – |
| 1985-1986 | 1173051 | – | – | – | – |
| 1990-1991 | 1086578 | 2305 | 1042 | 16544 | 1131 |
| 1995-1996 | 953026 | 2776 | 1638 | 14994 | 2463 |
| 2000-2001 | 751328 | 2361 | 1582 | 5472 | 1605 |
| 2009-2010 | 598339 | 1177 | 492 | 4449 | 226 |

*Source :* Department of Economics and Statistics, TVM, Government of Kerala, May 2011.

## Plantation Crops

Kerala also accounts for 91 per cent of natural rubber production of the country. Kottayam district has extensive areas producing and processing rubber. Apart from rubber, other plantation crops likes plantains or bananas are also grown in plenty. The area of production and productivity of rubber have been increasing continuously during the time period 1960 to 2010.

In the case of tea is an another major plantation crop in the state, the area has been steadily falling over the years. However, a slight increase in the absolute area was witnessed in the period between 1960-1976 and the Tea production and productivity had been increased between the period of 1980 to 1990, but its rate was falling in the first half of nineties.

Under the area of coffee plantations has been increasing in the state both absolutely and relatively. In the eighties the total production of coffee was declined, but after the period, the production of coffee was slightly improved.

In the case of cardamom, the production and productivity trends had declined from the period between 1961 to 197, and thereafter a continuous increase in production and productivity. After the post-reforms period the production and productivity of the cardamom was continuously increasing. The given below Table 2 shows the production of plantation crops in Kerala.

**Table 2. Production of Plantation Crops in Kerala (in million Tonnes)**

| *Year* | *Rubber* | *Tea* | *Coffee* | *Cardamom* |
|---|---|---|---|---|
| 1960-1961 | 23040 | 40370 | 7410 | 1280 |
| 1965-1966 | 46950 | 39150 | 9880 | 1610 |
| 1970-1971 | 78730 | 41450 | 12570 | 1250 |
| 1975-1976 | 128769 | 43264 | 14395 | 2050 |
| 1980-1981 | 140333 | 50716 | 36475 | 3100 |
| 1985-1986 | 184700 | 52628 | 23550 | 3340 |
| 1990-1991 | 307521 | 63416 | 35700 | 3450 |
| 1995-1996 | 474555 | 64794 | 45000 | 5380 |
| 2000-2001 | 579866 | 69132 | 70550 | 7580 |
| 2009-2010 | 745510 | 57809 | 59250 | 7800 |

***Source :*** Department of Economics and Statistics, TVM, Government of Kerala, May 2011.

## Garden Crops

The state like Kerala, occupies the predominant position for coconuts among the garden crops. It accounts for 53 per cent of the area and 38.34 per cent of the total cropped area in the year of 2009-2010. The production of coconut increased in the period between 1960-1970 and declined from the period between 1970 to 1980 after a period between 1980 to 2011, its total production was continuously increased.

Another important crop which is known as tapioca and is cultivated mainly in the drier regions. Tapioca is a major food of the Keralites. Besides production of the main crop, Kerala also a major producer of spices that form the cash crops of the state Kerala. Spice trade is about 3000 years old and it is wellknown how the fresh aroma of the superb quality Kerala Spices lured foreigners into this country in the medieval ages. Kerala Produces 96 per cent of the country's national output of pepper. The important Spices are cardamom, cinnamon, clove, tumeric, nutmeg and vanila. Cardamom is exported and bring great revenues to the country.

**Table 3. Production of Garden Crops in Kerala (in million Tonnes)**

| Year | Sugarcane | Pepper | Chillies | Ginger | Turm eric Other Planta ins | Areca nut | Banana | Cashe wnut | Tapioca | Sweet Potato | Ground Nut | Seasa mum | Cocount | Cotton | Tobacco |
|---|---|---|---|---|---|---|---|---|---|---|---|---|---|---|---|
| 1960-1961 | 38090 | 27030 | NA | 11270 | 4190 | 7737 | 327850 | 84630 | 1683000 | NA | 13800 | 2590 | 3220 | 1970 | 1010 |
| 1965-1966 | 40950 | 21650 | NA | 11190 | 3770 | 9681 | 361120 | 98030 | 3095660 | NA | 25220 | 2370 | 3293 | 1250 | 910 |
| 1970-1971 | 37630 | 25030 | 2730 | 19680 | 5340 | 12738 | 368980 | 115240 | 4617190 | NA | 16090 | 3900 | 3981 | 1290 | 1630 |
| 1975-1976 | 41831 | 24580 | 2442 | 22840 | NA | 11387 | 395042 | 122360 | 5390217 | NA | 35268 | 4571 | 3439 | 10273 | 1230 |
| 1980-1981 | 48178 | 28519 | NA | 32039 | 6141 | 10805 | 317405 | 81900 | 4060911 | 32967 | 8225 | 3833 | 3008 | 9847 | - |
| 1985-1986 | 42560 | 33121 | 984 | 44466 | 6201 | 10664 | 361126 | 80203 | 3276877 | NA | 6001 | 3702 | 3377 | 9624 | 935 |
| 1990-1991 | 51977 | 46802 | 544 | 45685 | 5123 | 13074 | 491935 | 102771 | 2803001 | 21611 | 9527 | 2063 | 4232 | 1732 | 472 |
| 1995-1996 | 28313 | 68568 | 495 | 46455 | 9559 | 19204 | 592410 | 82760 | 2500113 | 21775 | 9663 | 2131 | 5155 | 17206 | 285 |
| 2000-2001 | 27555 | 60929 | 222 | 42699 | 9037 | 87947 | 731650 | 66178 | 2586903 | 8963 | 2733 | 797 | 5536 | 6209 | 1186 |
| 2009-2010 | 28497 | 37899 | 1302 | 28605 | 6065 | 127893 | 408405 | 364501 | 2525383 | 4875 | 992 | 210 | 5687 | 1324 | 47 |

**Source :** Department of Economics and Statistics, TVM, Government of Kerala, May 2011.

Other cash crops that constitute the agricultural sector include tea, coffee, cashew coconut, arecanut, ginger and coconut. In fact coconut provides the principal source of income in Kerala from coir- industry to coconut shell artifacts, coconuts bring most of the economic gains to Kerala. Approximately, Kerala provides about 70 per cent of Indian output of coconuts.

Cashew is also an essential cash crop. Raw cashew is seasoned with salt and spices and it also a hot favourite with everybody. Almost every tourist buys a packet of Kerala cashews and love gorging on them. The home gardens of Kerala also adds to the states agrarian economy with a large number of vegetables spices, coconuts, fruits grown locally. The production of garden crops in Kerala is shown in Table 3.

## Impact of Climate Change on Agricultural Sector

Agriculture is the mainstay of Indian economy and provides food and livelihood security to a substantial section of the Indian population. The impact of climate change as witnessed in recent times of immense potential to adversely affect agriculture in this country in a variety of ways. As a large part of the arable land in India is rain fed, the productivity of agriculture depends on the rainfall and its pattern. Agriculture will be adversely affected not only by an increase or decrease in the over all amounts of rainfall but also by shifts in the timing of the rainfall. Any change in rainfall patterns poses a serious threat to agriculture and therefore to economy and food security. In this sector, relatively small climate changes can cause large water resources problems and other related problems. The productivity of most crops may decrease due to increase in temperature and decrease in water availability.

The impact of climate change on agriculture could result in problems with **food security** and may threaten the livelihood activities upon which much of the population depends. Climate change can affect crop yields (both positively and negatively), as well as the types of crops that can be grown in certain areas, by impacting agricultural inputs such as water for irrigation, amounts of solar radiation that affect plant growth, as well as the prevalence of pests. This is depicted in the below chart.

## Impact of Climate Change on Agriculture

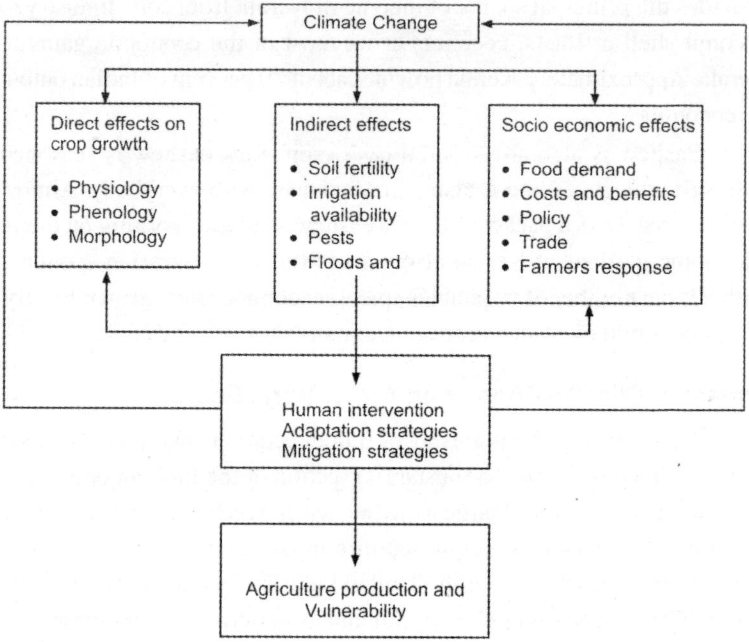


## Interrelationship between Climate Change and Agriculture

Climate change and agriculture are interrelated process, both of which take place on a global scale. Global warming is projected to have significant impacts on conditions affecting agriculture including temperature, carbon dioxide, glacial run-off, precipitation and the interaction of these elements. These conditions determine the carrying capacity of the biosphere to produce enough food for the human population and domesticated animals. The overall effect of climate change on agriculture will depend on the balance of these effects. Assessment of the effects of gobal climate changes on agriculture might help to properly anticipate and adapt farming to maximise agricultural production.

## Annual Greenhouse Gas Emissions by Sector

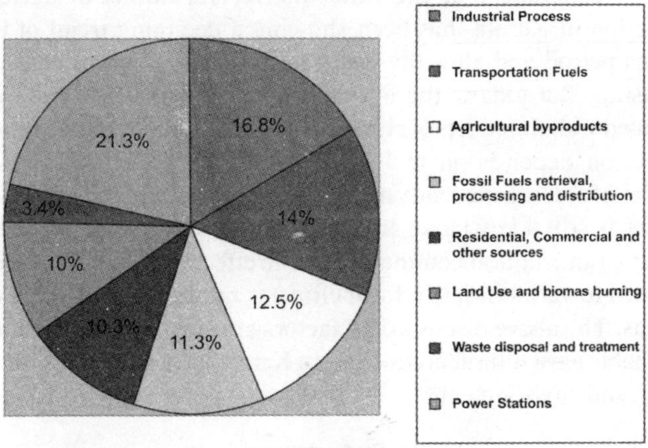


At the same time, agriculture has been shown to produce significant effects on climate change, primarily through the production and release of **greenhouse** gases such as carbon dioxide, methane and nitrous oxide, but also by altering the Earth's land cover, which can change its ability to absorb or reflect heat and light, thus contributing to radiative forcing. Land use change such as deforestation and desertification, together with use of fossil fuels, are the major anthropogenic sources of carbon dioxide; agriculture itself is the major contributor to increasing methane and nitrous oxide concentrations in Earth's atmosphere.

## Needs for Further Research

The complex interaction of climate impacts are combined with varying irrigation techniques, regional factors, and differences in crops, the detailed impacts of these factors need to be detailed study.

*The following are the major suggestions*

- Linking of predictions with agricultural productions systems to suggest suitable options for sustaining agricultural production;
- Preparation of a database on climate change impacts on agriculture ; and
- Evaluation of the impacts of climate change in selected locations.

## Conclusion

To conclude that the inter-district variations of agricultural production in Kerala has been showing a declining trend of the pre-reforms period and after the post-reforms period, it was continuously increasing. But today, the agricultural production in Kerala directly correlated with the effects of climate change. The variations of agricultural production depends on technological advances, such as improved varieties of seeds, genetically modified organisms, and irrigation systems, weather is still a key factor in agricultural productivity, as well as soil properties and natural communities. The effect of climate on agriculture is related to variabilities in local climates rather than in global climate patterns. The above discussed all factors are clearly pointed out that the sustainable agricultural production in Kerala is intertwined with climate change and environment.

## References

1. Anshu Rahal and Y.S. Shivay, *Effect of Global Warming on Crop Productivity*, Kurukshetra, July 2008, p.19.
2. Climate change : Challenges to Sustainable Development in India, Report of Government of India, New Delhi, 2008.
3. Elsamma Job; Yield Gap of Rice in Alappuzha District of Kerala, *Journal of Tropical Agriculture* 44 (1-2) : 88-90, 2006.
4. Government of Kerala, Agriculture Statistics, Department of Economics and Statistics, TVM, 2011.
5. P.A. Oram, *Sensitivity of Agricultural Production to Climate Change*, Reidel Publishing Company, Holland, Vol. 7, 2008, pp. 129-152.
6. Climate Change impacts on Agriculture in India, www.iari.res.in
7. http://dx.doi.org/10.1038/NCLIMATE1449
8. www.Thinktosustain.com

# 24

# Climate Change and Food Security

*Biju Kumar, A.*

*"Humanity must learn to live with climate change. But we cannot allow climate change to become one more aggravating factor for hunger in the world, one more dividing factor between the rich countries and the poor countries. It is our duty to help the poorer countries and, in those countries, the more vulnerable populations at risk, to deal with this new challenge."*

***Jacques Diouf, Director-General, FAO***

## Introduction

**Climate change** is emerging as one of the most challenging problems facing the mankind, with impacts percolating to every sector. Scientists and policy makers have become embroiled in extensive debates about potential changes brought about by an increase in anthropogenic greenhouse gas emissions, along with strategies for mitigation and adaptation. It is now accepted that environmental stress, often the result of global environmental change, coupled with increasingly vulnerable societies, may contribute to insecurity and even conflict. Changes in mean temperatures and rainfall, increasing weather variability and rising sea levels will affect the suitability of land for different types of crops and pasture, the health and productivity of forests, the incidence of pests and diseases, biodiversity and ecosystems. Climate change will worsen the living conditions of farmers, fishers and forest-dependent people who are already vulnerable and food insecure. Hunger and malnutrition will increase. Rural communities dependent on agriculture in a fragile environment will face an immediate risk of increased crop failure and loss of livestock. Mostly at risk are people living in developing countries, particularly along coasts, in floodplains, mountains and drylands. Food insecure people are already vulnerable to the impacts and pressures of fluctuating food and fuel prices, population growth and environmental degradation. Climate change is an additional threat and generates a profound impact on global hunger. In general, poor people will be at risk of food insecurity due to loss of assets and lack of adequate insurance coverage.

In a climate constrained world there is huge challenge to supply adequate resources to meet the needs of growing world population which quadrupled during the 20th century, increasing from about 1.5 billion in 1990 to about six billion in 2000 and expected to increase more than nine billion by 2050 (UN, 2005). During period of 1990 to 2000, consumption of natural resources increased by sixteen times and per capita consumption is projected to increase, putting even greater pressure on natural resources. According to living Planet Report 2006 we are using the planet's resources and producing waste faster than they can be renewed and regenerate by the earth's natural system. The latest data available (for 2003) indicate that humanity's Ecological Footprint, our impact upon the planet, has more than tripled since 1961. Our footprint now exceeds the world's ability to regenerate by about 25 per cent. This means that it took approximately a year and three months for the Earth to produce the ecological resources we used in that year.

In the coming decades, global agriculture faces the prospect of a changing climate, as well as the known challenge of continuing to feed the world's population, projected to more than 9 billion by the year 2050. Under these circumstances the impact of climate change on agriculture could result in problems with food security and may threaten the livelihood activities upon which much of the population depends. Climate change can affect crop yields (both positively and negatively), as well as the types of crops that can be grown in certain areas, by impacting agricultural inputs such as water for irrigation, amounts of solar radiation that affect plant growth, as well as the prevalence of pests.

## Human Development and Climate Change

The global scientific community views climate change as the most significant environmental threat of the 21st century - endangering the sustainability of the world's environment, its agriculture and consequently the health and well being of its people. During the past 200 years, human influence on the functioning of the Earth's systems has reached unprecedented levels. Massive burning of fossil fuels and widespread land conversions has altered the global carbon pools. As a result, carbon dioxide concentrations in the atmosphere have increased by over 30 per cent since 1800 and concentrations of methane, another important greenhouse gas, have doubled. According to the **Intergovernmental Panel on Climate Change (IPCC)**, increases in **greenhouse gas** emissions have been associated with an increase in the mean global temperature of 0.3°C–0.6°C since the late 19th century; by the end of the 21st century, according the IPCC, greenhouse gas emissions could cause the mean global temperature to rise by another 1.4°C–5.8°C.

Increases in mean global temperature will have numerous effects on agricultural production, chief among them being changes in growing seasons - the length of time that soil temperature and soil moisture conditions are suitable for crop growth. The Earth's oceans will expand, raising sea levels and reducing the amount of land available for agriculture. Extreme weather events, such as storms and floods, may increase in frequency.

Among the feedbacks that characterise such coupled human and natural systems, land use is affected by climatic change as well as by socioeconomic trends and population dynamics. In the complex chain of events from population pressures on land use to land pressures on the regional and global environment, policy may also intervene, for instance, by setting standards for local water and air quality, or by developing rules for greenhouse gas emission limitations or the trading of sequestered carbon. **Global warming** will alter **agro-environmental** conditions and thus affect the suitability and productivity of crops. On the one hand, it will increase the risk of pest and disease infestations. On the other hand, the increasing atmospheric concentration of carbon dioxide will enhance plant photosynthesis and contribute to improved water-use efficiency.

## Agriculture, Climate and Food Security

Production of food and other agricultural commodities may keep pace with aggregate demand, but there are likely to be significant changes in local cropping patterns and farming practices. There has been a lot of research on the impacts that climate change might have on agricultural production, particularly cultivated crops. Some 50 per cent of total crop production comes from forest and mountain ecosystems, including all tree crops, while crops cultivated on open, arable flat land account for only 13 per cent of annual global crop production. Production from both rainfed and irrigated agriculture in dryland ecosystems accounts for approximately 25 per cent, and rice produced in coastal ecosystems for about 12 per cent (Millennium Ecosystem Assessment, 2005).

**FOOD SECURITY:** According to Food and Agriculture Organization (FAO) food security exists when all people at all times have physical or economic access to sufficient, safe and nutritious food to meet their dietary needs and food preferences for an active and healthy life. Food security is the outcome of food system performance at global, national and local levels. It is often directly or indirectly dependent on agricultural and forest ecosystem services, such as, soil and water conservation, watershed management, combating land degradation, protection of coastal areas and mangroves, and biodiversity conservation.

The evaluation of climate change impacts on agricultural production, food supply and agriculture-based livelihoods must take into account the characteristics of the agro-ecosystem where particular climate-induced changes in biochemical processes are occurring, in order to determine the extent to which such changes will be positive, negative or neutral in their effects. The so-called "**greenhouse fertilisation effect**" will produce local beneficial effects where higher levels of atmospheric $CO_2$ stimulate plant growth. This is expected to occur primarily in temperate zones, with yields expected to increase by ten to 25 per cent for crops with a lower rate of photosynthetic efficiency (C3 crops), and by 0 to ten per cent for those with a higher rate of photosynthetic efficiency (C4 crops), assuming that $CO_2$ levels in the atmosphere reach 550 parts per million (IPCC, 2007); these effects are not likely to influence projections of world food supply. The impacts of mean temperature increase will be experienced differently, depending on location. For example, moderate warming (increases of 1 to 3°C in mean temperature) is expected to benefit crop and pasture yields in temperate regions, while in tropical and seasonally dry regions, it is likely to have negative impacts, particularly for cereal crops. Warming of more than 3°C is expected to have negative affects on production in all regions (IPCC, 2007). The supply of meat and other livestock products will be influenced by crop production trends, as feed crops account for roughly 25 per cent of the world's cropland.

For **climate variables** such as rainfall, soil moisture, temperature and radiation, crops have thresholds beyond which growth and yield are compromised. For example, cereals and fruit tree yields can be damaged by a few days of temperatures above or below a certain threshold. In the European heat wave of 2003, when temperatures were 6°C above long-term means, crop yields dropped significantly, such as by 36 per cent for maize in Italy, and by 25 per cent for fruit and 30 per cent for forage in

France (IPCC, 2007). Increased intensity and frequency of storms, altered hydrological cycles, and precipitation variance also have long-term implications on the viability of current world agro-ecosystems and future food availability.

Agriculture is important for food security in two ways: it produces the food people eat; and (perhaps even more important) it provides the primary source of livelihood for 36 per cent of the world's total workforce. In the heavily populated countries of Asia and the Pacific, this share ranges from 40 to 50 per cent, and in sub-Saharan Africa, two-thirds of the working population still make their living from agriculture (International Labour Organisation, 2007). If agricultural production in the low-income developing countries of Asia and Africa is adversely affected by climate change, the livelihoods of large numbers of the rural poor will be put at risk and their vulnerability to food insecurity increased.

Agriculture, forestry and fisheries are all sensitive to climate. Their production processes are therefore likely to be affected by climate change. In general, impacts are expected to be positive in temperate regions and negative in tropical ones, but there is still uncertainly about how projected changes will play out at the local level, and potential impacts may be altered by the adoption of risk management measures and adaptation strategies that strengthen preparedness and resilience.

The **food security** implications of changes in agricultural production patterns and performance are of two kinds:

- Impacts on the production of food will affect food supply at the global and local levels. Globally, higher yields in temperate regions could offset lower yields in tropical regions. However, in many low-income countries with limited financial capacity to trade and high dependence on their own production to cover food requirements, it may not be possible to offset declines in local supply without increasing reliance on food aid.
- Impacts on all forms of agricultural production will affect livelihoods and access to food. Producer groups that are less able to deal with climate change, such as the rural poor in developing countries, risk having their safety and welfare compromised.

## Climate Change Impacts on Food Security

Significant changes in climatic conditions will affect food security through their impacts on all components of global, national and local food systems. More frequent and more intense extreme weather events and droughts, rising sea levels, and increasing irregularities in rainy season patterns are already having immediate impacts on food production, food distribution infrastructure, incidence of food emergencies, livelihood assets and opportunities and human health, in both rural and urban areas. Impacts of gradual changes in mean temperatures and rainfall are likely to be disruptive, whether positive and negative, and may include:

- Changes in the suitability of land for different types of crops and pasture,
- Changes in the health and productivity of forests,
- Changes in the distribution, productivity and community composition of marine resources. Changes in the incidence and vectors of different types of pests and diseases,
- Loss of biodiversity and ecosystem functioning of natural habitats,
- Changes in the distribution of good quality water for crop, livestock and inland fish production,
- Loss of arable land due to increased aridity and associated salinity, groundwater depletion and the rise in sea level,
- Changes in livelihood opportunities,
- Changes in health risks, and
- Internal and international migration.

The warming is in turn producing dramatic changes in climatic conditions that affect agricultural production and ultimately our food security. Major potential changes that can alter our food production and cause impact on food security are given below.

**Increase in global mean temperature:** (Increase in maximum temperature on hot days, increase in minimum temperature on cold days, increase in annual occurrence of hot days and increase in frequency, duration and intensity of heat waves.)

- Reduced production of food crops and livestock products in affected areas.
- Local losses could have temporary effect on local markets.
- Reduction in global supplies likely to cause market prices to rise.
- Impacts on incomes, prices and affordability uncertain.
- Changes in preference uncertain.
- Risk of dehydration.
- Risk of ill health from eating food that is spoiled.
- Ability of body to process food reduced due to heat stress or diseases.
- Higher cost for storing grain and perishable products.

**Change in precipitation:** (Increase in frequency, duration and intensity of dry spells and droughts, changes in timing, location and amounts of rain and snowfall.)

- Declines in food production
- Less availability of wild foods
- Pressure on grain reserves
- Decrease in food exports /increase in food imports
- Increased need for food aid
- Local increase in food prices in drought-affected areas
- Loss of farm income and nonfarm employment
- Preferred foods not available or too costly
- Greater instability of food supply, food prices and agricultural-based incomes.

**Increase in frequency and intensity of extreme weather event:** (Increase in annual occurrence of high winds, heavy rains, storm and flash floods, often associated with tropical storms and tornados).

- Possible decrease in surplus production in flooded agricultural areas.
- Increased need for emergency distribution of food rations.
- Possible increase in food prices.
- Possible loss of farm income and non-farm employment, depending on extent of asset loss.
- Food safety is compromised by water pollution and damage to stored food.
- Ability of body to process food reduced due to diseases.

**Grater weather variability:** (Greater instability in seasonal weather patterns, change in start and end of growing seasons).

- Some local losses virtually certain, but their likely geographic distribution is not known.
- Likely impact on global supplies, trade and world market prices is not known.
- Reduced yields may lead to loss of farm income, but this depends on market conditions.
- Greater instability of food supply, food prices and agricultural-based incomes is likely.

**Carbon dioxide enrichment effect:** (Increase in availability of atmospheric carbon dioxide for plant growth).

- Increased food production in major exporting countries would contribute to global food supply but diversion of land from food to more economically attractive cash crops could negate this benefit.
- Increases in food production would limit price increases on world markets, but diversion of productive assets to other cash crops could cause food prices to rise.

## Climate Change Vulnerability on Agricultural Production and Food Security

Agriculture, forestry, and fisheries are all sensitive to climate. Therefore, their production processes - whether for food, feed, fibre, beverage, energy or industrial crops, or for livestock, poultry, fish or forest products - will be impacted by climate change. In general, impacts in temperate regions are expected to be positive, and those in tropical regions negative, although there is still considerable uncertainty about how projected changes will play out locally, and projected impacts could also be altered by adoption of risk management measures and adaptation strategies that strengthen preparedness and resilience. Changes in agricultural production patterns will affect food security in two ways:

- **Impacts on the production of food will affect food supply at both global and local levels.** Globally, higher yields in temperate regions could offset lower yields in tropical regions. However, in many low-income countries that have limited financial capacity to trade, and that rely heavily on their own production to cover their food requirements, it may not be possible to offset declines in local supply without increased reliance on food aid.
- **Impacts on all forms of agricultural production will affect livelihoods and ability to access food.** Producer groups less able to deal with climate change, such as the rural poor in developing countries, risk having their safety and welfare compromised. Besides food and agricultural production, other food system processes e.g., processing, distribution, acquisition, preparation and consumption are equally important for food security.

Overall, food system performance is much less dependent on climate today than it was two hundred years ago. Now, however, there is an increased risk of storm damage to transport and distribution infrastructure, with consequent disruption of food supply chains. Climate change is likely to make access to food more difficult for many currently vulnerable people and other low-income consumers, whether because of reduced own production, loss of employment opportunities as farm and non-farm production patterns shift, or lower purchasing power due to rising market prices for food. Additionally, the rising cost of energy and the need to reduce consumption of fossil fuels have given rise to a new calculus - that of "food miles" - which should be kept as low as possible in order to reduce emissions. The combination of all of these factors could result in a reversion to more local responsibility for food security in the future.

Agricultural-based livelihood systems that are already vulnerable to climate change risk increased crop failure, loss of livestock and fish stocks, increasing water scarcities and destruction of productive assets. They include small-scale rainfed farming systems, pastoralist systems, inland and coastal fishing/ aquaculture communities, and forest-based systems. Rural people inhabiting coasts, floodplains and low-lying river deltas, mountains, drylands and the arctic are most at risk. Moreover, the urban poor, particularly in coastal cities and floodplain settlements, also face increasing risks. Amongst those at risk, pre-existing socio-economic discriminations are likely to be aggravated, causing deterioration in nutritional status for women, young children, and elderly, ill and disabled people.

### Climate Change and Food Security: Some Facts

**Human society will face new risks and pressures.** Food security is unlikely to be threatened at the global level, but some regions are likely to experience food shortages and hunger. Water resources will be affected as precipitation and evaporation patterns change around the world. Physical infrastructure will be damaged, particularly by sea-level rise and by extreme weather events. Economic activities, human settlements, and human health will experience many direct and indirect effects. The poor and disadvantaged are the most vulnerable to the negative consequences of climate change.

**Global agriculture will face many challenges over the coming decades.** Degrading soils and water resources will place enormous strains on achieving food security for growing populations. These conditions may be worsened by climate change. While a global warming of less than 2.5°C could have no significant effect on overall food production, a warming of more than 2.5°C could reduce global food supplies and contribute to higher food prices.

**Some agricultural regions will be threatened by climate change, while others may benefit.** The impact on crop yields and productivity will vary considerably. Added heat stress, shifting monsoons, and drier soils may reduce yields by as much as a third in the tropics and subtropics, where crops are already near their maximum heat tolerance. Mid-continental areas such as the US grain belt, vast sections of mid-latitude Asia, sub-Saharan Africa and parts of Australia are all expected to experience drier and hotter conditions. Meanwhile, longer growing seasons and increased rains may boost yields in many temperate regions; records show that the season has already lengthened in the UK, Scandinavia, Europe and North America.

**Higher temperatures will influence production patterns.** Plant growth and health may benefit from fewer freezes and chills, but some crops may be damaged by higher temperatures, particularly if combined with water shortages. Certain weeds may expand their range into higher-latitude habitats. There is also some evidence that the poleward expansion of insects and plant diseases will add to the risk of crop losses.

**Soil moisture will be affected by changing precipitation patterns.** Based on a global warming of 1.4 – 5.8°C over the next 100 years, climate models project that both evaporation and precipitation will increase, as will the frequency of intense rainfalls. While some regions may become wetter, in others the net effect of an intensified hydrological cycle will be a loss of soil moisture and increased erosion. Some regions that are already drought-prone may suffer longer and more severe dry spells. The models also project seasonal shifts in precipitation patterns: soil moisture will decline in some mid-latitude continental regions during the summer, while rain and snow will probably increase at high latitudes during the winter.

**More carbon dioxide in the atmosphere could boost productivity.** In principle, higher levels of $CO_2$ should stimulate photosynthesis in certain plants. This is particularly true for so-called C3 plants because increased carbon dioxide tends to suppress their photo-respiration. C3 plants make up the majority of species globally, especially in cooler and wetter habitats, and include most crop species, such as wheat, rice, barley, cassava and potato. Experiments based on a 50 per cent increase of current $CO_2$ concentrations have confirmed that "$CO_2$

fertilisation" can increase mean yields of C3 crops by 15 per cent under optimal conditions. C4 plants would also use water more efficiently, but the effects on yields would be smaller in the absence of water shortages. C4 plants include such tropical crops as maize, sugar cane, sorghum and millet, which are important for the food security of many developing countries, as well as pasture and forage grasses. These positive effects could be reduced, however, by accompanying changes in temperature, precipitation, pests, and the availability of nutrients.

**The productivity of rangelands and pastures would also be affected.** For example, livestock would become costlier if agricultural disruption leads to higher grain prices. In general, it seems that intensively managed livestock systems will more easily adapt to climate change than will crop systems. This may not be the case for pastoral systems, however, where communities tend to adopt new methods and technologies more slowly and where livestock depend more fully on the productivity and quality of the rangelands, which may become degraded.

**Food security risks are primarily local and national.** Studies suggest that global agricultural production could be maintained relative to the expected baseline levels over the next 100 years with moderate climate change (below a 2°C warming). However, regional effects would vary widely, and some countries may experience reduced output even if they take measures to adapt. This conclusion takes into account the beneficial effects of $CO_2$ fertilisation but not other possible effects of climate change, including changes in agricultural pests and soils.

## Climate Change and Food Security in India

Climate change may have considerable impact on production of various crops in India that could result in problems with food security and may threaten the livelihood activities upon which much of the population depends. The impacts on agriculture could be of two major types. Firstly, by altering production adversely in the main food producing areas, climate change could enhance food scarcities. The secondly, there could be profound impacts on the physiological mechanisms regulating plant and animal productivity. The greatest impact is likely to come from changes in precipitation patterns. The crop production potentials of a place are largely determined by its climatic, crop properties and their interactions. Climate change can affect crop yields (both positively and negatively), as well as the types of crops that can be grown in certain areas, by impacting agricultural inputs such as water for irrigation, amounts of solar radiation that affect plant growth, as well as the prevalence of pests. The predicted changes to agriculture vary greatly by region and crop.

Predicted climate change impacts on wheat production:

- The study found that increases in temperature (by about 2°C) reduced potential grain yields in most places. Regions with higher potential productivity (such as northern India) were relatively less impacted by climate change than areas with lower potential productivity (the reduction in yields was much smaller).
- Climate change is also predicted to lead to boundary changes in areas suitable for growing certain crops.
- Reductions in yields as a result of climate change are predicted to be more pronounced for rain fed crops (as opposed to irrigated crops) and under limited water supply situations because there are no coping mechanisms for rainfall variability.
- The difference in yield is influenced by baseline climate. In sub tropical environments the decrease in potential wheat yields ranged from 1.5 to 5.8 per cent, while in tropical areas the decrease was relatively higher, suggesting that warmer regions can expect greater crop losses.

Predicted climate change impacts on rice production:

- Overall, temperature increases are predicted to reduce rice yields. An increase of 2-4°C is predicted to result in a reduction in yields.
- Eastern regions are predicted to be most impacted by increased temperatures and decreased radiation, resulting in relatively fewer grains and shorter grain filling durations.
- By contrast, potential reductions in yields due to increased temperatures in Northern India are predicted to be offset by higher radiation, lessening the impacts of climate change.
- Although additional $CO_2$ can benefit crops, this effect was nullified by an increase of temperature.

## Mitigation and Adaptation to Climate Change: Need for Food Security

**Mitigation of climate change:** It involves actions to reduce greenhouse gas emissions and sequestering or storing carbon and making development choices that will lead to low emissions. In the long term, mitigating climate change will be critical to avoiding future breakdowns in food and livelihood systems and sharp increases in the number of food-insecure people worldwide. Historically, land conversion from forest to pasture- or cropland, and intensive crop and livestock production practices have been important sources of greenhouse gas emissions. Food systems also have enormous potential to mitigate climate change, however, particularly at the production end of the food chain. Moreover, many of the most effective mitigation measures also represent highly effective adaptation strategies, especially for commercial agriculture.

Investing in wider adoption of best practices for mitigation in the food and agriculture sector could, therefore, have multiple payoffs for food security, including contributing to the stability of global food markets and providing new employment opportunities in the commercial agriculture sector, as well enhancing the sustainability of vulnerable livelihood systems. Such practices include:

- *Reducing emissions of carbon dioxide and other greenhouse gases,* such as through reduction in the rate of land conversion and deforestation, better control of wildfires, adoption of alternatives to the burning of crop residues after harvest, reduction of emissions from commercial fishing operations, and more efficient energy use by forest dwellers, commercial agriculture and agro-industries;
- *Reducing emissions of methane and nitrous oxide,* such as through improved nutrition for ruminant livestock, more efficient management of livestock waste and of irrigation water on rice paddies, more efficient applications of nitrogen fertilizer on cultivated fields, and reclamation of treated municipal wastewater for aquifer recharge and irrigation;
- *Sequestering carbon,* such as through improved management of soil organic matter, with conservation agriculture involving permanent organic soil cover, minimum mechanical soil disturbance and crop rotation (which also saves on fossil fuel usage); improved management of pastures and grazing practices on natural grasslands, including by optimising stock numbers and rotational grazing; introduction of integrated agroforestry systems that combine crops, grazing lands and trees in ecologically sustainable ways: use of degraded, marginal lands for productive planted forests or other cellulose biomass for alternative fuels; and carbon sink tree plantings.

**Adaptation to climate change:** Adaptation can be defined as adjustments in natural or human systems and behaviours that reduce the risks posed by climate change to people's lives and livelihoods. It involves learning to manage new risks and strengthening resilience in the face of change. Risk management focuses on preparing to deal with shocks. Change management focuses on modifying behaviours over the medium-to-long term to avoid disruptions or declines in global and local food supplies due to changes in temperature and precipitation regimes, and to protect ecosystems through providing environmental services. The following are the important practices for adapting to climate change in the food and agriculture sector.

- Protecting local food supplies, assets and livelihoods against the effects of increasing weather variability and increased frequency and intensity of extreme events through risk management in general and for risks specific to different ecosystems (marine, coastal, inland water and floodplain, forest, dryland, island, mountain, polar, cultivated), through research and dissemination of crop varieties and breeds adapted to changing climatic conditions and through introduction of tree crops to provide food, fodder and energy and enhance cash income.
- Avoiding disruptions or declines in global and local food supplies due to changes in temperature and precipitation regimes through more efficient agricultural water management in general, more efficient management of irrigation water on rice paddies, improved management of cultivated land, improved livestock management and use of new, more energy-efficient technologies by agro-industries.
- Protecting ecosystems through provision of environmental services, such as, use of degraded or marginal lands for productive planted forests or other cellulose biomass for alternative fuels, CDM carbon sink tree plantings, watershed protection, prevention of land degradation, protection of coastal areas from cyclones and other coastal hazards, preservation of mangroves and their contribution to coastal fisheries, and biodiversity conservation.

## Conclusions

At the global level, therefore, food system performance today depends more on climate than it did 200 years ago; the possible impacts of climate change on food security have tended to be viewed with most concern in locations where rainfed agriculture is still the primary source of food and income. Rising sea levels and increasing incidence of extreme events pose new risks for the assets of people living in affected zones, threatening livelihoods and increasing vulnerability to future food insecurity in all parts of the globe. Such changes could result in a geographic redistribution of vulnerability and a relocalisation of responsibility for food security - prospects that need to be considered in the formulation of adaptation strategies for people who are currently vulnerable or could become so within the foreseeable future. The potential impacts of climate change on foodsecurity must, therefore, be viewed within the larger framework of changing earth system dynamics and observable changes in multiple socio-economic and environmental variables. For combating with climate change and food insecurity concerted action is urgently required at both global and local levels.

## References

1. United Nations 2005, World population prospects: The 2004 revision. http//esa.un.org/unpp/p2k0data.asp
2. FAO, 2007, Climate change and food security: A framework document, Rome.
3. FAO, 2007, Adaptation to climate change in agriculture, forestry and fisheries: Perspective, framework and priorities. Report of the FAO Inter departmental Working Group on Climate Change, Rome.
4. Climate change and India-issues concerns and opportunities, 2002, Shukla P R, Sharma S K, Ramana P V (eds.), Tata McGraw-Hill Publishing Company Limited, Delhi, India.
5. ILO, 2007. Chapter 4. Employment by sector. In Key indicators of the labour market (KILM), 5 th edition.Available at: www.ilo.org/public/english/employment/strat/kilm/download/kilm04.pdf.
6. IPCC, 2001. Glossary of Terms used in the IPCC Third Assessment Report. Available at: www.ipcc.ch/glossary/index.htm.
7. IPCC, 2007. Climate Change 2007 the physical science basis. Contribution of Working Group I to the Fourth Assessment Report of IPCC. Cambridge, UK. Cambridge University Press.
8. Lobell David B, et al. 2008, Prioritizing Climate Change Adaptation Needs for Food Security in 2030, SCIENCE Vol. 319 1, pp 607-610.
9. Millennium Ecosystem Assessment. 2005. Ecosystems and human wellbeing: Synthesis. Washington DC, Island Press for WRI.

# Index

## H



## I

**R**

**T**

## U

**Y**



**Z**